We as Freemen

We as Freemen

Plessy v. Ferguson

By Keith Weldon Medley

PELICAN PUBLISHING COMPANY
Gretna 2003

The word "Pelican" and the depiction of a pelican are trademarks
of Pelican Publishing Company, Inc., and are registered in the
U.S. Patent and Trademark Office.

Library of Congress Cataloging-in-Publication Data

Medley, Keith Weldon.
We as freemen : Plessy v. Ferguson / by Keith Weldon Medley.
    p. cm.
Includes index.
ISBN 1-58980-120-2 (hardcover : alk. paper)
    1. Plessy, Homer Adolph—Trials, litigation, etc. 2. Segregation in
transportation—Law and legislation—Louisiana—History. 3.
Segregation—Law and legislation—United States—History. 4.
United States—Race relations—History. I. Title: Plessy v. Ferguson. II.
Title.
    KF223.P56 M43 2003
    342.73'0873—dc21
                                        2002154505

Printed in the United States of America

Published by Pelican Publishing Company, Inc.
1000 Burmaster Street, Gretna, Louisiana 70053

In memory of my parents,
Alfred Andrew Medley, Sr., and Veronica Rose Toca Medley

For my sons,
Keith and Kwesi

"We, as freemen, still believe that we were right and our cause is sacred."
—Statement of the Comité des Citoyens, 1896

Contents

Acknowledgments

I would like to thank Dr. Michael Sartisky, Jenifer Mitchel, John R. Kemp, and the Louisiana Endowment for the Humanities for their assistance in making it easier for me to complete this task. In that same frame, I am deeply indebted to my grant writer and daughter-in-law, Tia Medley, for her hard work and persistence in my grant efforts. I would also like to thank Carol Bebelle, James Borders, Andrea Benton Rushing, Dr. Lawrence Powell, and Beverly McKenna for their assistance in the grant process. I am grateful to Wayne Everard, Greg Osborn, and Dr. Colin Hamer and other staff of the New Orleans Public Library's Louisiana Division. I am also grateful to past and current staff at the Amistad Research Center at Tulane University for their assistance. These include Florence Borders, Lester Sullivan, Brenda Square, Dorinda Phillips, Dr. Clifton Johnson, and Dr. Donald Devore. Lester Sullivan is currently the resident archivist at Xavier University in New Orleans and he is also to be thanked for his cataloging of articles from the *Crusader* found on Xavier University's shelves. I would also like to thank the University of New Orleans Library and the staff in the Louisiana and Special Collections area for their valuable assistance. Other sites in Louisiana that were of assistance include the Historic New Orleans Collection, the Orleans Parish Notarial Archives, Tulane University's Louisiana Division, the Louisiana State Archives, and the Louisiana State University Special Collections.

Outside of Louisiana, I am indebted to Nancy Brown at the

Chautauqua County Historical Society in western New York for helping me navigate the Albion W. Tourgee Collection. I also would like to thank the staff at the Boston Public Library, the Massachusetts Historical Society, the National Archives, and the Library of Congress for their professionalism and assistance. I am very appreciative of the experience of having worked with Timothy Foote and Marian Smith Holmes of *Smithsonian* magazine and their efforts and advice to me in preparing my 1994 article for their publication. I am also thankful to Louise Mouton Johnson for her illustrative work and Richard Sexton and Phillip Gould for their photographs in the *Smithsonian* article.

A special thanks goes to those who offered me lodging and sustenance during my research expeditions, in particular, the family of Jackie Knightshade in Washington, DC, and my cousin Shelia and her husband, George Platt, in Martha's Vineyard. I would also like to acknowledge the many people I have met in my research of the Plessy saga, including Dr. Lawrence Powell of Tulane University and the late Dr. Joseph Logsdon of the University of New Orleans. I also enjoyed meeting the extended relatives of Homer Plessy, including Keith Plessy, the late Russell Plessy and his family, and many other relatives at the 1996 Plessy Conference in New Orleans. The Plessy centennial was also an occasion to restore the grave of Homer Plessy with Robert Florence, Gregory Osborn, Fr. Jerome Ledoux, and other members of the Friends of New Orleans Cemeteries. I am also appreciative of the reference material on shoemaking forwarded to me by Rusty Moore of the Plimoth Plantation in Plymouth, Massachusetts, where he still makes shoes by hand. Also, Bobby Duplissey was kind enough to share his genealogical research on the Plessy family in Louisiana. I am especially indebted to the staff of the *New Orleans Tribune,* which has published many of my historic reports, including my first Plessy article. I thank the publishers Dr. Dwight and Beverly McKenna for allowing me the space to write about New Orleans' history and culture. Scholars such as Otto H. Olsen, for his documentary work on the case in *The Thin Disguise* and his comprehensive *Carpetbaggers Crusade,* provided me with enormous insight into the life and times of Albion Tourgee, Sr. Dorothea McCants' translation of Rodolphe Desdunes 1911 book, *Nos Homes et Notre Histoire,* opened the doors to the world of free people of color in New Orleans. Civil-rights attorney Nils Douglas's paper on Louis A. Martinet was invaluable. Dianne Baquet provided me with information on Rudolph Baquie. Finally, I would like to lovingly acknowledge all those who gave me inspiration and moral support, including my grandchildren Emily Rose and Adam Guillaume Medley; my brother, Alfred Medley, Jr.; and my sister, Marilyn Vandergriff, her husband, Larry, and daughter, Brittany.

Finally, I am pleased to see the efforts by the students at Frederick Douglass High School in New Orleans and the Crescent City Peace Alliance in their drive to erect a civil-rights memorial at the site where Homer Plessy was arrested.

CHAPTER 1

A Negro Named Plessy

> On Tuesday evening, a Negro named Plessy was arrested by Private Detective Cain on the East Louisiana train and locked up for violating section 2 of act 111 of 1890, relative to separate coaches. . . . He waived examination yesterday before Recorder Moulin and was sent before the criminal court under $500.00 bond.
> —*New Orleans Daily Picayune,* June 9, 1892

Homer Plessy arrived at the Press Street Depot for his date with history. June 7, 1892, was warm and cloudy. The temperature reached eighty-six degrees. That day, he challenged Louisiana's Separate Car Act. That was his moment. Standing at the depot looking north, Plessy could view the New Orleans Northeastern Railroad's Queen and Crescent line heave down the tracks and then through swampy woods, on its way to Northern destinations far removed from the travails of the post-Reconstruction South. However, it was Plessy's mission to board the East Louisiana Railroad's local line, which never left Louisiana but crossed a seven-mile bridge over Lake Pontchartrain, rolled past Lewisburg, Mandeville, and Abita Springs, and then terminated at the depot in Covington, Louisiana. Unlike his fellow travelers, Plessy was not there as a commuter or on a one-dollar excursion to the beaches across Lake Pontchartrain. He was there to test the constitutionality of "that infamous contrivance known as the 'Jim Crow Law,'" according to a statement by the group that engineered Plessy's act of civil disobedience. Later in 1892, Plessy appeared before John Howard Ferguson, a judge whose criminal-court ruling launched *Plessy v. Ferguson* on its journey to America's highest judicial tribunal. Over 20,000 passengers annually traveled the East Louisiana Railroad.[1] Only Plessy had cause to wonder what the Supreme Court might think about his trip.

Before there was Linda Brown versus the board of education, and before there was Rosa Parks and the Montgomery Improvement Association, there was Homer Plessy and a New Orleans group of eighteen men called the Comité des Citoyens (Committee of Citizens). Far from being happenstance, Plessy's actions resulted from a last-ditch, almost desperate effort by this contingent of civil libertarians, ex-Union soldiers, Republicans, writers, a former Louisiana lieutenant governor, a French Quarter jeweler, and other professionals. In September 1891, they came together to challenge act 111 of the 1890 Louisiana legislature, a law that segregated railroad trains. Their objective was to obtain a United States Supreme Court ruling preventing states from abolishing the suffrage and equal-access gains of the Reconstruction period. In a year's time, the Comité des Citoyens formulated legal strategy while raising money from the people of New Orleans' neighborhoods, small towns throughout the South, and in cities as far away as Washington, DC, and San Francisco. They published their views in attorney Louis Martinet's Republican *Crusader* newspaper, held rallies in churches and fraternal halls, and garnered support wherever they could. Finally, they organized two cases to test the law and solemnly vowed to bring the matter into the chambers of the United States Supreme Court. "We find this the only means left us," one Comité des Citoyens pamphlet stated. "We must have recourse to it or sink into a state of hopeless inferiority."

Their six-year quest through America's political and legal system traversed many crucial issues in American jurisprudence: states' rights, federal authority, individual liberties, rights of association, racial classification, the regulation of interstate and intrastate commerce, and the central question of the Supreme Court's role in defending the individual rights of American citizens. Citizen Plessy's one-block-long, illegal

train trip brought before the court many of the debates, sentiments, and divisions that had visited the country since its birth.
Could states regulate people based on race? Didn't the Fourteenth Amendment's equality clauses prohibit such discrimination? Who was qualified to assign racial categories? Could
states intrude into such intimate decisions as marriage and
relationships because of the races of the betrothed? Were people
of color citizens, slaves, or something in between? Were they
less than human? Did the United States Constitution guarantee
them any rights at all? The Supreme Court's 1857 *Dred Scott
Decision* said no. Would America's future rise to the "created
equal" high ideals of the Declaration of Independence? Or
would it be mired in antagonism? *Plessy v. Ferguson* joined the
1857 *Dred Scott Decision* and 1954's *Brown v. Board of Education*
as three watershed cases in the Supreme Court's treatment of
civil rights. The matter concerning Plessy's place in America
has persistently stuck in the craw of United States jurisprudence since its inception. Even today, it reverberates across the
national landscape.

And what of Homer Plessy and John Ferguson, two names
forever coupled in American history? Consider Homer
Plessy—a racially mixed, young shoemaker who volunteered as
a test case for equal rights. Consider John Ferguson—a son of
New England and so-called carpetbagger who married into an
abolitionist New Orleans family but owed his political life to a
former Confederate general. What winds of history brought
these two relatively minor historical figures to confront each
other on an autumn day in a late nineteenth-century New
Orleans courtroom? Oddly—given the nature of the case—
skin color was one common characteristic that Plessy and Ferguson shared.

Over a century has elapsed since this nineteenth-century
shoemaker named Plessy rose from obscurity and became the
pivotal figure in one of the most controversial and far-reaching
Supreme Court cases in American civil-rights history. In many
ways, his actions echoed the disobedience of conscience of

Henry David Thoreau and a series of 1860s sit-ins that integrated
New Orleans' mule-drawn streetcars. Plessy sought to challenge
an unjust law, bring a cause before the public eye, and seek
redress before the courts of the land. In that light, his actions
also portended elements from Rosa Parks 1954 refusal to relin-
quish her seat to a white man on a Montgomery bus. It also
employed the sentiments of Dr. Martin Luther King's 1957 Montgomery bus boycott, the 1961 freedom rides, and the NAACP's
legal fights to desegregate schools across America. But unlike the
widely honored Rosa Parks and Dr. King, Plessy's name became
associated with the painful era of Jim Crow. While some criticized
the Comité des Citoyens for initiating a chain of events that
could possibly lead to an adverse Supreme Court ruling, our
journey to the era of Plessy and the Comité des Citoyens will
show that state-mandated racial separation had already spread
across the Deep South and beyond. Far from causing separate-
but-equal policies, Plessy and his compatriots were among the
foremost to mount a legal and civil disobedience campaign in
the 1890s at great risk to their livelihoods and safety.

How did a historically obscure Homer Plessy become a focal
point in American history? One of Plessy's twenty-first century
relatives, Dr. Boake Plessy, described Homer as a "relatively
quiet, ordinary citizen who got involved, and beyond that,
there were no other events in his life which would have
marked him for history."[2] Homer Plessy's occupations
included shoemaker, clerk, laborer, and collector for a black-
owned insurance company. He lived in the downtown Creole
section of New Orleans. He was literate and spoke French. In
a region with a population defined largely in terms of black
and white, he was the exception that defied the rule. He had
fair skin. His genealogy was not found in dusty, plantation,
breeding books, but in the city-records room. His father was
not a slave during pre-Civil War times, but a free person of
color with access to education, property, and wages. Members
of his pre-Civil War ancestry were not the anonymously
enslaved, but property-owning blacksmiths, carpenters, and

shoemakers. Still, his African ancestry subjected him to the same discriminatory laws visited upon the formerly enslaved.

At age thirty, shoemaker Plessy was younger than most members of the Comité des Citoyens. He did not have their stellar political histories, literary prowess, business acumen, or law degrees. Indeed, his one attribute was being white enough to gain access to the train and black enough to be arrested for doing so. This shoemaker sought to make an impact on society that was larger than simply making its shoes. When Plessy was a young boy, his stepfather was a signatory to the 1873 Unification Movement—an effort to establish principles of equality in Louisiana. As a young man, Plessy displayed a social awareness and served as vice president of an 1880s educational-reform group. And in 1892, he volunteered for a mission rife with unpredictable consequences and backlashes. Comité des Citoyens lawyers Albion Tourgee, James C. Walker, and Louis Martinet vexed over legal strategy. Treasurer Paul Bonseigneur handled finances. As a contributor to the *Crusader* newspaper, Rodolphe Desdunes inspired with his writings. Plessy's role consisted of four tasks: get the ticket, get on the train, get arrested, and get booked.

With Reconstruction and its advances toward equal rights, it may have seemed at one time that racial restrictions would become a relic of pre-Civil War America. But thirty years after emancipation, Plessy prepared to be arrested. His was a crime of ethnicity in that if he would have been white and performed the same activity, his actions would have been legal. Shouldn't he have been judged as Plessy and not as a man of a certain race of people? Had he done something wrong? The legislature did not pass a law regulating the rail travel of murderers or rapists. The Civil War, constitutional amendments, civil-rights acts, social movements, and politicians of the 1860s and 1870s promised a life free from the limits of the caste system of his parents' era. What did his young wife think? Was she proud, or did she think him somewhat quixotic? Plessy stood in many ways as an everyman, or everyperson, representing individuals discriminated against not because of behavior or character, but because of the group into which they were born. Could Plessy have known—as he stood at that depot looking like a white guy, neatly dressed with his first-class ticket—that his name would be on a court decision that would become a part of every discussion about Jim Crow? That instead of being thanked for taking this burden, he would be often pilloried? Or that he would be slurred on the front page of a New Orleans newspaper as a "snuff colored descendant of Ham"? Or that his name would be bantered about in countless legal journals, appeals courts, and the *Brown v. Board of Education* decision in 1954? Because, after all was said and done, he was, quite simply, Homer Plessy—Homere Adolphe Plessy, to be exact—a son of old New Orleans.

Before they are filled with the high moments and lengthy pronunciations, the High Court's civil-rights cases invariably rise from communities and people far removed from the power and politics of Washington, DC. Many times, the histories, lives, and simple wants of individuals seeking redress become overshadowed by legalese, the passions of any given era, and the social impact of their judicial journey. Cases often emerge from cities and small towns, individual circumstances, and simple motivations that the Court's justices never see. For Dred Scott, the plaintiff of the 1857 *Dred Scott Decision,* a Missouri courtroom provided the setting for his insistence that he, his wife, and two daughters were free people, not slaves. For Linda Brown, the plaintiff in the 1954 *Brown v. Board of Education* decision, a Topeka, Kansas, parent's desire to send a child to a neighborhood school triggered massive social change. For Homer Plessy, train tracks a block away from the Mississippi River set the stage for his plea before the United States Supreme Court. The venue was New Orleans, Louisiana, where Plessy was born in 1863. That was one year after Union navy gunboats stormed down the Mississippi River, overran the city's defenses, and took control of this strategic port location in an early Civil War battle.

La Ville de la Nouvelle-Orléans

Established as a French military garrison colony in 1718 by Jean Baptiste Le Moyne, Sieur de Bienville, New Orleans' proximity to the Gulf of Mexico provided a strategic location as a rare piece of high ground near the mouth of the Mississippi River.[3] Its environment would always be a double-edged sword that exposed its inhabitants to the whims of a watery, wind-whipped, hot, humid, hostile terrain. In 1721, the first of many hurricanes destroyed every structure.

So arduous was the environment, France punished its social outcasts with forced labor there. Between the years 1718 and 1721, the seven thousand Frenchmen arriving in Louisiana included salt smugglers, vagabonds, drunks, murderers, prostitutes, and deserters who suffered for their transgressions with exile to the Louisiana colony.[4] In the same period, ships, with names such as *l'Aurore, le Ruby, le Marechal, l'Expedition, le Fortune, la Venus,* and *le Courrier de Bourbon* traded for slaves and then sailed to Louisiana from the West African ports of Gore and St. Louis.[5] For both groups—the indentured French and the African slaves—their unenviable task was to construct a defensible outpost from the inhospitality of the Louisiana marshes. For the French prisoners, their term of servitude was a grueling three years, after which they were given part of the land they worked.[6] For most Africans, their sentence was life. Upon arrival in Louisiana, Africans cleaned and drained swamps, constructed levees and buildings, dug canals, hacked trees, and assisted with public-works projects. Rations consisted of one and a half pounds of corn and a half-pound of lard per day.[7] From its beginning, New Orleans also housed a sizable number of free people of color who participated in the economic life of the colony.

Spain acquired Louisiana from France in 1763. The Spanish crown envisioned a more far-reaching vision of New Orleans than that of military outpost. With New Orleans as the capital, a series of ten Spanish governors ruled from the Cabildo next to the Church of St. Louis (St. Louis Cathedral). During the forty-year Spanish reign, the number of Africans quintupled. By 1800, there were 25,000 slaves and 20,000 free people of color.[8] In 1802, France reacquired Louisiana and dealt it to the United States in the Louisiana Purchase of 1803. In New Orleans, on December 29, 1803, soldiers lowered the French flag and hoisted the American flag in the Place des Armes (Jackson Square).[9] The deal dramatically increased the size of the United States by 140 percent, gave it dominion of the Rocky Mountains, and added a half billion acres of land to the public domain.[10] In 1812, Louisiana gained statehood as the eighteenth state of the fledgling Union. In 1815, the Battle of New Orleans thrust the city into the national spotlight when Andrew Jackson's troops routed the British just downriver from the city. Two battalions consisting of free men of color participated, and it is believed that a free black rifleman shot British general Sir Edward Pakenham.[11] A fourteen-year-old black drummer boy named Jordan Noble set the cadence for the victory over the British when he served "as a guidepost in the 'hell of fire' by keeping up the drumbeat."[12]

Free People of Color

Homer Plessy's parents, Adolphe Plessy and Rosa Debergue, belonged to New Orleans' free-people-of-color caste. A fixture in New Orleans since its earliest days, free people of color obtained their status from purchase by a relative or themselves, manumission by a white parent or owner, or migration from other countries such as Martinique, Haiti, or Cuba, which countenanced free-black populations. Typically French-speaking and Roman Catholic, free people of color possessed property rights but could not vote, frequent many of the city's public places, or establish organizations without permission. Section 40 of the Louisiana Black Code stated that "free people of color ought never to insult or strike white people nor presume to think of themselves equal to the white, but on the contrary they ought to yield to them on every occasion, and never speak to them or answer them, but with respect."[13] Though officially banned in Louisiana, a number of relationships called *placages* developed between white males and black women. In some instances, children received family names, inheritances, and free status. A number of free people of color received European educations and achieved prominence in science, music, literature, and philanthropy.

Homer Plessy's paternal grandfather was Germain Plessy, a white Frenchman who was born in Bourdeaux circa 1777. He and his brother, Dominique Plessy, arrived in New Orleans from Sainte Domingue (now Haiti) in the wake of the Toussaint L'Ouverture-led slave revolution, which wrested the island from Napoleon in the 1790s. The brothers Plessy made their way to New Orleans with thousands of other Haitian expatriates. City directories listed Germain as operator of Germain Plessy and Co. His name appeared as a plaintiff in three civil-court cases in the First Judicial Court in 1827.[14] He was also identified in St. Louis Cathedral records as a godfather during a christening.[15]

The union of Germain Plessy and a free woman of color named Catherina Mathieu produced eight children, including Homer's father.[16] Catherina was born in 1782—the child of a free woman of color named Agnes and a white Frenchman named Mathieu Deveaux. Domingo was born in 1804, Honore in 1806, Gustave in 1809, Claris in 1815, Jean Livie in 1818, Marie in 1820, and Catherine in 1824. Homer Plessy's father, Joseph Adolphe Plessy, was born on March 19, 1822. Adolphe and his younger sister were both baptized at St. Louis Cathedral in New Orleans. Between 1812 and 1816, Germain's brother, Dominique, had moved to Avoyelles Parish, where he married a white woman named Nancy Roe and had three sons. This branch of the family subsequently went under the name Duplissey. Dominique died in 1820 or 1821.[17]

Homer Plessy's mother, Rosa Debergue, was a descendant of Michel Debergue and Josephine Blanco. Rosa was born circa

1835. She too was described as a free person of color and a native of New Orleans. City directories of 1870 listed her occupation as seamstress. In the 1880 census, she was enumerated as a forty-five-year-old mulatto who kept house. With the exception of Germain Plessy, most of the pre-Civil War New Orleans Plessy entries in the state archives' indexes have a *C*, for colored, associated with them. Rosa Debergue's family also had a *C* by their names in Louisiana birth and death indexes. Adolphe Plessy and Rosa Debergue produced a daughter named Ida Plessy, who was born at a residence on Union Street (now Touro Street) in the Faubourg New Marigny in downtown New Orleans. Her November 9, 1855, birth record described Homer's father, Adolphe Plessy, as a free man of color (f.m.c.), a native of New Orleans, and a thirty-three-year-old carpenter. Rosa Debergue was listed as his wife and also a native of New Orleans. Carpentry was a popular occupation among the Plessy men in the nineteenth century, and by 1890, they operated under the name Plessy Builders. The Plessys and Debergues generally lived in the downtown French-speaking sections of the city. The Debergues had a family house at 105 Union Street. In 1855, seventy-three-year-old Plessy patriarch Germain Plessy and Gustave Plessy, his son, were listed as living on Elysian Fields Avenue, at the corner of Craps Street (now Burgundy).

Despite legal and political limitations, free people of color played a large role in New Orleans' development. There were 11,000 such people in New Orleans right before the Civil War. A number of institutions begun by free people of color exist in New Orleans until this day. One is St. Augustine's Catholic Church in the 1200 block of St. Claude Street in Faubourg Tremé. It was here in the 1840s that the Sisters of the Holy Family recited their vows as the first African-American group of nuns in the United States. In the 1840s, seventeen free people of color produced *Les Cenelles*, a 210-page book of poems written in the French romantic tradition. The following year, a New Orleans-born scientist named Norbert Rillieux invented a vacuum cup that revolutionized the refining of sugar, but he relocated to Paris in order to obtain a patent. Rillieux, incidentally, was a relative of the French impressionist Edgar Degas.

One of the most interesting examples of institution-building among free people of color before the Civil War was the Catholic School for Indigent Orphans, also popularly called the Couvent School. This school is a ubiquitous fixture throughout the Plessy saga, as many members of the Comité des Citoyens would serve the school as administratiors, teachers, and legal advisors. After Plessy's mother remarried in the 1870s, a member of Plessy's stepfamily served as president of the institution. Plans for the school began in 1848 with the last will and testament of West African native Marie C. Couvent, who bequeathed a school for the "colored orphans of the faubourg Marigny." All of its teachers were of African descent and had been educated in France or Haiti. The stellar faculty included Paul Trevigne and Joanni Questy (writers and poets), E. J. Edmunds and Basile Crockere (mathematicians), and Adolphe Duhart (dramatist). Paul Trevigne, who taught at the school for forty years, edited the *l'Union* newspaper after the war, while Duhart's play *Lelia* showcased at the Theatre d'Orleans. The school's math teacher and master swordsman, Basile Crockere, also operated a premiere fencing academy at his Salle d'Armes in a city where dueling under oak trees was an acceptable way for men to settle questions of honor. Madame Couvent's legacy is still alive today in the form of the Bishop Perry Middle School—still at the corner of Dauphine and Touro Streets in Faubourg Marigny.

While a number of prominent New Orleanians emerged from Adolphe and Rosa's community of free people of color, the primary trades of this caste were carpenters (257), laborers (145), cigar makers (171), shoemakers (151), and draymen (101). Free women of color operated boarding houses and worked as seamstresses. Repression of this group's limited freedoms increased in the years before the Civil War. Many set sail for Haiti or other less-threatening shores.

> M. Adolphe Plessy native of New Orleans residing on Union street 3rd District in this city who hereby declares that on the seventeenth of March of this present year was born in this city (17th March 1863) a male child named Homere Patris Plessy issue of the legitimate marriage of deponent with Rosa Debergue native of New Orleans.
>
> —Homer Plessy's birth certificate, April 1863
> Louisiana State Archives

Homer Plessy was born on St. Patrick's Day in 1863. His middle name on the birth record reflects the patron saint of his natal day but later records show his middle name as either Adolph or the French equivalent, Adolphe, after his father. Homer's grandfather, Germain Plessy, died the month after his birth. One can hardly imagine a more volatile era in American history than that into which Plessy was born. Lincoln's Emancipation Proclamation had been in effect for less than three months and New Orleans was under the occupation of the Union army. The Civil War was underway. On the day after Homer's birth, the papers reported news from the Battle of Port Hudson and the sinking of the Confederate ship *Webb* by the USS *Monongahela*.[18] While the Civil War spared New Orleans much of its architecture and culture, it ripped its social, political, and caste fabric with the emancipation of enslaved Africans and a fifteen-year occupation by Federal troops. With Union forces occupying the city, Plessy's early childhood was framed by a decade resplendent and tragic. It was filled with heroic war battles, jubilant processions, mass movements, grand orations, and violent reactions. Unlike his parents, who were limited and defined by the pre-Civil War caste system, the formative years of Homer Plessy's life paralleled the Civil War, emancipation, and the Reconstruction era.

On January 5, 1869, the French-language *New Orleans Bee* reported the death of Homer's father, Adolphe Plessy. A burial notice invited his friends and acquaintances to assist in the final preparations. At 3:00 in the afternoon, Adolphe Plessy's funeral procession departed from the Debergue-Blanco family home at 105 Union Street, near the corner of what are now Touro and Marais Streets in Faubourg New Marigny.[19] Before Homer Plessy's father died at forty-six years old, he must have felt a bright future ahead for his five-year-old son. Indeed, Homer Plessy spent his growing years in a Louisiana where he was free to vote, engage in politics, and catch any streetcar he chose without legal molestation. In 1868, adult males, regardless of ethnicity or previous condition of slavery, could become eligible to vote by paying a $1.50 poll tax, the proceeds earmarked for schools and charities. In 1869, Louisiana became the only Southern state to introduce an integrated school system, and in 1870, a Louisiana statute removed the state's ban against interracial marriages. One by one, legal barriers to public accommodations, suffrage, and education fell. In the last forty years of the nineteenth century, Louisiana's African-descent community produced an interim governor, three lieutenant governors, six state officers, thirty-two state senators, and ninety-five state representatives.[20] Additionally, the people of the state elected nineteen black sheriffs, thirteen black tax collectors, twelve parish assessors, thirteen parish coroners, two parish judges, and four town mayors.[21] Male suffrage became enshrined in the Constitution in 1870.[22]

Plessys, Debergues, and Duparts

In the 1870s, despite the personal and social gravity of the era, life for Homer Plessy went on. On May 3, 1871, when Homer was eight years old, his mother married Victor M. Dupart, a thirty-six-year-old clerk at the post office. Victor M. Dupart, born on February 22, 1835, was the son of shoemaker Martial Dupart and Josephine Olivella. Victor also had a *C* by his name in the birth indexes, as did most Duparts. Both of Victor's parents were natives of the city. Victor Dupart's previous wife, Louise Demazillere, had died at the age of thirty-five in 1869, the same year that Homer's father passed away.[23] Rosa must have been pleased to have Victor Dupart as a father figure to Homer. Victor must have welcomed a helpmate. At the time of their marriage, he had his hands and house full with six children under his roof: Formidor, 12, and little Victor L., 10, who both attended Straight College's elementary school; and Victoria, 13, who stayed at home with Augustine, 8, Lionel, 3, and Valdes, 1.[24] The entire household was classified as mulatto. Joining them would be Homer, Ida, and Rosa.

Rosa Debergue Dupart became a recipient of the property at 105 Union Street upon the death of Josephine Blanco on December 23, 1871. Josephine was the widow of Debergue patriarch Michel Debergue.[25] In 1872, Homer's mother appeared in the city directory as "Rosa D. Dupart, widow Plessy." In 1873, she bore Victor Dupart another son, and Homer a little brother, when Charles Dupart joined the brood. Among the Duparts, Homer found himself in a family setting that was socially and politically engaged. The Duparts had been active in the military, in traditional occupations, in community interaction, and in politics. There was Sgt. Pierre Dupart, listed on the roster of the First Battalion of Free Men of Color in the 1815 Battle of New Orleans.[26] Leon Dupart served as a corporal M.P. assigned to the Fifth Precinct. Cabinetmaker Henry Dupart lived on Marais Street in Tremé, near the corner of St. Phillip Street. Other Duparts listed as shoemakers, a blacksmith, a cigar maker, and a butcher. The Duparts also participated in the benevolent, social, religious, and masonic societies that were bedrock to New Orleans social groupings. A group called the Societe des Jeunes Amis (Society of Young Friends) listed F. M. Dupart and V. L. Dupart among its members. Like Formidor and Victor L., in his adult life, Homer also participated in a number of these organizations: the Societe des Francs Amis (Society of French Friends), Cosmopolitan Mutual Aid Society, Scottish Rites Masons, and the Justice, Protective, Educational, and Social Club. Homer was an officer in each of those groups.

While none of the Plessys, and only one Debergue, is listed on the Orleans Parish voters' poll tax rolls for 1869 and 1870, Victor M. Dupart was one of ten Duparts who paid the Orleans

Parish poll tax, necessary to ensure a vote to exercise newly granted suffrage.[27] There were three Victor Duparts who appeared in the 1870 city directory. All lived on the same block, at 47 Annette Street in New Marigny between Urquhart and North Villere Streets. One Victor Dupart was president of the Couvent School. In fact, the principal of the Couvent School, playwright Adolphe Duhart, stood as the witness when Rosa and Victor M. Dupart married.

Unification

It was probably the Duparts more than the Plessys who influenced Plessy's social, activist, and occupational future. When Homer Plessy was ten years old, in 1873, Victor and Marcelle Dupart joined the Unification Movement—an early civil-rights construction that included at least five members who later joined the Comité des Citoyens.[28] Victor M. and Marcelle Dupart were among the approximately eight hundred names appearing in the *New Orleans Times* as supporters of the Unification platform. One thousand other names went unprinted because of space. Indeed, Aristide Mary, the man who initiated the formation of the Comité des Citoyens was a Unification Movement cochairman.[29] The Unification Movement was not noted for its longevity or success but for its ambition, boldness, and vision to even attempt such a thing in such a time. And considering the venom of the era, it was quite an accomplishment to get 1,800 black and white people to sign their names to a document calling for racial equality. Coordinated by a group of fifty blacks and fifty white in New Orleans, its "Appeal for the Unification of the People of Louisiana" called for political equality, racial unity, and an end to discrimination. Its statements were sentiments later expressed by the Comité des Citoyens.

Plessy the Shoemaker

Homer Plessy was fourteen years old when Reconstruction

ended in 1877. Plessy and family still resided in the Debergue family home at 105 Union Street. In 1880, New Orleans, a city mainly below sea level, suffered incessant rains that left unpaved streets like Union impassable for days. Wooden boards served as sidewalks over interminably muddy streets. Goats, chickens, and mules would invariably lose their tether and scurry about the neighborhood.[30] City directories also listed Formidor Dupart at the 105 Union Street address along with Victor M. Dupart. The census of 1880 listed Homer's mother, Rosa Dupart, as a mulatto housekeeper. Census takers noted the presence of Homer and his twenty-five-ear-old sister, Ida Plessy, who kept house. Homer's little brother, Charles Dupart, now seven, had already started school.[31]

In 1879, at age sixteen, Homer Plessy worked as a shoemaker along with his stepbrother Formidor Dupart. Indeed, in the 1880s, with the exception of Homer, all Plessys in the city directory were carpenters. Though the building trades remained the primary occupation of the Plessy men in the latter nineteenth century, Homer followed in the footsteps of a Dupart family trade. Marcelle, Gustave, and L. V. Dupart all worked as shoemakers—a profession shoe historian June Swann called "the gentle craft." Swann also noted that shoemakers were "early literates among craftsmen and also showed a strong interest in politics."[32]

To succeed at shoemaking, Plessy was required to have a keen intellect as well as a certain brawn. Shoemaking primers of the era not only dealt with shoe construction, but also contained detailed anatomical illustrations of the human foot. In the century before Homer and Formidor Dupart began their shoemaking professions, the traditional tools, implements, and processes had not changed much since the fourteenth century. For Homer, the shoemaker's hammer employed the carpentry skills of his natural father's family, while the sewing needles and thread utilized elements of his mother's work as a seamstress. The traditional shoemaker spent his days hunched at a workbench that contained the bevy of tools used in the craft. The tasks could be tiring and monotonous and came with their own set of injuries. Homer's hands risked broken thumbs, scars, and needle pricks. Laslo Vass and Magda Molnar wrote of the typical shoemaker's hands: "marked by cuts from knives and thread, shaped by many thousand of hammer blows and stitches, they bear the traces of their past labor."[33]

In the mid-1800s, traditional shoemaking principles and methods began to feel the hot breath of American industrial capitalism. During Homer and stepbrother Formidor's shoemaking days, the craft had already seen its most prestigious years. In 1846, Elias Howe invented the sewing machine. Then, in 1858, Lyman R. Blake invented a machine that sewed the upper part of the shoe to its sole. One by one, the craftsmen's talents and experience in shoemaking that had protected the steps of mankind for 15,000 years would be taken over by machines. At best, a shoemaker could produce no more than three pairs of shoes in a day. By the 1890s in New Orleans, there were 366 black shoemakers out of a total of 1,469 shoemakers. By 1910, the total number of shoemakers dipped to 422, with sixty-five percent of those being black.[34] "Small shoemaking workshops, unable to compete with the speed of industrial manufacturing or to keep up with falling prices, suffered heavy losses," according to Vass and Molnar.[35] "The shoemaker was downgraded to a mere cobbler who mended shoes."

Plessy the Young Activist

"The shoemaker should look no higher than the sandal," according to Pliny the Elder, Roman writer in the first century A.D. Pliny the Elder was repeating what the Roman artist Apelles once said to a shoemaker who criticized more of Apelles' art than Apelles wanted to hear.[36] Perhaps "look no higher than the sandal" seemed a tempting axiom to question as Homer Plessy contemplated challenging segregation. It would be safer and more secure just to concentrate on shoemaking or some other career and ignore the instinct to get involved. Had anyone mentioned to Homer during shoemaking training that Crispin and

Crispinian, two shoemaking Catholic saints of the third century A.D., wound up being tortured with their own tools and beheaded for standing up for their convictions?[37] Circumstances or temperament, or both, led Homer Plessy on a quest to make more of a mark on society than the quality of its footwear. Homer's activism may have peaked at the Press Street Depot in 1892, but it did not begin there. In 1887, still in his early twenties, he waded into the crisis issue of education reform in New Orleans and became vice president of a fifty-member organization called the Justice, Protective, Educational, and Social Club. This group demanded changes to the school system as they witnessed a large number of children in the city "of school age . . . growing in idleness and ignorance."[38]

If the Civil War and Reconstruction framed Homer Plessy's early life, it was the Hayes-Tilden Compromise and the resultant return to Democrat rule in Louisiana that complicated his young adulthood and thrust him into activism. According to Donald E. Devore and Joseph Logsdon in *Crescent City Schools,* the Democrats in Louisiana increased attacks on traditional Republican initiatives such as universal education. "The educational collapse may have been most dramatic for black New Orleanians," Devore and Logsdon wrote. "But all groups suffered after Democratic Redeemers launched their determined attack on the reforms in public education that had occurred during Reconstruction. . . . By the early 1880's, the school board had to close the schools for several months of the year and even beg Northern foundations for outright charity. It was a humiliating and sad spectacle for an urban system once ranked among the nation's best."[39]

Along with transportation, education has always been a racially charged flash point in civil rights. When Homer was younger and the Republicans held power, the state mandated that schools have free textbooks and be free from racial discrimination, and it devoted five mills of property-tax revenue to adequately fund public education. Additionally, the 1868 Louisiana Constitution's Article 135 declared quite clearly "there shall be no separate school or institution of learning established exclusively for any race by the State of Louisiana." However in 1877, two months after a new school board assumed control as part of the details of the Hayes-Tilden Compromise, members hastened to resegregate the Orleans Parish schools. In 1877, respected Republican activist Aristide Mary, from the Unification Movement, led a large delegation to the school-board meeting to protest. Mary's followers believed that separate schools led to separate trains, bans on interracial marriages, ad infinitum. In addition to a return to segregated public schools, by 1883 the lack of finances closed all the schools for most of the semester and many of the city's youth joined the "ungoverned gamin of the streets," according to the Orleans Parish superintendent. Of course, for those with money, there were 205 private schools.[40]

Plessy's Justice, Protective, Educational, and Social Club published their statement of principles in English and French. As vice president in 1887, Homer ranked second only to club president L. J. Joubert, who later become business manager of the *Crusader* and a member of the Comité des Citoyens. Based in the downtown Creole section of New Orleans below Canal Street, the Justice, Protective, Educational, and Social Club's leaflet entitled "To All Who May Be Concerned" lamented that "our young men and women will grow up in ignorance and immorality, thereby crumbling our societies, and prove themselves unworthy citizens of the State and the United States of America." They further protested that, "Our population of school children exceeds twenty (20) thousand in the Districts. And of the eighteen (18) Public Schools we cannot claim five (5) for one class, of which the accommodations are good." The leaflet further called for action and intellectual attainment:

> We will promote education by all the limiting means in our power; we shall try and collect a Library, to be located and placed at our convenience; and shall make lawful demand to the Government for our share of public education; and ask the same shall be protected and placed in the hands of proper representatives,

proofs against fraud and manipulations, thereby insuring good teachers, a full term and all the necessary articles for the maintenance of schools, which at this moment we have not.

We shall build a Social Circle, where our intellectual welfare, both social and moral, will be promoted by inculcating the best principles and virtues.

We shall unite ourselves and bring our influence to bear in one solid mass, only where we are respected, our rights protected, and our interest and welfare connected.

Then our support will be given by a solid pledge and guarantee in denouncing all treachery, and the protection and rights of Labor.

With these principles in view, we demand the unanimous aid and support of the class and the approbation of all honest, intelligent and just men."[41]

Plessys in Tremé

In 1888, Homer Plessy was working at Patricio Brito's French Quarter shoemaking business on Dumaine Street near North Rampart in the French Quarter.[42] In July 1888, twenty-five-year-old Homer married nineteen-year old Louise Bordenave, the daughter of Oscar Bordenave and Madonna Labranche.[43] Fr. Joseph Subileau, the bearded French-born pastor of St. Augustine's Church, performed the ceremony.[44] Plessy's employer, Patricio Brito, served as witness. In 1889, Homer and Louise moved to Faubourg Tremé, just north of the French Quarter. Today, the Tremé area is known for its brass bands, second-line funerals, and social and pleasure clubs. In Plessy's era, Tremé also bubbled with diversity, culture, politics, and music. Developed in 1812, many free people of color settled there following migrations from Haiti and Cuba. Down the street from the Plessys' home, the Ida Club, on North Claiborne between Dumaine and St. Ann Streets, advanced music, literature, and the drama. Grand-dancing festivals—given by benevolent and social organizations such as the Big Three Social Club or a "committee of gentlemen"—raised money to benefit widows or improve libraries. Social and benevolent clubs met monthly at

Economy Hall, Hope Hall, and Congregation Hall (where the Comité des Citoyens would hold their protests and fund-raising rallies). Musicians such as Professor Moret, Tio and Doublet, and the Onward String Band performed at these same halls on weekends.[45] And according to the authors of *New Orleans Architecture Volume VI: Faubourg Tremé and the Bayou Road,* "A roster of the names of musicians who played in New Orleans Dixieland, brass, and jazz bands between 1880 and 1915 indicates that well over half lived in the creole suburbs, primarily Faubourg Tremé."[46]

The Plessys' strip of Faubourg Tremé was brick-paved North Claiborne Avenue near Bayou Road—a ridge that Native Americans once used to access a waterway named Bayou St. John, which flowed into Lake Pontchartrain. Homer and Louise rented a recently built shotgun-double-styled house at 1108 North Claiborne, between Hospital (now Governor Nicholls) and Ursulines Avenue.[47] Still a predominant housing style in New Orleans, shotgun houses were characterized by rooms lined one behind another, with transom windows and high ceilings. One version of the origin of the shotgun house has it receiving its name because one could theoretically fire a blast through open doorways from the front of the house through the back without hitting anything. Shotgun houses allowed more airflow during the sticky New Orleans summers. Outside of Homer and Louise's front door, every four minutes, mule-powered yellow streetcars of the Canal and Claiborne line clopped by en route to open-air fruit and vegetable markets at St. Bernard Circle, about a half-mile downriver from the Plessys' house.[48] Outside Homer and Louise's bedroom window, Congregation Hall hosted Saturday-night grand-dancing festivals where New Orleanians swayed to the sounds of Professor Joseph A. Moret's String Band. Right across Claiborne and down the Bayou Road stood the Bayou Road Boys School (colored). Plessy's walks home from Patricio Brito's shoe shop took him down the cobblestones of Ursulines Street, past a lumberyard, stables, corner grocery stores with second-story residences, and Economy Hall, where Louis Armstrong would later trumpet New Orleans music with crafted abandon.[49] In Tremé, townhouses with wrought-iron second-story balconies, and villas with stately center halls, stood next to petite plastered-brick Creole cottages and former slave quarters that were converted into backyard apartments.

While Homer Plessy was a native-born American citizen who registered to vote in the Sixth Ward's Third Precinct, his fellow voters and neighbors were as varied as the neighborhood's architecture.[50] Black and white native New Orleanians lived side by side with immigrants from Germany, Mexico, West Indies, Scotland, and France. Scotland native Robert Morial lived on the other side of Congregation Hall. Further down the block, at 1122 North Claiborne, was a black barber. Many of Plessy's neighbors still practiced the trades that built New Orleans and kept this weather-beaten city afloat. Occupations of Plessy's neighbors included carpenters, a physician, a grocer, a baker, masons, laborers, slaters, clerks, cigar makers, a blacksmith, and, this being New Orleans, a bartender. Integrated though it was, Homer and Louise's neighborhood witnessed its share of deplorable ethnic hatred. At the edge of Tremé stood Congo Square and the imposing Orleans Parish Prison, which would be the site of the shooting and lynching of eleven Italian immigrants in 1891. To the other side of Parish Prison stood the Tremé market, St. Louis Cemetery #1, and the sporting houses of the City Commons, an area that became Storyville, the nation's first red-light district. Beyond the City Commons, toward Lake Pontchartrain, St. Louis Cemetery #2 enclosed the burial spot for Marie C. Couvent and other notable people of color.

It was 1890 when the Louisiana legislature voted on a law that separated people by race on railroad trains. After a lifetime of relative freedom from state-mandated segregation, the C for colored was once again being suggested. Homer Plessy spent the first half of his life exercising the newfound rights that were denied his parents. He would spend the 1890s trying to keep those rights. At the beginning of the last decade of the nineteenth century, Homer was not even thirty years old. Still, the future of civil rights in America would ride on his day in court.

CHAPTER 2

John Howard Ferguson

At half-past-ten in the office lately occupied by Judge Marr, in the presence of Judge J. O. Baker, District Attorney Butler and Assistant District Attorney Adams, Mr. Robert C. Upton administered to Hon. John H. Ferguson the oath of office as judge of a criminal district court.

—*New Orleans Daily Picayune*, July 6, 1892

The man whose name followed Plessy's throughout American history was born in Massachusetts in the late 1830s. Unlike Homer Plessy's Louisiana, which was purchased from France in 1803, John Howard Ferguson's Massachusetts played a crucial role in actually creating and defining the United States of America. Massachusetts's residents—white and black—lived and died for the young republic's continued existence and ideals. Massachusetts was also a one-time home to half of the eight Supreme Court justices that ruled on Homer Plessy's case.[1] Like South Louisiana, Massachusetts thrived as a watery world, containing over four thousand miles of rivers and over one thousand lakes and ponds. Lighthouses along its eastern shore have long guided the way for fishing vessels and other boats seeking a snug harbor along its nearly two thousand miles of ocean shoreline.[2] Moving westward, the Atlantic's rocky shores and beaches transform into rolling hills and valleys. Massachusetts once stood at the center of a vast whaling industry that brought fortunes to ship captains and inspiration to writers such as Herman Melville, who penned the classic *Moby Dick*. In 1620, the Pilgrims arrived from Europe at Massachusetts's Plymouth Rock. Ten years later, the Puritans followed and established the town of Boston. The Puritans held a stringent ethic that widely influenced early American institutions.

Massachusetts led the charge in the War for Independence. Framingham native and former slave Crispus Attucks became the first martyr in the American Revolution at the Boston Massacre. In addition to its American Revolution legacy, the Commonwealth of Massachusetts spawned numerous American literary figures, politicians, and forward thinkers. There was Phillis Wheatley, who was born in 1753 in Senegal, brought to America as a slave at the age of seven, raised in Boston by the Wheatley family, and achieved prominence as America's first black female poet of note. William Lloyd Garrison became one of the country's pioneer abolitionists. Tousled native son Henry David Thoreau's *On the Duty of Civil Disobedience* fueled civil-rights movements well into the twentieth century. Author Albert J. Von Frank stated: "Massachusetts was not just any state, but arguably the home of anti-slavery and the capital of culture in the North."[3]

While different from Plessy's Louisiana, the problem of race also infused Massachusetts. As ground zero for America's revolution, Ferguson's Massachusetts emerged as an early passionate opponent of slavery. The ignoble institution upbraided the Commonwealth's religious and political underpinnings and only rarely did a Massachusetts jury side with slave owners. Article 1 of the Massachusetts 1780 Constitution declared that "all men are born free and equal, and have certain natural, essential, and unalienable rights." It took a ruling in a 1783 case called the Quock Walker Case—*Commonwealth v. Jennison*—to give it meaning. The chief justice of the Massachusetts Supreme Court, William Cushing, lent judicial expression to the Preamble's words on behalf of escaped slave Quock Walker, whose master wanted to reclaim him as bondage:

> Whatever sentiments have formerly prevailed in this particular or slid in upon us by the example of others, a different idea has taken place with the people of America, more favorable to

the natural rights of mankind, and to that natural, innate desire of Liberty, with which Heaven (without regard to color, complexion, or shape of noses-features) has inspired all the human race. And upon this ground our Constitution of Government, by which the people of this Commonwealth have solemnly bound themselves, sets out with declaring that all men are born free and equal—and that every subject is entitled to liberty, and to have it guarded by the laws, as well as life and property—and in short is totally repugnant to the idea of being born slaves."[4]

In 1790, Massachusetts reported zero slaves.[5]

Born in Martha's Vineyard

John Ferguson was born in 1838 on the island of Martha's Vineyard.[6] Now known as a New England getaway, this island achieved prominence in the 1800s for its view of the fleets of whaling ships that charged headlong into icy-rough Atlantic seas scouring the area for whales, harpooning them, and bringing their meat back to shore. John Ferguson's father made his living as a one of the many shipmasters of the area—an occupation that led to wealth for many New England seamen. Today, many of the streets and landmarks of Martha's Vineyard take their name from these ship captains in the old towns of Edgartown, Vineyard Haven, and Chilmark. As in Puritan Boston, an ethic of temperance prevailed in Ferguson's place of birth, which he embraced throughout his life. Forbearance emerged as a constant theme. One 1847 article in the island's newspaper, the *Vineyard Gazette*, entitled "Temperance" touted the advantages of water over wine at dinner, stating, "the use of Cider, as a drink, is considered highly deleterious to the morals of man" and "nothing but water is needed for the use of man. It will preserve the strong man's strength and the fair woman's beauty."[7]

In the late 1850s, shortly after turning twenty-one, John Ferguson began the study of the law in Boston. Called the Athens of America, Boston enveloped Ferguson in its intellectually stimulating and historically enlightening climate. As a law student, the young Mr. Ferguson resided at Samuel J. Taft's Boarding House at 93 Summer Street. He studied four blocks away in the offices of Benjamin Franklin Hallett at 33 School Street in Room 11 of the Niles Block Building, next door to Boston's city hall.[8] John Ferguson must have been wide-eyed as he walked Boston's streets, past historic sites and buildings that marked the Revolution's beginnings. If Massachusetts gave birth to visionary people, Boston nurtured them. How must it have felt to study the American constitutional and legal system in a city where dreams of individual freedoms had turned that city's streets bloody? What better locale to hone his oratorical skills than in the capital of free speech? There were the graveyards, churches, and meeting halls that found strength and prominence during the early struggles for liberties codified in the Bill of Rights. On Ferguson's walks home from school, he passed the Old South Meeting House at the corner of Washington and Milk Streets, where the Sons of Liberty gathered in 1773 to start the Boston Tea Party and where slave and poet Phillis Wheatley attended church. Not too far away, the Old North Church of the "one by land, two by sea" fame held the story of Paul Revere's famous ride. On nearby Tremont Street, John Ferguson could wander through the Granary Burial Grounds Cemetery and contemplate the spirits of Paul Revere, Crispus Attucks, Samuel Adams, and other eighteenth-century American patriots who took their

John H. Ferguson (Courtesy *Daily Picayune*)

final rest there. A few blocks from his place of study, Ferguson could sit in one of the benches at Faneuil Hall. Dubbed the Cradle of Liberty, this meeting hall echoed the orations of Pres. George Washington, Frederick Douglass, William Lloyd Garrison, and even Ferguson's teacher and mentor, Benjamin Hallett.[9]

Under the Tutelage of Benjamin Franklin Hallett

Benjamin Franklin Hallett was a major national Democratic Party powerbroker. When Ferguson began his studies, sixty-six-year-old Hallett had already lived a full life as a journalist, ideologue, lawyer, temperance advocate, emancipationist, politician, and United States attorney—and was now a mentor to ambitious law students such as John Ferguson.[10] Like Ferguson's father, Hallett's father was also a shipmaster. In his early years, the younger Hallett was a firebrand editorial writer for the *Boston Advertiser* before becoming editor of the *Boston Daily Advocate,* an Anti-Masonic journal. As a lawyer, the Brown University graduate argued for individual rights, espoused suffrage, and published *Rights of the Marsaplee Indians* and *The Right of the People to Establish Forms of Government.*[11] In 1837, Hallett participated in a meeting at Faneuil Hall to protest the murder of Elijah P. Lovejoy. Lovejoy was an Illinois abolitionist newspaper editor who was killed as he tried to prevent his opponents from throwing his printing press into the Mississippi River.[12] When the *Boston Daily Advocate* merged with the *Boston Post,* Hallett became the head of New England's foremost Democratic newspaper. In 1849, he argued before the Supreme Court in the case of *Luther v. Borden* in support of Rhode Island's Dorr's Rebellion. As a frequent delegate to Democratic Party conventions, Hallett rose to the position of chairman of the National Democratic Committee. In the late 1840s, he convinced Democrats to adopt a platform resolution stating, "We are opposed to slavery in every form and color, and in favor of freedom and free soil wherever man lives throughout God's heritage."[13] He supported Franklin Pierce, who appointed him United States attorney for Boston in 1853. He also supported James Buchanan—the *Dred Scott Decision* president. Hallett also authored the 1856 platform for the Democratic Convention.

Benjamin Hallett's transition from visionary to politician ensnarled him in the issue of race during a case similar to that which John Ferguson would face in the Plessy case. In the 1850s, Hallett's quandary came in the person of Anthony Burns—a victim of the Fugitive Slave Act, which was enacted as part of the 1850 compromise to hold the North and South together. Contrary to the law's intention, the Fugitive Slave Act's application drove even further the wedge between abolitionists and supporters of slavery. Under the Fugitive Slave Act, persons suspected of being escapees could be taken away, sent before a federal government commission, and returned to the South based simply on the word of a claimant. It even *required* ordinary citizens to assist the government in rounding up fugitive slaves. For the alleged slave, there would be no trial by jury—only the judgment of special federal commissioners who, incidentally, received five dollars extra if they returned the accused to the claimant. Hallett's son was one of those commissioners.

But many in Massachusetts viewed their state as the birthplace of freedom. The case of Anthony Burns—a stowaway in his early twenties seeking an end to his slavery in Richmond—stoked rage among abolitionists. For them, the thought of sending a man back into slavery desecrated the city's very heritage. The fact that the United States government—of "all men are created equal"—assisted the slave catchers infuriated them. And the fact that the act could be applied against the wishes of the Commonwealth turned moderates into militants. The abolitionist Vigilance Committee held an emotional meeting at Faneuil Hall then stormed the jail, determined to rescue Anthony Burns by force. In the ensuing melee, a policeman was shot.

Whatever Benjamin Hallett's personal feelings, as United States district attorney, the law and Democratic Party politics pressured him to support those who would repatriate Burns back to slavery. As the author of Democratic national platforms, Hallett had to be able to sell the Democratic Party to the planter class in the South and keep the coalition of Southern and Northern Democrats from dissolution. He had once championed the cause of emancipation but he now was part and parcel of the Democratic Party, including their Southern brethren. And, in the end, Hallett participated in the chain of events that sent a twenty-two-year-old young man back to slavery. Albert J. Von Frank wrote, in *The Trials of Anthony Burns,* "Hallett seemed to his contemporaries to have exchanged the fire of his youthful radicalism for the dubious security of political advancement."[14]

In the end, neither the militant vigilantes nor the pacifist abolitionists could save Anthony Burns. Pres. Franklin Pierce dispatched troops to Boston to seize Burns and return him to his former life of slavery in Virginia. According to the book *Holy Warriors,* the soldiers crooned "Carry Me Back to Old Virginia" as they brought Burns through the phalanx of troops that led to the wharf. According to James Brewer Stewart, this civil-rights case sparked outrage in the Boston community and added to tensions that would lead to the Civil War:

> Stark in its drama and frightening in its implications, the sight of armed federal troops occupying the streets of Boston against its own "freedom-loving" citizens greatly intensified long-accumulating fears of the "slave power's" intentions. [President] Pierce's actions . . . suggested strongly that the office of the President itself, the army he commanded, the powers of executive order and veto he enjoyed, and the party system that supported him, had all been placed at the exclusive disposal of the planter class. Northerners in both major parties wondered increasingly whether any civil liberties remained under firm guarantee, or whether republican freedom existed at all apart from the generosity of the slaveholders. Militants like [Theodore] Parker challenged their audiences: "We are the vassals of Virginia. It reaches its arm over the graves of our mothers, it kidnaps men in the city of Puritans, over the graves of Samuel Adams and John Hancock."[15]

On the Fourth of July, 1854, in Framingham, Massachusetts,

the hometown of Revolutionary War martyr Crispus Attucks, an exasperated Henry David Thoreau condemned men such as Hallett, whom he viewed as complicit in Anthony Burns' repatriation: "The judges and lawyers . . . and all men of expediency, try this case by a very low and incompetent standard," Thoreau stated. "They consider, not whether the Fugitive Slave Law is right, but whether it is what they call constitutional. . . . They persist in being the servants of the worst of men, and not the servants of humanity."[16]

But with the outbreak of the Civil War, Boston witnessed political affiliation give way to staunch Unionism. Hallett and other Democrats staunchly supported the Union, as did William Lloyd Garrison and many of the abolitionists.[17] Hallet even signed a letter to raise money for Unionists in Tennessee under attack by secessionists.[18] Boston newspapers daily called on volunteers, gave updates of campaigns and casualty figures, reported on pro-Union meetings at Faneuil Hall, and oftentimes published news items from New Orleans newspapers—such as the *Era* and the *New Orleans Tribune*—on the movement of troops and the price of cotton. Newspapers referred to the Confederate States of America as rebels and traitors and the Civil War as a rebellion. Benjamin Franklin Hallett called for an end to party politics: "Let Massachusetts be a unit in supporting the Union. And let there be no division as to men in this election."[19]

Benjamin Hallett died on September 30, 1862. John Ferguson had completed his course of study, and in 1863, his lawyer's shingle now hung at an office at 20 Court Street, not far away from where Hallett's office stood.[20] He also worked as a counselor in the partnership of Fitz and Ferguson, with Daniel F. Fitz. Ferguson remained in Boston as the Emancipation Proclamation took effect, Jefferson Davis surrendered at Appomattox, and grief and uncertainty followed President Lincoln's assassination. It was Massachusetts's regiments that had occupied New Orleans during the Civil War and two Massachusetts residents—Nathaniel Banks and Benjamin Butler—had governed the occupation.

Ferguson learned from returning soldiers of the vast opportunities in the defeated South. To the victors went the spoils. Eager for new adventure, Ferguson left Boston for a new life in an old city.

South to New Orleans

When John Ferguson arrived in New Orleans, the city was under Federal occupation. Homer Plessy was but a toddler. Confederate sympathizers looked upon men such as Ferguson as carpetbaggers, Northerners who "came in droves to take possession of commerce and politics, to whatever extent it was possible."[21] John Ferguson married into the family of an outspoken New Orleans Unionist, Thomas J. Earhart, who strongly denounced slavery and the Confederacy. "Hereafter," Earhart declared at an 1863 Canal Street rally of the Loyal National League of Louisiana, "man is man, be the shade of his skin white, green, or black." In April 1863, Earhart addressed Unionists at New Orleans' Lyceum Hall to layout plans for a civil government. Earhart wanted Louisiana to be a free state with a constitution that did not "recognize and protect slavery."[22] Later that year, the Workingmen's Union National League of Louisiana selected Earhart as a delegate to the National Convention of the Friends of Freedom.[23] In October 1865, Earhart was among a group of sixty attorneys who took the congressional loyalty oath to the Union, attesting that he never took up arms against the Union and "pledged to defend the Constitution of the United States against all enemies, domestic and foreign."[24] In July 1866, John Ferguson married Earhart's daughter, Virginia. Ferguson began his law practice shortly thereafter, working at the Morris Building in the uptown commercial district of New Orleans.

New Orleans of the 1860s was a world apart from Ferguson's Boston. Boston was born under the king of England, New Orleans the king of France. When Boston began America's revolution against Britain, New Orleans was then a colony of

the Spanish crown. Massachusetts had been a leader in indus-
trialization; New Orleans had been "the least industrial of the
large cities of the nation."[25] Boston was north; New Orleans
was geographically deep south and culturally diverse. Boston
had been virtually free of slavery for over seventy years, New
Orleans only for a moment. Boston was Protestant, New
Orleans Catholic. Boston's character invoked Puritanism with
solemn observance of Sunday Sabbaths. Baptist Ferguson's
new city contained little evidence of the Puritan ethic to which
he had been accustomed. "Drinking was widespread, prostitu-
tion was accepted and even advertised, and gambling was a way
of life."[26] Ferguson must have shared the sentiments of an earlier, fellow New England traveler, Christian Schultz, who, after
taking a jaunt around the city in the years following the 1803
Louisiana Purchase, chronicled:

> Our Yankees feel not a little foolish upon their first arrival in
> this city, where the manners and amusements are so very differ-
> ent from their own. Their delicacy is first offended, at finding
> most of the billiard tables placed in the front room on the lower
> floor, with all the doors and windows . . . entirely subject to the
> view of every passenger in the street. Yet, this is but a trifle, in
> comparison to the shock their piety receives on the first Sunday
> morning after their arrival, by finding these tables surrounded
> by a much larger company, and the stroke of the cue and mace
> resounding from one end of the city to another. . . . I heard a
> gentleman from the eastward exclaim on returning from a Sun-
> day tour through the city, "O where are our selectmen of
> Salem?"[27]

In New Orleans, Ferguson set up shop as a civil lawyer. He
worked in the city's warehouse district but moved quickly to
distance his family life from the turmoil of post-Civil War New
Orleans. Ferguson built a cottage outside the city limits in an
upriver town called Burtheville and became one of the first
settlers on Henry Clay Street—not far from the Mississippi
River. There, John and Virginia raised three children: Walter,
Milo, and Donald Ferguson. As fate would have it, New
Orleans annexed Burtheville in 1870 as its Fourteenth Ward.

Although he avoided the city's intricate webs of social circles, Ferguson did join the Knights of Pythias—a benevolent organization chartered by Congress in 1864, during the Lincoln presidency. Abraham Lincoln called the Knights of Pythias "one of the best agencies conceived for the upholding of government, honoring the flag, for the reuniting of our brethren of the North and of the South, for teaching the people to love one another, and portraying the sanctity of the home and loved ones."[28] On Sundays, Ferguson worshiped at the nearby St. Charles Avenue Christian Church. His original cottage still stands at 1500 Henry Clay.[29]

ıdge Ferguson's former cottage in uptown New Orleans at 1500 Henry Clay

1877: Ferguson as Legislator

> I, Francis T. Nicholls, Governor of the State of Louisiana,
> have thought proper to issue my proclamation, convening the
> General Assembly of this State to meet in extra session at Odd
> Fellows' Hall, in the city of New Orleans, on Friday the second
> day of March, A. D., 1877 at 12 o'clock m.[30]

With this statement, the former Confederate general Francis
T. Nicholls assumed control of Louisiana. His governorship
came as the result of the Hayes-Tilden Compromise of 1876-77.
Thus began Ferguson's political alliance with Louisiana
Democrats. An anathema for Homer Plessy and his compatriots in the Comité des Citoyens, the Hayes-Tilden Compromise
presented an opportunity for John Ferguson. The Nicholls legislature, backed by a militia called the White League, allowed
Louisiana to become one of three Southern states that established a competing legislature and negotiated for power with
Congress. One of the Nicholls legislature's first orders of business was to purge members who did not follow their lead. On
the second day of the conference, a resolution passed stating,
"Every member of this House whose name is regularly on the
roll, who, by Tuesday, sixth March, 1877, does not answer roll
call, take the oath required by the constitution and laws as a
member, and take and occupy his seat on the floor as a regularly sitting member, shall then and there, on Tuesday the
sixth of March, 1877, by twelve meridian of said day . . . be regularly proceeded against for expulsion or vacancy, with a view
of having a new election ordered."[31]

Ferguson's seat in Nicholls' rival legislature came at the
expense of uptown black representative Aristide Dejoie, who
the Nicholls forces expelled on the second day of the session.
The chairman of the Committee on Elections and Qualifications
presented the following report on March 5, 1877, installing
thirty-nine-year-old Ferguson as a representative of uptown New
Orleans: "To the Honorable Speaker and Members: The Committee on Elections and Qualifications, to whom was referred

the contestation of J. H. Ferguson vs. A. Dejoie for a seat in this House, respectfully report that . . . contestant, J. H. Ferguson, is legally and justly entitled to a seat in this House, as a Representative of the Thirteenth, Fourteenth, Sixteenth and Seventeenth wards, parish of Orleans. . . . Messrs. Sartain and Ferguson presented themselves to the Speaker's stand, took the constitutional oath of office and were seated as Representatives of their respective parishes."[32]

It could be that having Yankee John Ferguson as a representative put a more diverse spin on a legislative body that Governor Nicholls pledged would respect the rights of all citizens. Ferguson's legislative initiatives reflected a bend toward efficiency, reform, procedure, and constituent needs rather than any ideological or racial agenda.[33] He served out the 1877 session introducing bills to establish a justice's court in Carrolton, exempt his district from a prohibition of slaughterhouses, and streamline legal proceedings. Similar to Hallett's early defenses of individual rights, Ferguson proposed a procedure that would allow defendants to speak on their own behalfs at trial. His measure was narrowly defeated but later adopted. After Aristide Dejoie regained his seat in 1878, Ferguson returned to his civil-law practice.

Ferguson on the Bench

In 1891, John Ferguson entered the criminal-attorney arena as defense attorney, along with F. Armant, for Charles Paterno, an Italian man (who never came to trial) accused in the assassination of New Orleans police chief David Hennessy.[34] By 1892, Ferguson had been a practicing Louisiana lawyer for almost twenty-five years. Throughout his life, Ferguson had always found himself under the umbrella of powerful and noted men—Benjamin Hallett in Boston, Thomas J. Earhart in his early New Orleans days, and Francis T. Nicholls in 1876. During the 1892 elections, Ferguson traveled to twenty different Louisiana parishes to speak in support of state senator

Murphy Foster's successful gubernatorial campaign and against the Louisiana Lottery Company.[35] Though his brother-in-law Ferdinand Earhart received an 1890 appointment as New Orleans United States attorney from Republican president Benjamin Harrison, Ferguson attached his political career to the Democratic coattails of former governor Nicholls and Gov. Murphy J. Foster. And on June 30, 1892, Governor Foster tapped Ferguson for a judgeship vacancy in Orleans Parish Section A. Ferguson was to fill the term of Robert H. Marr, who disappeared under mysterious circumstances on Election Day in May 1892. Section A was one of only two criminal courts in Orleans Parish and was established by the 1879 Constitutional Convention.[36]

The Criminal Courts Building where Ferguson held court was located at the corner of Lafayette and Camp Streets in uptown New Orleans. It was from the balcony of this building—then called St. Patrick's Hall—that Francis T. Nicholls was inaugurated as governor in 1877. The surrounding area was not unlike the Boston setting where Ferguson first studied law. With a statue of Benjamin Franklin in the center, Lafayette Square housed a busy and eclectic mix of commercial, educational, governmental, and professional offices. Across from Ferguson's court stood Gallier Hall—New Orleans' seat of government. (The location of the city's seat of government in the Uptown sector of New Orleans also displayed the declining role of Creole leaders in New Orleans.) The casket of the former Confederate president, Jefferson Davis, once laid in state at Gallier Hall as did that of assassinated police chief David Hennessy. To the left of Ferguson's court building, on South Street, stood the First Presbyterian Church, with its spire reaching to the heavens. The square also housed hook-and-ladder companies, a carriage shop, a soda-water factory, and the First District court and police station.

Ferguson's swearing-in took place on July 5, 1892, less than a month after Homer Plessy's attempt to ride the train. Ferguson's ascent to judge of Section A also installed him as the senior criminal-court judge for the four remaining years of Judge Marr's term. As part of the first day's proceedings, district attorney Charles A. Butler presented his commission to Judge Ferguson, as did Butler's assistant district attorney, Lionel Adams who would prosecute the Plessy case.

As in his legislative days, Ferguson gave no indication of a racial agenda. The man from Martha's Vineyard would make his early reputation as the antigambling judge. Early on, he decided to use the power of his office to inject a strong dose of Massachusetts Puritanism into the city's easy culture. In September, he embarked on what could be considered a Herculean mission to clean New Orleans of gambling. He composed a charge to the grand jury that strongly implied police complicity in, or at least tolerance of, vice as Ferguson took the grand jury on a written, street-by-street account of illegal gambling:

> I desire to bring to your knowledge, as forcibly as possible, that there are numerous gambling houses in the city of New Orleans located in the central or business portion of the city.
>
> To be more specific
>
> On Royal Street between Canal and Customhouse, where there are at least three such houses. Between St. Charles and Carondolet Streets, on Gravier Street, one or more.
>
> On Common Street, between St. Charles and Carondolet streets, and on Canal Street and on other principal thoroughfares, gambling is carried out in all of these places such [games] as dice and roulette, and have been for many years without concealment and in open defiance of the law and those whose business is to suppress it.
>
> In the rear of a barroom and oyster saloon on Dryades Street, between Erato and Thalia streets, a game is operated every Saturday night, where [minors] are allowed to play, in violation of law.
>
> Dice and other gambling games are conducted near the Dryades market in a one story frame building in the rear of the coffee stand. This place is patronized by black and white and minors at least every Saturday and Sunday night.
>
> The question naturally presents itself. Why were the proprietors and others not arrested and dealt with according to law?"[37]

Judge Ferguson then boldly summoned the chief of police

from the station across Lafayette Square to the grand-jury room for answers. The chief left with instructions to "close up all gambling institutions according to law; to arrest all persons found therein, and to seize all paraphernalia which may be used in playing such games." The chief dutifully sent a copy of the grand-jury report to the district commanders.

Oyez, oyez, oyez. The court of Judge Ferguson was now in session.

CHAPTER 3

Albion W. Tourgee

TO THE PRESIDENT

Sir, We, the undersigned citizens of the United States, being actuated by none other than patriotic motives, do respectfully suggest to you the name of ALBION W. TOURGEE of Mayville, New York, for consideration in the election of a successor to the late Justice Lamar upon the Bench of the United States Supreme Court.

Judge Tourgee's ripe scholarship, large experience of men and affairs, legal acumen and ability as a Constitutional lawyer eminently qualify him for the discharge of the duties as a Justice of the Supreme Court.

—A group of twenty Tourgee supporters
writing to President Cleveland in an unsuccessful effort
to secure an appointment of Albion W. Tourgee
to the United States Supreme Court on January 27, 1893[1]

Plessy and Ferguson were local figures. The case, however, would attract a prominent national figure before the Supreme Court— that being Plessy's lawyer. Ohio native Albion W. Tourgee was a Union soldier, Reconstruction-era North Carolina judge, and noted and perennially controversial nineteenth-century writer and social commentator. An advisor and critic to American presidents, Tourgee had been an outspoken supporter of the cause of black equality. In *Carpetbagger's Crusade,* biographer Otto H. Olsen described Tourgee as "the nation's most persistent and outspoken white champion of racial justice during the last decades of the nineteenth century."[2] Tourgee intersected with the Comité des Citoyens in the passage of the Separate Car Act of 1890 but more importantly in their declaration in the *Crusader* to challenge the law in court. A month after the Comité des Citoyens made known its intentions to challenge segregation, Tourgee offered his services to represent them.

Albion Tourgee's America was seen through a different prism than that of Plessy or Ferguson. Tourgee may have obtained his sympathy for the downtrodden through the plight of his ancestors, who were persecuted based on religion rather than ethnicity. He was a descendant of the Huguenots, French Protestants violently suppressed by the Catholic Church and the French crown in the sixteenth, seventeenth, and eighteenth centuries. Between the years 1618 and 1725, some five thousand to seven thousand Huguenot refugees arrived in New England, including the Tourgees and the family of Paul Revere, whose family name was actually the French *Rivoire*. The first Tourgees eventually settled in Kingston, Rhode Island and subsequently moved to Framingham, Massachusetts, then to Lee, Massachusetts, in the Berkshire mountains. There, Albion's father, Valentine Tourgee, Jr., met and wed Louise Winegar, a descendant of the *Mayflower* pilgrims. The couple moved to Williamsfield in Ashtabula County, Ohio, where Albion Winegar Tourgee (Toor-zhay) was born on May 2, 1838.

The life of Albion Tourgee experienced many ups, downs, dramas, and near-death situations that would have waylaid the spirit of a less-driven soul. The product of a strict Methodist upbringing, Tourgee's father loved argument and debate, engaging Albion in polemics from his boyhood. Albion's mother died when he was only four years old. Valentine remarried in 1847 then reconstituted the Tourgee clan forty miles north of Williamsfield in Kingsville, Ohio, putting them closer to the Lake Erie coastline. Albion grew to be intellectually insatiable, rebellious, righteous, and persistent—a person seemingly oblivious to scorn and able to disburse it with equal force. "To be in the world, yet not of it was not for him," according to Roy F. Dibble in his 1921 biography entitled *Albion W. Tourgee*. "He hated with perfect hatred anything that savored of dandyism or of a dilettante attitude toward life, and attacked it with unrelenting acerbity."[3] Early on, a farm accident left him blind in one eye. At age fourteen, disagreements with his stepmother spurred him to run away from home. He made his way to Lee, Massachusetts, where he lived with maternal relatives for two years. In the industrial town of Lee, near the robust Berkshire mountains, Albion the farm boy indulged his thirst for reading and further cultivated his taste for the literary. At sixteen, he returned home to Kingsville, Ohio, attended Kingsville Academy, taught at an elementary school, and met his lifelong partner—the talented and sociable Emma Kilbourne, a descendant of the Tories from New England. It was Emma Kilbourne who sensitized Albion to the evils of slavery.

Albion Winegar Tourgee (Courtesy Smithsonian/ Culver Pictures)

For Union Suffer, Toil, or Die

In the fall of 1859, at age twenty-one, Albion Tourgee enrolled in the University of Rochester. There, he participated in debates, mastered the study of logic and language, and immersed himself in poetry and Shakespeare. On the eve of the Civil War, in October 1860, Tourgee captained the Rochester Wide Awake Club, a campus organization that promoted the ideals of Abraham Lincoln's Republican Party. Albion Tourgee belonged to the same Civil War generation of John Ferguson—they were born in the same year. While Ferguson spent the Civil War in Boston, Tourgee enlisted in the Twenty-seventh New York Volunteers. Within two months, he found himself as part of an attack force in the ill-fated July 1861 Battle of Bull Run near Manassas in northern Virginia. As the Union army beat a hasty retreat to Washington, DC, a wagon wheel struck Tourgee at full force, sending him into a coma. When he recovered, he found his legs paralyzed and the army declared him unfit for military service. Unable to walk, apparently for life, he returned to Ashtabula County and Emma Kilbourne.

With treatment by a back specialist in Cleveland, Ohio, however, Tourgee recovered use of his legs but pain remained as a lifelong reminder of his military duty. While walking on crutches, he began the study of law at the firm of Sherman and Farmer in Ashtabula, Ohio, and in the spring of 1862, he started recovering the full use of his legs. Thus rehabilitated, Tourgee rejoined the Union army in July 1862 to the chagrin of Emma Kilbourne. As a first lieutenant in Company G of the 105th Ohio Volunteers, he marched back off to war. He took a shell to his hip at the Battle of Perryville, served four months as a prisoner of war at three Confederate prison camps, and engaged in battles in Kentucky, Georgia, and Tennessee at Tullahoma, Chickamauga, Chattanooga, Lookout Mountain, and Missionary Ridge. "Let Union be your battle cry. / For Union suffer, toil, or die," he wrote.[4]

Tourgee's army service galvanized his religious faith and his sympathy for the enslaved. According to Otto H. Olsen, "While Tourgee was recovering from the injuries received at Bull Run, anti-slavery sentiments pervaded his poetry and oratory."[5] Tourgee's writings recalled escaped slaves who furnished Union troops with water and other supplies on Union "hell marches" to Southern battlefields. In constant disputes with superiors, Tourgee once unsuccessfully applied for command of a black regiment. In September 1862, he was placed under arrest after he refused to "surrender a colored man who had saved [his] company."[6] Tourgee came to view the Civil War as a fight not only to save the Union, but also for the higher cause of racial equality. "I don't care a rag for the Union as it was," he wrote. "I want and fight for the Union better than it was."[7] Tourgee's regiment once skirmished with Tennessee men at bayonet point to prevent them from claiming escaped slaves. He and Emma Kilbourne married on May 14, 1863. In May 1864, he was admitted to the bar in Ohio and began working for Sherman and Farmer's law firm. In the fall of 1864, at age twenty-six, Albion and Emma settled in Erie, Pennsylvania, where he became principal of Erie Academy.

In 1865, after the last shot had been fired in the Civil War, just as John Ferguson and thousands of Northern carpetbaggers had done, the Tourgees ventured to the defeated Confederate states for opportunities in the South. The Tourgees decided on Greensboro, North Carolina, and established a botanical nursery business. But adverse treatment of Southern Unionists and blacks pulled Albion Tourgee into the simmering politics of this troubled region. Theodore L. Gross, who authored a literary biography named *Albion W. Tourgee* in 1963, asserted that Tourgee "established himself as one of the most controversial figures ever to live in North Carolina—a carpet-bag-lawyer who intended to help the freedmen obtain justice in the South."[8]

As editor of the *Union Register* newspaper in Greensboro in 1867, Albion Tourgee increased his involvement in the South's

political future. Idealistically, Tourgee and many other Northerners thought that the South would emulate the North in a
relatively short period of time. Tourgee opposed the presidential plan of reconciliation between Union and Confederacy
that favored the antebellum ruling hierarchies of the South.
He preferred plans that uplifted the political status of landless
whites while educating blacks and moving them to citizenship.
In the 1868 North Carolina Constitutional Convention,
Tourgee authored planks that eliminated property requirements for voting and holding office. Historian George M.
Fredrickson wrote in 1966 that Tourgee "wished to eradicate
caste and class prerogatives by . . . improving public education
. . . and extending democratic procedures to include direct
election of judges and local officials. . . . His proposals reveal . . .
that he was as much concerned with lower-class whites as with
the Negroes."[9]

As a politician, Tourgee won a six-year term as a superior-
court judge. He was loved and loathed for his willingness to
lampoon the Southern-plantation way of life and challenge
the emerging violent power of the Ku Klux Klan. According to
Theodore L. Gross, "Because of his ceaseless preference for
the Negro and condemnation of the South in toto . . . attempts
were made to take his life and by 1870 the Klan was constantly
following him."[10] Many in North Carolina scorned Tourgee
for his views, intransigence, and attitude toward the Old
South. His self-righteous style and Northern chauvinism made
him a poster child for the stereotypical carpetbagging Yankee.
A North Carolina governor called Tourgee "the meanest Yankee
who ever settled among us."[11] But he engendered admiration
and deep loyalty among those who, heretofore, had few voices
to speak on their behalf. On the Fourth of July, 1867, Tourgee
addressed a group of 1,500 blacks and their supporters at Lin-
colnton, North Carolina, speaking his message that all men
were free and equal.[12] Eventually, he won respect in North Carolina for his competence and fairness on the bench. He also
coauthored a universally praised rewrite of the North Carolina

Civil Code. In 1879, Democrats regained power in North Carolina, and Tourgee and Emma returned to the North to raise their child, Aimee, born to them in North Carolina.

Tourgee the Author

While in North Carolina, Albion Tourgee had already begun his career as a writer, having published *'Toinette a Novel* under the pseudonym Henry Churton in 1874. Like Harriet Beecher Stowe with *Uncle Tom's Cabin*, Tourgee employed fictional settings as a conduit to social and political issues. "A novel without a purpose is the counterpart of a man without a purpose," Tourgee stated. "One written for mere amusement may be either good or bad, but at the very best, is only the lowest form of art."[13] In 1879, shortly after leaving North Carolina, *Figs and Thistles* appeared in bookstores, as did his signature novel, *A Fool's Errand*—a semiautobiographical fictionalized account on efforts to change hearts and minds in the South. In Tourgee's writings, fools were those idealists who believed in liberty and equality despite the negativity and protestations of others who thought that people of different classes, races, or regions were incapable of unity or racial progress. According to George M. Fredrickson, *A Fool's Errand* reflected Tourgee's fictionalized look at the nation's attempt to "build a bridge from Negro emancipation to Negro equality," a task that Tourgee relentlessly pursued for most of his adult life.[14] *Bricks without Straw* also succeeded commercially, bringing Tourgee a degree of wealth and exposure.

In 1880, the nonfictional *Invisible Empire* was appended to reprints of *A Fool's Errand*. Tourgee was, perhaps, at his most compelling, politically and historically, in factual works. Instead of couching his points and beliefs in fictional characters, fictional settings, and Southern dialect, *The Invisible Empire* plainly laid out the hard, cold case against the Ku Klux Klan, the facts behind the fictional *A Fool's Errand*. He employed congressional testimony to detail the origins, rise, and modus operandi of the Ku Klux Klan through the words of victims, ex-Klansmen, and other witnesses. In the chapter documenting the Klan's ruthless attacks on black education, Tourgee quoted Caroline Smith a colored woman of Walton County, Georgia: "They went to a colored man, whose son had been teaching school, and took every book they had and threw them into the fire, and said they would dare any other nigger to have a book in his house."[15]

Another chapter, entitled "The New Book of Martyrs," listed page after page of testimony from those who had been what Tourgee called "ku-kluxed." Two examples were "a White man . . . ku-kluxed for having sold a pistol to a negro" and "Abram Coley (colored), fifty-two years old, member of Legislature from Greene, Co., Ga . . . taken out of his night by 60 disguised men, and beaten with sticks and straps until insensible."[16] The Methodists reported, "Not less than twenty churches and school-houses belonging to the Methodist Episcopal Church have been burned in Georgia."[17]

In another chapter, called "Southern Sensibilities," *The Invisible Empire* delved into the deep-seated views about Southern blacks that fueled the Klan. Consider the raw observations of Hon. Henry C. Dibble of 1877 New Orleans, reprinted in *The Invisible Empire:*

> Taught by the laws of caste to look upon himself and his class as alone entitled to exercise the prerogatives of citizenship, he [the Southern White] resented the disposition of the black man to claim his franchise about in the same spirit in which a man will shoot a dog which has climbed upon the table and will not get down.

Also targeted were Northern white sympathizers. Dibble further stated:

> The ostracism of Republicans in business became a tenet of the Democratic party in the South. . . . [Republicans] were guilty of the greatest social offense known in these slave-holding communities; they had affiliated with negroes—had fallen into the caste of Pariahs.[18]

As an energetic writer, Albion Tourgee expounded his views in a wide variety of outlets. He wrote for the *National Anti-Slavery Standard,* the *North American Review,* the *Congregationalist,* and New York Tribune and frequently appeared in newspapers' letters to the editor. He lectured extensively—often dismissing prepared texts for passionate extemporizations. He published over twenty books—nonfiction, fiction, poetry, and even a play based on A *Fool's Errand.*

As one of the few writers of the Reconstruction era who actually lived in the South, Tourgee was called on by American presidents. Former president Ulysses S. Grant even referred to Tourgee's work in a speech, entitled "Why I Am a Republican," on September 28, 1880. "Once started," President Grant foresaw, "the Solid South will go as Kukluxism did before, as is so admirably told by Judge Tourgee in his 'Fool's Errand.' . . . [A] desirable solution can only be attained by the defeat, and continued defeat, of the Democratic party as now constituted."[19] Similarly, Grant's successor, Pres. James A. Garfield, summoned Tourgee to the White House. Commenting on A *Fool's Errand,* President Garfield expressed hope that America would be a "paradise for all such fools."[20] Garfield met for two hours with Tourgee for a perspective of national policy after Reconstruction. "But for the publication of your work, I do not think my election would have been possible," Tourgee quoted Garfield as stating to him.[21] He responded to Garfield's request for guidance with another nonfictional book, though Garfield had then since been assassinated. In *An Appeal to Caesar,* Tourgee outlined a plan for incorporating blacks into citizenship that called for a national education program and a permanent Freedmen's Bureau. Former president Rutherford Hayes also read Tourgee. In his diary, President Hayes wrote, "Finished reading Tourgee's *Murvale Eastman.* It is his best book; puts the question of our time admirably. He has hit the nail on the head. More that is good and less that hurts than in any book I have seen on the question."[22]

At Thorheim in Mayville

In 1881, Albion Tourgee was on a train trip from Pennsylvania to Chicago. At a rest stop in Westfield, in New York's northwestern Chautauqua County, an insistent newspaper boy sold him a local newspaper. An illustration of a house for sale in the neighboring village of Mayville caught Tourgee's eye and he returned for a visit. Tourgee embraced the house and its environs as the perfect writing setting—removed from the day-to-day distracting pulls of cities and the volatility of living amongst the Ku Klux Klan.[23] Located on placid Chautauqua Lake and near Lake Erie, Mayville was only seventy-five miles from his boyhood home of Kingsville and a comfortable 600 miles from his Reconstruction home of Greensboro, North Carolina. A carriage ride or brisk walk away stood the Chautauqua Assembly, or Chautauqua Institute, a religious camp meeting ground that became a center of art, culture, and social debate—a place where Tourgee would often be called on to speak. Tourgee dubbed his new home Thorheim, or Fool's House, after his best-selling novel and his self-proclaimed title as "one of the fools."

Tourgee wrote prolifically during the 1880s. He published *John Eax* and *Mamelon* in 1882 and a newspaper called *Our Continent*. In 1884, Tourgee began writing a column called "A Bystander's Notes" for the *Chicago Inter-Ocean* newspaper. "A Bystander's Notes" kept his views on current events before the public eye. Though mellower, Tourgee remained committed to the "all men are created equal" tenet of the Declaration of Independence and equal-rights clauses of the Fourteenth Amendment. In the 1890 *Murvale Eastman, Christian Socialist*, Tourgee put forth a doctrine of Christian Socialism—combining Christ's teachings with politics and good works, where "all classes and conditions, shall make the welfare of their fellows the first and highest object in life, after their own wants and the comfort of those dependent on them."[24] Historian George M. Fredrickson described Tourgee as a "true believer who did

Tourgee's home in Mayville, New York, which he called Thorheim, or fool's house, after his successful novel *A Fool's Errand*

not shy away from the hard choices which history requires of the faithful."[25] However, by the 1890s, his books sold less, while Southern mistreatment of blacks escalated along with governmental and Northern indifference. "Tourgee . . . was heard by an ever-narrowing circle," Fredrickson noted. Tourgee stood among the old guard of equal-rights advocates—a declining political presence, as time, death, and disinterest decreased their ranks. He continued to write novels but none reached the commercially successful plateau of *A Fool's Errand* and *Bricks without Straw*. According to Theodore L. Gross, his earlier works "proved popular because they were the only complete fictional accounts of Reconstruction until that time. . . . But it was curiosity rather than sympathy that led people to

Books by Albion Tourgee

read Tourgee's best novels. When that interest had been satisfied by subsequent writers—writers who described the South in
a more conciliatory and hence more agreeable fashion—the
general response to Tourgee was one of hostility, or, at best, of
indifference."[26] Tourgee seemed to be evolving into *The Man
Who Outlived Himself* (the title of a later novel). But seen
through a contemporary lens, Tourgee and the Comité des
Citoyens may actually have been before their time as they
sought an interracial grass-roots campaign to protect the rights
of America's black citizenry.

The Comité des Citoyens' opposition to the Separate Car
Act exemplified the issue Tourgee lectured and wrote about—
equality and the rights of citizens. A fight against a segregation
law could be a dead-end journey for him. Then again, it could
be Tourgee's dragon-slayer battle against inequality, one last
stab, and, perhaps, a sweeping victory for the ages. Would he
represent Homer Plessy and the Comité des Citoyens? Of
course he would. Would the Comité des Citoyens approve
Tourgee's involvement? With enthusiasm, they did. For
Tourgee and the Comité des Citoyens, this was the one opportunity for a group of Reconstruction fellows to stop segregation, perhaps the last chance. Tourgee expressed that a
number of Supreme Court justices on the bench in 1890 had
misgivings about the Court's conclusions in previous civil-
rights cases. Therein laid a window of opportunity.

CHAPTER 4

One Country, One People

> That on the 1st day of January, A. D. 1863, all persons held as slaves within any State or designated part of a State the people whereof shall then be in rebellion against the United States shall be then, thenceforward, and forever free.
>
> —Emancipation Proclamation,
> issued by Pres. Abraham Lincoln
> September 22, 1862

> Fellow citizens, this is the first time for eighty seven years that the son of Africa is permitted to join in a public celebration of the Fourth of July. . . . We have passed through trials and persecutions—we have been chained and handcuffed for two hundred and fifty years. . . . Tonight the son of Africa holds his head up to the public. Our country has given us our rights—we have now but to defend them.
>
> —Rev. James Keelan
> Loyal National League of Louisiana rally on Canal Street
> Fourth of July, 1863

The issue that brought Plessy, Tourgee, Ferguson, and the Comité des Citoyens onto the stage of history was racial regulation. During New Orleans' colonial era, it was done through edicts and black codes. In 1724, the French implemented the *Code Noir*—or Black Code. These were the first mandates in Louisiana's colonial history that regulated caste and race. They additionally established guidelines on religion in the colony as well as the manumission, treatment, and punishment of the enslaved population. The Black Code demanded a curious mix of cruelty and compassion in dealing with the colony's

67

enslaved population and those of religions other than Catholic. Articles 1, 2, and 3 respectively expelled Jews from the colony, made religious instruction of slaves mandatory, and prohibited any form of worship other than Roman Catholicism. Article 4 mandated the confiscation by the authorities of any slave who was supervised by someone other than a Catholic, while Article 5 confiscated slaves who were forced to work on Sunday from their owners. Article 10 stated that if a husband was a slave and the wife free, the children would be free. But if the father is free and the mother a slave, the children would bear her condition of servitude. Articles 20 and 21 allowed for slaves "not properly fed, clad, and provided for" or "abandoned" to file complaints. Article 43 forbade selling slave husbands and wives separately. Article 50 allowed masters to free their slaves pending review by the Superior Council. Article 54 granted freed slaves "the same rights, privileges which are enjoyed by free-born persons." Article 6 forbade intermarriage by whites and blacks. Slaves involved as concubines would be confiscated and "be forever incapable of being set free," while the master would be simply fined. Article 12 authorized the whipping of slaves who carried "offensive weapons or heavy sticks." Article 15 prohibited slaves from selling products on their own, and Article 22 barred slaves from property rights. Article 27 authorized capital punishment to the slave who struck members of a master's family and "produced a bruise, or the shedding of blood in the face." Similarly, Article 28 authorized execution of slaves who committed violence against free people of color, while Article 34 punished free people of color who harbored slaves. Article 32 provided the penalty of cutting off the ear of runaway slaves who did not return within thirty days. Being hamstrung and branded awaited second offenders. Third offenses brought death. Article 38 prohibited masters from mutilating slaves. However, it did allow them "to put their slaves in irons, and to have them whipped with rods or rope."[1]

However, as the city became part of the fledgling American

democracy, suppression became more complicated. For a young America, the Louisiana Purchase opened wounds in the ongoing tension over slavery, class, and caste. Obviously, the high ideals reflected in the nation's earliest documents represented a future journey to democracy rather than a state of being. In the constitutional conventions, compromises over slavery brought forth unity but not necessarily unanimity. For an embryonic abolitionist sentiment, chattel slavery seemed hopelessly incongruous with the Bill of Rights and the Declaration of Independence. The seeds of conflict could be seen in the nuances of language that crafted the Constitution. Nowhere in the document are the words slave, slavery, black, or white mentioned. Even the infamous Three-fifths Compromise, which counted populations of Southern states for purposes of taxation and representation, avoided the mention of the term slave or black in favor of clauses such as "person held to service or labor."[2]

Before the Civil War, political battles over slavery centered on expansion versus containment. For the Southerners, one slave state had to exist for each free state or else their political balance in Congress would be overwhelmed. As time went on, hashing out compromises over race and slavery became increasingly contentious and then impossible. The battles over race were largely congressional, since the early United States Supreme Court was, in many ways, a separate-but-unequal branch of government. Its consignment to a clerk's office in the Capitol basement attested to its virtual irrelevance. But then, in the 1803 case of *Marbury v. Madison,* the Supreme Court gave itself the power to evaluate and invalidate acts of Congress and state legislatures.

Though it was different from slavery in other parts of the South, New Orleans' slavery still violated fundamental human rights. One need only look at advertisements in the daily paper to sense slavery's dehumanizing nature. One ad in an 1837 newspaper announced "HORSES AND NEGRO LOST."[3] Still another told of a runaway: "A tall slender Negro woman,

Hannah, about forty years of age, with but one eye."[4] One man offered a five-hundred-dollar reward for Mariah, aged twenty-eight to thirty years, about five feet five inches, "heavy made, a dark griffe, large mouth, and in the habit of laughing when spoken to. She speaks French a little, and is slightly pitted with the small pox. She will probably try to pass herself off as a hair dresser, or as a boy. . . . She will doubtless deny to whom she belongs."[5] Still another told of "NEGROES FOR SALE: Just arrived, 72 young and likely Virginia Negroes; among which are field hands, wood choppers, plough boys, house servants, cooks, washers, and little nurses. Also, a first rate blacksmith."[6] A twenty-dollar reward went out for the capture of "Leroy—12 years old, slender built, high cheek bones and sharp chin; has a down look when spoken to, but sprightly."[7]

From the *Dred Scott Decision* to Civil War

Before Homer Plessy challenged the concept of racial regulation, in 1846, Dred Scott made his rise from obscurity when he went to court in Missouri to validate his free status. But as anti-slavery tensions reached a boiling point in the 1850s, Dred Scott's case evolved from a procedural matter to a flash point in the ongoing political and social battles of the definition of people of African descent. During this time, the national debate over the expansion of slavery reached fever pitch. National and international pressures against American slavery came from many quarters. By 1850, New World slavery was confined to Brazil, Cuba, Puerto Rico, some Dutch colonies, and the American South.[8] Abolitionists became more aggressive, freeing fugitives from jail, and in some places, open warfare broke out between so-called "free soilers" and slavers. Amidst this backdrop, when in 1852 the Missouri Supreme Court reversed a lower court order and ruled against him, Dred Scott's lawyers drafted an appeal to the United States Supreme Court that resulted in the suit *Scott v. Sanford*. Meanwhile, in 1856, at its first-ever, national convention, the Republicans harnessed the growing sentiment against slavery's expansion. They nominated John C. Frémont and ran their campaign with the slogan of "Free Speech, Free Soil, Frémont." The party garnered a surprisingly high thirty-three percent of the vote while losing to Democrat James Buchanan, who received forty-five percent, with another party receiving the balance.[9]

In contesting Scott's appeal to the Supreme Court, Sanford's lawyers widened the case to question whether Congress had any power whatsoever to regulate slavery. President Buchanan wanted the Supreme Court to settle the question in favor of slavery and wrote them to tell them so. After being elected, he called stopping "the agitation of the slavery question in the North" the "great object of my administration."[10] In March of 1857, in a seven-to-two decision that split along regional lines, the seven justices from slave-holding states not only ruled against Dred Scott but also declared that black people are not entitled to *any* federal constitutional protections whatsoever. It ruled that black people, whether slave or free, could *never* become constitutional citizens. It stripped Congress of any authority to regulate slavery in any United States territory. In one fell swoop, it overturned all of the compromises dating back to the founding of the Republic and allowed slavery in all states and territories. By abolishing the concept of free states, slave owners now received constitutional protections to bring their slaves anywhere—California, Massachusetts, Rhode Island, wherever they wished—with full impunity. The decision denied all the military and social accomplishments of people of color. It indeed rendered that people of African descent—regardless of class or amount of property— had no more rights under the Constitution than did a piece of furniture and could *never* aspire to those rights. Roger Brooke Taney of Maryland, the chief justice, himself a former slaveholder, read the decision that Pres. James Buchanan hoped would settle once and for all the question of slavery:

> They had for more than a century before been regarded as beings of an inferior order; and altogether unfit to associate

with the white race, either in social or political relations; and so far inferior that they had no rights which the white man was bound to respect; and that the negro might justly and lawfully be reduced to slavery for his benefit.

Dred Scott was not a citizen of Missouri within the meaning of the Constitution of the United States, and not entitled as such to sue the courts. He was bought and sold and treated as an article of merchandise and traffic.[11]

In his dissent, Benjamin Curtis pointed out that free blacks in at least five of the original thirteen states were granted citizenship, thus making them citizens of the United States. A few months after the *Dred Scott Decision*, John Appleton, judge of the Maine Supreme Court, issued a decision that refuted the logic and facts of the Supreme Court majority. Justice Appleton pointed out that "there are no historic facts more completely established, than that during the revolution they were enlisted, and served as soldiers; that they were tendered and received as substitutes, that they were required to take, and took the oath of allegiance."[12] Indeed, there were similar contributions and accolades about black military service from Pres. Andrew Jackson during the Battle of New Orleans. Dred Scott did eventually obtain his freedom but doing so would require a white person to acquire possession of his title. Taylor Blow did just that. This ended Scott's grueling eleven-year legal battle. His legal freedom was short-lived, however, for Scott died of tuberculosis the following year on September 17, 1858, in St. Louis, buried in an unmarked grave. Taylor Blow later had a marker placed on his grave.

After the *Dred Scott Decision*, militant abolitionists who wanted slavery destroyed turned to violence. For the slaves who dreamed of escaping to go North, there would be no quarter, no hope of freedom, and no place to run. In October 1859, John Brown led a ragtag band of slaves and abolitionists and briefly seized an arsenal at Harpers Ferry, West Virginia, for which he and his compatriots were hung. In 1857, the Louisiana legislature passed a law prohibiting manumission.

For free people of color like the Plessy family, the decision stripped them of any claims to any constitutional rights. In New Orleans, one newspaper called for their expulsion.

For those opposed to slavery's expansion, the decision meant that America had gone from being a nation with slave states to a slave nation. Abraham Lincoln, in a speech before the Illinois legislature, declared the *Dred Scott Decision* an erroneous ruling and stated the Republican view, seeing the "negro as a man; that his bondage is cruelly wrong, and that the field of his oppression ought not to be enlarged."[13]

Dred Scott's journey to the United States Supreme Court inflamed passions over human rights in the most volatile time in United States history. Abraham Lincoln was elected president on November 6, 1860, with only forty percent of the popular vote but with a sizable majority of electoral votes. On the twentieth of the following month, South Carolina seceded. Because of assassination plots, Lincoln had to be secreted in to Washington, DC, for his inauguration. There, the *Dred Scott Decision*'s author, Roger Taney, Supreme Court chief justice, administered the oath of office on March 14, 1861. One month later, on April 12, 1861, Confederate general P. G. T. Beauregard commenced firing on Fort Sumter in South Carolina, beginning what Lincoln termed an "insurrection," but what history called the Civil War. Twentieth-century Supreme Court justice Felix Frankfurter wrote, "Dred Scott . . . probably helped to promote the Civil War, as it certainly required the Civil War to bury its dicta."[14]

In 1861, Louisiana joined other Southern states in passing the ordinance of secession. But thirteen months later, in April 1862, Union navy gunboats barreled down the Mississippi to quickly capture the Port of New Orleans. One of the first acts of the occupation's general, Benjamin Butler, was to affix a stern quote from the Battle of New Orleans hero, Andrew Jackson, to Jackson's statue in front of St. Louis Cathedral: "The Union must and shall be preserved."[15]

For the next fifteen years, New Orleans became somewhat of a laboratory for one of the great democratic experiments in history. Ex-slaves now relished their newfound freedoms of speech, religion, association, and mobility. They heartily pursued their right to increased citizenship, access to education, and reconstruction of family. Legal pronunciations, constitutional amendments, and American politics became intimate and personal. For them, the Bill of Rights proved the theme of the 1860s as American democracy embarked on a promising journey.

Emancipation!

Abraham Lincoln's Emancipation Proclamation recognized the freedom of all enslaved people in the Confederate states. Former slave, abolitionist lecturer, and newspaper editor Frederick Douglass declared, upon the proclamation taking effect, "We shout for joy that we live to record this righteous decree."[16] On the Fourth of July in 1863 in New Orleans, the Loyal National League of Louisiana—a group of Southerners who retained their loyalty to the Union despite secession—held the first integrated political rally ever on Canal Street.[17] Torches, banners, and American flags waved in the nighttime breeze as, according to the league's minutes, "white men and women, black men and women, shouting aloud in concert" gave three cheers for Abraham Lincoln. From New Orleans' abolitionist German community, Dr. Maas told the cheering crowd "whenever freedom comes in conflict with despotism, the former is bound to triumph." Then, all became quiet as a black man named Rev. James Keelan strode to the lectern and, according to the minutes of the Loyal National League, "before that audience stood for the first time in any Southern State, a man whose skin of ebon blackness proclaimed him of the former chattels of earth":

> For the first time a colored man stands before you, to appeal to your senses as men and lovers of our country. . . . Fellow citizens, this is the first time for eighty-seven years that the son of Africa is permitted to join in a public celebration of the Fourth of July—yet he had a right, according to the Declaration of Independence. There never was a field of battle in this country that their bones

were not bleached upon the soil—when General Washington's army failed for the lack of reinforcements, the black man came and fought side by side with the white man, and in every battle they fought like men. We now, thank God, are permitted to speak our minds and pay our tribute to the great men who contributed so much to the nation's glory."

"We have passed through trials and persecution—we have been chained and handcuffed for two hundred and fifty years. All we want now is our rights and religious privileges—to live as Christians in a Christian country. We like our rebel friends, and we don't want to hurt them. We want them to give us our rights and to receive us as distant brothers. . . . But they can't be good Christians while slavery stands.

Let us go. We have raised your children, cleaned up your grounds and enriched you. Now let us go.[18]

Across town in Congo Square—the site of African dance and rituals before the Civil War—processions, politics, fiery oratory, free-soil meetings, and sit-ins replaced the dancing of old. A week after the Loyal National League's event, on July 11, 1863, thirty-seven black societies and the Forty-seventh Massachusetts Regiment led a funeral procession that carried the body of Union captain Andre Cailloux through Congo Square. Cailloux was considered the first black hero in the Civil War for his actions at the Battle of Port Hudson. The next year, celebration enlivened the once-dusky Congo Square expanse as Lincoln's armies gained the upper hand militarily and politically. And as General Sherman's Union forces forged southward toward the bloody pounding of Atlanta, on June 11, 1864, dressed in red, white, and blue, thousands in New Orleans' black community freely gathered in Congo Square to cheer the Louisiana Constitutional Convention's official adoption of the Emancipation Proclamation. With American flags waving, 100 gun salutes, and the city's church bells ringing, the Fourth Colored U. S. Calvary and black veterans of the 1815 Battle of New Orleans led an array of social-aid societies, political clubs, dignitaries, teachers, first-time students, and marching bands through the city streets. "Is not Emancipation a fixed fact?" queried the *Era* newspaper as it reported on the proceedings:

> In the Square a large platform, rising in the form of an amphitheater, had been erected, with a stand for the speakers. The platform was decorated with flags and evergreens. . . . [T]he speaker's stand was covered by a large awning, underneath which we found a number of ladies, teachers of the colored schools established by General Banks. Among those on the platform, we noticed old Jourdan [Jordan Noble] and fifteen or sixteen colored veterans of 1815.
>
> About 12:00, Captain Pearson's battery fired a salute of one hundred guns, and one hundred taps were struck by the Alarm Telegraph on the city bells. . . . The procession began to file out of the square on Rampart Street.
>
> First came the military—three regiments of colored soldiers—looking extremely well. . . . Then came the different societies, each with its appropriate banner; then the pupils of the public schools; then the veterans of 1814 and 1815; City and State authorities, and Free State Committee. Then the different clubs—Republican, Radical, Economy Association, Arts and Metiers, . . .United Brothers, Congregation and other societies. Then came carriages with Capt. Cailliou's [*sic*] family, ex-officers and privates of the First, Second, Sixth, and Seventh Regiments, Louisiana Native Guard, Societies—Artisans, Amis, Francais Amis, Mechanics in wagons.
>
> The procession arrived at Canal Street, and moved up Canal to Carondolet, to Triton Walk, up Triton Walk to St. Charles, up St. Charles to Fourth, and at the corner of Prytania and Fourth, in front of General Bank's residence."[19]

In 1865, the *New Orleans Tribune* reported a somber observance in Congo Square. Mourners gathered to ponder the assassination of Republican Abraham Lincoln and an uncertain but hopeful future in an expanding American democracy. "Go on any plantation," spoke the Reverend George W. Levere, who was chaplain of the Twentieth Regiment of the United States Colored Troops, "and you will see every man of African descent with tears in his eyes, saying his prayers to God, and lamenting this national calamity and affliction. Let the name of Abraham Lincoln be blessed forever."[20] Out of respect for President Lincoln, mourning badges were worn for the next thirty days. Recently emancipated slaves stood among the mourners on that pivotal day in Congo Square. Many had poured in from surrounding plantations to fight on the side of the Union army. For them it was finally their right to demand control of their lives, respect for their being, and compensation for their hours of toil. Similarly, New Orleans' sizable free-black community sought to prove themselves as capable at citizenship as they had proved themselves to be in literature, science, business, and on battlefields. To be sure, there existed stark class differences between the free men and the freedmen of color. But for now, the African in their veins united them. Later in the decade, P. B. S. Pinchback proclaimed, "I am a citizen. [We are] proud of our manhood and perfectly content to stand where God has placed us in the human scale; and would not lighten or darken the tinge of our skins, nor change the color or current of our blood."[21]

The1860s forged men who shaped the black leadership of Louisiana throughout the remainder of the nineteenth century. Representing the First District at the Lincoln memorial were future lieutenant governor and future Comité des Citoyens member Caesar C. Antoine. Also active were Battle of Port Hudson veteran Capt. James H. Ingraham, future lieutenant governor Oscar Dunn, and former drummer boy in the Battle of New Orleans Jordan R. Noble, who was president of the Fourth Ward committee during the Lincoln memorial.[22] Lincoln's presidency spawned a most profound legacy. When he took office, millions of people were legally held in bondage. By December in the year of his death, legal slavery had ended. Congressional programs emerged to assist in the monumental task of assimilating millions of people who had been denied freedom into American life. In the span of years between 1865 and 1869, the Freedmen's Bureau allotted 21 million rations, operated forty-six hospitals, and treated nearly five hundred thousand cases of illness. The Freedmen's Bureau also coordinated the operation of educational facilities and aided the establishment of Howard University, Hampton Institute of Virginia, Atlanta University, and others. By 1870, with the assistance of the Freedmen's Bureau, nearly two hundred fifty thousand students received formal education in almost five thousand schools.[23] In December 1865, the Thirteenth Amendment was ratified to forever abolish slavery in the United States. The amendment read: "Neither slavery nor involuntary servitude, except as punishment for crime whereof the party shall have been duly convicted, shall exist within the United States, or any place subject to their jurisdiction."

In April 1866, Congress passed the Civil Rights Act of 1866 to eliminate all state-enforced "black codes." This legislation also granted citizenship and rights of commerce to all persons born in the United States without regard to race, color, or previous condition of servitude.[24] The following year in March, Congress approved the Reconstruction Act, which divided the ten states of the Confederacy into five military districts and authorized steps for each of the rebellious states to rejoin the Union. These steps included convening electors to frame a constitution that guaranteed voting rights to all males, submitting the state constitution for congressional approval, and voting to ratify the Fourteenth Amendment, proposed by Congress in 1866.[25]

Star Cars and Civil Disobedience

Interestingly, Homer Plessy's manner of civil disobedience on public conveyances occurred on a more massive scale in the 1860s. While railroad trains provoked Plessy in the 1890s and buses sparked Rosa Parks in 1954, in the late 1860s it was segregated mule-powered streetcars, called "star cars," that engendered civil disobedience. In 1867, one-third of the mule-drawn streetcars that clumped along the city's thoroughfares were painted with a huge black star. While black Union soldiers could ride in the car of their choice, most blacks were confined to the star cars. In addition, newspapers reported that whites would use the star cars in addition to their own when it was convenient. So, in the spring of 1867, a coordinated effort to defy the regulations began in what the *New*

Orleans Crescent called a "pre-concerted design on the part of a number of colored men."[26]

On April 28, 1867, a black rider named William Nicholls alighted onto a nonstarred car, tussled with the driver, and was arrested. Trying to downplay the controversy, the streetcar company dropped the charges, frustrating Nicholls, who sought to test the policy in court. The company adopted a strategy of their own and ordered their drivers to refuse to move the car if a black person sought access to a nonstarred car. However, on May 4, 1867, Joseph Guillaume led a group of downtown residents a block from the Plessy home to confront the separate-streetcar policy and the companies' new strategy.

> The impending crisis was illustrated on Love St. [now North Rampart] at half past 11:00 yesterday morning in the car no. 148 allotted for whites by the entrance of a dusky son of Africa, rejoicing in the name of Joseph Guillaume, who insisted upon riding therein. When remonstrated by the driver, he coolly took the reins in his own hands and was about transforming himself from a loyal citizen to a regular Jehu and a bruiser to anyone who dared to interfere with him."[27]

The situation escalated. The next Sunday morning broke with two black women sitting in a whites-only car, engaging in a battle of patience with a driver who refused to move. On another car not far away, a white man and a black man argued over the latter's right to board. All over the city, in varying stages of defiance, blacks were on cars previously intended for whites' use only. A citywide sit-in was in progress. Things grew more heated as the day progressed, particularly in the Congo Square environs:

> About 500 of them congregated on Rampart, near Congo Square, and after stringing themselves out into line on each side of the road along which the cars had to pass, called upon the negroes who were passing in the 'star cars' to get out and ride in the other; that they had the same right to ride them as the white man had. A colored man jumped aboard a white car. The driver told him to get off. He was about to go when the crowd

> ran pell-mell towards the car with cries of 'stay on. stay on.' . . .
> Colored men got into white cars on Canal and adjacent streets
> and all times between 1 and 8 o'clock."[28]

The next day, the streetcar companies abolished the star-car system. Thomas Adams, chief of police, issued an edict: "Have no interference with negroes riding in cars of any kind. No passenger has a right to reject any other passenger, no matter what his color. If he does so, he is liable to arrest for assault, or breech of the peace."[29]

The Legacy of Emancipation

One by one, legal barriers to public accommodations, suffrage, and education fell. In April, the Louisiana Constitutional Convention of 1868 granted equal access to public conveyances licensed by the state, eliminated racial discrimination in juries, and granted suffrage to black males. The convention also mandated that state-supported schools accept all applicants between the ages of six and twenty-one without regard to color.[30] On June 25, 1868, Louisiana rejoined the Union and approved the Fourteenth Amendment two days later. The following month, the Fourteenth Amendment granting equal protection of the law to all citizens, regardless of color, became part of the United States Constitution. This amendment in effect nullified the Supreme Court's 1857 *Dred Scott Decision* and would serve as the constitutional basis for Homer Plessy's appeal to the United States Supreme Court:

> All persons born or naturalized in the United States are citizens of the United States and of the State wherein they reside. No State shall make or enforce any law which shall abridge the privileges or immunities of citizens of the United States; nor shall any State deprive any person of life liberty, or property, without due process of law; nor deny to any person within its jurisdiction the equal protection of the laws."

In March 1870, the Fifteenth Amendment, which extended the right to vote to those previously held in bondage, was ratified.

This amendment affirmed that "the right of citizens of the United States to vote shall not be denied or abridged by the United States or by any State on account of race, color, or previous condition of servitude."

In 1870, the Enforcement Act of 1870 passed Congress and outlawed conspiracies to prevent American citizens from pursuing rights and privileges granted under the Constitution. Congress also approved the act of 1871, which established mechanisms to ensure fair voting procedures and gave federal courts jurisdiction over voting-rights cases. Later that year, the act of 1871 (the Ku Klux Klan Act), gave the president the authority to use troops to protect an individual's constitutional guarantees.[31] In a historic event full of symbolism in June 1872, three African-Americans addressed the Republican National Convention. Ralph B. Elliott chaired the South Carolina delegation, Joseph H. Rainey represented South Carolina, and John R. Lynch represented Mississippi. In December 1872, P. B. S. Pinchback, the lieutenant governor of Louisiana, became the first black governor in United States history after the suspension of the sitting governor during an impeachment.[32]

Freedmen in Louisiana applied themselves to political participation, family reconstruction, and education of their children. By 1880, black males were heads of household in eighty percent of black homes in New Orleans and represented over fifty percent of Louisiana voters.[33] Many black families sacrificed considerably to provide their children access to the knowledge that was denied so many generations. United Presbyterian minister Rev. Thomas Calahan documented this phenomenon as he toured Louisiana after the Civil War: "Go out in any direction," he observed. "And you meet negroes on horses, negroes with oxen, negroes on foot, . . . men, women, and children, negroes in uniform, negroes in rags; all hopeful, everyone pleading to be taught, willing to do anything for learning. They are never out of our rooms, and their cry is for 'Books! Books! And 'when will school begin?'"[34] School integration proceeded relatively peacefully in New Orleans. The principal of Bienville School reported that "[it is] seldom that the usual peace and good order of the school are disturbed by any exhibitions of prejudice." At the Mason school, three black males rose to the top of their classes in grammar and arithmetic.[35]

Civil War did not end civil unrest. With each move toward civil rights came a backlash. In 1866, disgruntled Confederates attacked the headquarters of the Federal occupation and killed forty-four blacks. In 1868, more violence preceded national elections. In the aftermath of that riot, leaflets of the newly formed Ku Klux Klan blanketed city streets. Elected black officials also faced personal violence. A Massachusetts-born schoolteacher and candidate for state representative, Franklin St. Clair, was killed while returning from a speaking engagement in Morehouse Parish. State Rep. Alexander Francois was brutally murdered.[36]

A Monument to Unity, Accord, and Justice

In 1873, the Unification Movement formed with the purpose of uniting Louisiana. Its membership contained Republicans and Democrats, blacks and whites, Jews and Gentiles, and ex-Confederate and Union soldiers. Former Confederate general P. G. T. Beauregard was a founding member, as was Louisiana's black lieutenant governor C. C. Antoine, a former captain in the Seventh Louisiana Colored Infantry of the Union army. The Committee of One Hundred (fifty blacks and fifty whites) selected a Jewish businessman named Issac Marks as chairman of the Unification Movement. Speaking of the provisions of the Unification's "Appeal for the Unification of the People of Louisiana," Marks stated: "As opportunity presents itself, I intend to put into practical operation every recommendation in the manifesto. It is my determination to continue to battle against these abstract, absurd and stupid prejudices and to bring to bear the whole force of my character, and all of the little talent I possess, to break them down. They must disappear, they will disappear. It is only a question of time. It is our political duty to hasten it, if we desire to redeem the State."[37]

In addition to being a grocery owner and insurance-company

president, Marks chaired the fire department's board of commissioners. Like Marks, many of the other whites on the committee came from the New Orleans business community. Their professions included insurance-company president James Day, bank president Auguste Bohn, and Beauregard, who presided over a railroad company. The committee's black complement included Dr. Louis Roudanez, the Paris-educated founder of the *New Orleans Tribune*, the first black daily paper in the United States. Other black members included state senator George Kelso, Orleans Parish school-board member Charles H. Thompson, and Civil War regiment leader James Lewis, who became the New Orleans administrator of public works. On June 16, 1873, after finalizing the manifesto, their names and their platform appeared in area newspapers. Their visionary "Appeal for the Unification of the People of Louisiana" called for a statewide commitment to civil rights:

> First—That henceforward we dedicate ourselves to the unification of our people.
>
> Second—That by "our people", we mean all men, of whatever race, color or religion, who are citizens of Louisiana, and who are willing to work for her prosperity.
>
> Third—That we shall advocate by speech, and pen, and deed, the equal and impartial exercise by every citizen of Louisiana of every civil and political right guaranteed by the constitution and laws of the United States, and by the laws of honor, brotherhood, and fair dealing.
>
> Fourth—That we shall maintain and advocate the right of every citizen of Louisiana to frequent at will all places of public resort, and to travel at will on all vehicles of public conveyances upon terms of perfect equality with any and every other citizen.
>
> Fifth—That we pledge our honor and good faith to exercise our moral influence to bring about the rapid removal of all prejudices heretofore existing against the colored citizens of Louisiana.[38]

Other recommendations included a commitment to nonviolence and the removal of racial barriers to public education, public conveyances, banks, and employment, and the "cultivation of a broad sentiment of nationality which shall embrace the

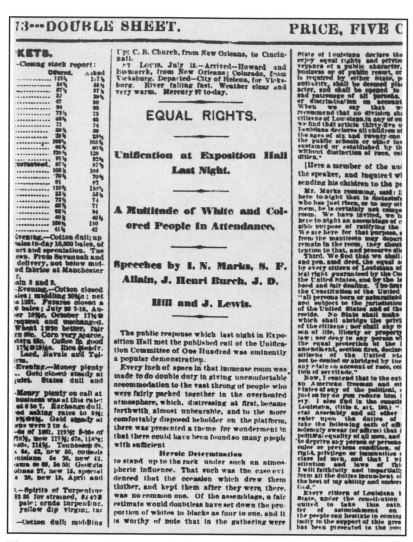

The Unification Movement's biracial appeal for the unification of Louisiana in 1873

whole country and uphold the flag of the Union." The document further called upon news outlets to join in "erecting this monument to unity, accord, and justice, and like ourselves to forever bury beneath it all party prejudices."

On July 15, 1873, the Unification Movement met its public. On a hot muggy evening in crowded Exposition Hall, a large biracial crowd gathered in stifling heat. In an outer gallery, a group of musicians played inspirational tunes while waiting for the meeting to commence. Inside the hall, the Committee of One Hundred took their seats on the platform. Above their heads, between two American flags, a canvas displayed the phrase "Equal Rights, One Flag, One Country, One People."[39] At 8 P.M., Issac N. Marks took the podium and faced his fellow citizens, an array of colors. He spoke with fervor of a Louisiana being the example for unity in the rest of the nation:

> I desire to impress every man here tonight with the same solemnity of feeling that fills my bosom tonight. This is no ordinary occasion. This is no political gathering. This is no outpouring of the adherents of a political party, or worshippers of a political leader. It is the quiet, earnest, determined counsel of a portion of the people of the State of Louisiana coming together.
>
> We come here tonight, I hope—I trust in God—that we come here tonight to lay upon the altar of our country all of the prejudice of the past, to recognize all citizens of the United States as equals before the law, and we come here tonight to unanimously ratify the manifesto.

Marks also predicted the dawn of a new era: "not only in our own state but through the length and breadth of our entire land."[40]

But as he read the resolutions, it became clear that many in attendance came not to praise the Unification Movement, but to bury it. One man interrupted Issac Marks' speech to blast the notion of integrated schools. Hisses and heckles soon followed from others in the crowd. The last speaker, a black Republican from Connecticut, ended the meeting by castigating Democrats in attendance with a lengthy lecture on their past evils. The next day, many who supported unification quickly bailed. The *Picayune* accused black members of killing the movement. The *Republican* newspaper accused the white members of reneging on their promises. One newspaper opined that, "the Democratic politicians and the Republican politicians will oppose any movement that will break up their political organizations, and thrust them into retirement."[41]

T. Harry Williams wrote in 1945 that the Unification Movement's leadership barred "professional politicians from their organization. The worst effect of excluding the politicians was to cause those of both parties to fight unification." Other cynics stated that many in the movement's white contingent supported the Unification Movement only as a ruse to rid the city of the Federal occupation. Rodolphe Desdunes, a member of the Comité des Citoyens, saw the Unification Movement as a vision of America's best future in his 1911 book *Nos Hommes et Notre Histoire:* "The movement failed but we have retained the memory of it. If it did not succeed, it was because it was premature."[42] The Unification Movement's inability to take root left a void in state leadership. Furthermore, its decline strengthened the hand of white supremacists who lacked lofty goals but had no qualms about using violence to obtain political ends. In 1874, in the Battle of Liberty Place, members of the White League ambushed and killed eleven members of the city's integrated metropolitan police force. Later that year, an emboldened White League urged white students to forcibly remove their black classmates from the schools. The *New Orleans Bulletin* asserted in December 1874 that "the white race rules the world—the white race rules America—and the white race will rule Louisiana—and the white race shall rule New Orleans."[43]

In March 1875, Congress passed the Civil Rights Act of 1875, prohibiting discrimination in public accommodations such as public conveyances and places of amusement. It also granted aggrieved individuals the right to sue for damages and placed those suits in federal court.[44] But as the country tired of the federal occupation and former Confederates rejoined Congress, this would be the last congressional civil-rights legislation until 1957. In the contested, most disputed presidential election in American history, Democrat Francis T. Nicholls gained the governorship as the result of the Hayes-Tilden

Compromise. This congressional deal conceded control of legislatures to Democrats in Louisiana, Florida, and South Carolina. In exchange, the Democrats agreed to protect black voting and civil rights. Thus ended Reconstruction. The Federal troops withdrew from the South shortly thereafter and signaled a retreat by the Federal government from the civil-rights arena. Louisiana's first post-Reconstruction governor, Francis T. Nicholls, assuaged anxieties by pledging "to obliterate the color line in politics and consolidate the people on the basis of equal rights and common interests." Likewise, with John Ferguson as a member, Nicholls' Democratic legislature pledged to support "kindly relations between the white and colored citizens of the state upon a basis of justice and mutual confidence."[45]

CHAPTER 5

The Separate Car Act of 1890

> BE IT FURTHER ENACTED THAT the officers of passenger trains shall have power and are hereby required to assign each passenger to the coach or compartment used for the race to which such passenger belongs; any person insisting on going into a coach or compartment to which by race he does not belong, shall be liable to a fine of Twenty Five Dollars or in lieu thereof to imprisonment for a period of not more [than] twenty days in the Parish Prison.
>
> —The Separate Car Act, Section 2, Act 111
> 1890 Louisiana legislature

> We'll make a case, a test case, and bring it before the Federal Courts.
>
> —Louis Andre Martinet, editor
> *Crusader*

Francis Nicholls was elected governor for a second term in 1888. But in 1890, a olitical battle over a lottery bill in the Louisiana legislature triggered a retaliatory law that separated blacks from whites on railroad trains. Much had changed since the "equal rights and common interests" days of 1877. This Separate Car Act marked year one of the Plessy saga.

The United States Supreme Court

Ineffectual during the war, the United States Supreme Court in the 1870s ushered in a long procession of rulings that limited the scope of the Reconstruction laws and constitutional amendments. In April 1873, in the *Slaughterhouse Cases,* a five-to-four Supreme Court ruling narrowed the Fourteenth Amendment's definition of national-citizenship rights.[1] In March 1876, in *United States v. Reese,* by a vote of eight to one, the Supreme Court invalidated part of the Enforcement Act of 1870.[2] In this Kentucky case, the Supreme Court established a legal platform for states to later adopt literacy tests, poll taxes, grandfather clauses, and other mechanisms that excluded large numbers of African-Americans from elections. In January 1878, in another Louisiana case, *Hall v. DeCuir,* the United States Supreme Court overturned a judgment in favor of Josephine DeCuir, a black woman denied entrance into a steamship restaurant until the white diners finished eating. Citing federal preeminence in interstate commerce, the Court declared the Louisiana law that guaranteed equal access in public transportation to be unconstitutional.[3] In 1880, in *Virginia v. Rives,* the Supreme Court stated that no matter how pervasive the absence of blacks jurors, the process remained constitutional unless evidence showed that explicit discrimination occurred.[4]

As the Supreme Court overturned or narrowed civil-rights statutes, states enacted more discriminatory laws. In 1881, Tennessee passed laws that segregated its railroad cars. Between the years 1887 and 1889, legislatures in Florida, Mississippi, and Texas followed suit. In the *Civil Rights Cases of 1883,* the Court declared the 1875 civil-rights laws that granted equal access to public accommodations to be unconstitutional.[5] Also in 1883, in *Pace v. Alabama,* the Supreme Court upheld an Alabama law that punished adultery more severely if the offending parties were of different races.[6] In *United States v. Harris,* the Supreme Court declared part of the act of 1871 (the Ku Klux Klan Act) unconstitutional when it was applied to a lynch mob that beat a black prisoner to death. The Court ruled that the Fourteenth Amendment only applied to state action and not individual action.[7]

In March 1890, in *Louisville, New Orleans & Texas Railway Co.*

v. Mississippi, the Supreme Court upheld a Mississippi law that forced railways to provide separate accommodations for black and white passengers. Unlike the Plessy case, which opposed such laws on the basis of the Fourteenth Amendment, the railroad that brought the suit argued that such laws constituted unfair regulation of interstate comm[erce.[8] Within a year after that decision, five additional states passed laws that segregated railroad cars.[9] In August, the Mississippi Constitutional Convention of 1890 enacted a two-dollar poll tax and barred people who could not read and interpret the state constitution from voting. The sole black convention delegate, Isiah Montgomery, predicted the move would disenfranchise over 123,000 black voters.[10]

New Orleans after Reconstruction

In Louisiana, there were progressions and setbacks for blacks beyond Reconstruction in an ambiguous racial climate. In 1888, blacks registered to vote comprised half of Louisiana's electorate and the legislature contained eighteen black members that year.[11] Meanwhile, streetcars and train stations remained integrated. In New Orleans in 1890, blacks constituted twenty-seven percent of New Orleans' population. There was interracial dating. The *New Orleans Lantern* commented on the "surprising amount of cohabitation of White men with Negro women." The *New Orleans Mascot* stated, "This thing of white girls becoming enamored of Negroes is becoming too common."[12] The World's Fair of the 1880s was open to all. According to C. Vann Woodward, "In the spring of 1885, Charles Dudley Warner, Mark Twain's friend, neighbor, and onetime collaborator from Hartford, Connecticut, visited the International Exposition at New Orleans. He was astonished to find that 'white and colored people mingled freely, talking and looking at what was of common interest,' that blacks 'took their full share of the parade and the honors,' and that the two races associated 'in unconscious equality of privileges.'"[13]

In New Orleans, a civil-rights group called the American Citizens' Equal Rights Association monitored the growing impetus toward race-based legislation. Similar to the Unification Movement, ACERA worked toward a nonracial political alignment. Its constitution sought to "better secure the free and full exercise of every political and civil right as guaranteed to the American citizen by the constitution and laws of this government and the improvement of the moral, intellectual, and material interests of the people of the United States of America."[14] The New Orleans chapter was part of an effort to create a functional, national, civil-rights organization dedicated to protecting blacks' civil rights. Former Louisiana lieutenant governor P. B. S. Pinchback presided over the national organization. Activist Methodist minister Rev. A. E. P. Albert presided over the state association. ACERA was an attempt to mobilize grassroots sentiments across the country into a national force. In New Orleans, ACERA chapters were established in various wards throughout the city with the purpose of choosing delegates for a national convention. In the Tremé neighborhood, the organization met at the Globe Hall on St. Peter and St. Claude Streets.

The Louisiana Lottery Company

By 1890, New Orleans reigned as a deepwater port with access to Latin America. Engineering changes to the mouth of the Mississippi River engendered a surge in economic activity. Twelve wood-planked wharves serviced a river teeming with coal boats, barges, schooners, steamers, ferryboats, and every imaginable seaworthy vessel. Tonnage on the city's fifteen railway systems linking the New Orleans port with the North American continent doubled between the years 1862 and 1892.[15] New Orleans exported more cotton than any other port. But if New Orleans was the South's queen city, it also maintained its reputation as the region's wayward sister. Nine temperance societies and a number of Catholic convents competed for souls against eight breweries and over 650 city saloons.[16] An 1890 law sought to prohibit "all dance houses, free and easy gambling dens, barrel houses, and shandangoes."[17]

The city also housed the Louisiana Lottery Company, a multimillion-dollar private enterprise chartered by the 1868 Louisiana legislature. It was a legislative battle over this uniquely Louisianan institution that created the political context for the Separate Car Act, as Louisiana's white-supremacist contingent sought an alliance with the antigambling forces. At the time of Louisiana's 1890 legislative session, the Louisiana Lottery Company was on the last spins of a twenty-five-year lease to sell lottery tickets nationwide. According to one estimate, the Louisiana Lottery Company accounted for forty-five percent of New Orleans' postal receipts. In the city of New Orleans, the company operated over 108 shops that were sometimes no more than tables set up outside of bars. As a tax-exempt entity, its sole legal requirement was to give $40,000 a year to New Orleans' Charity Hospital. The Louisiana lottery proved to be a lucrative enterprise. Dividends to stockholders reached 125 percent. Its drawings were quite the ritualistic spectacle and took place in the St. Charles Theater. The lottery enlisted ex-Confederate generals P. G. T. Beauregard and Jubal Early to lend the proper degree of solemnity and honor to the drawings, as described by New York newspaper correspondent Dr. William Shaw Bowen: "There were 840 cylinders contained in the small brass drum over which Croupier Beaureguard presided and one-by-one the boy, his assistant, drew forth from each the roll of paper which decided the fate of many a man's or woman's aspirations and hopes." Most were waiting for the chance that their twenty-dollar tickets would result in a winning monthly drawing for $300,000.[18] "The monotonous voices of the two old generals . . . went on like clockwork," Dr. Bowen described.

> The audience . . . became restless. An old woman, evidently one who scrubbed floors for a living, sat near me. Whenever a

number was called she turned her eyes in a mechanical manner toward the number on the precious slip . . . Precious [only] until the last cylinder had been removed from the brass drum. Then I heard her groan and she tore the paper in fragments and flung them on the floor. . . . At exactly 12:30 Croupier Jubal unrolled a slip of paper and called 8,132. . . . No. 8,132 draws the capital prize of $300,000. The audience remained as still as death for a moment; then a sound of murmur expressive of disgust went up and half of those present hastened out of the theater.

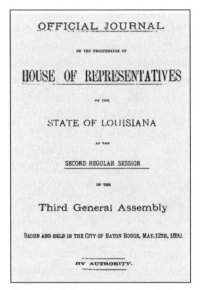

Journal of the 1890 House of Representatives for the State of Louisiana (Courtesy Louisiana Supreme Court Library)

The Louisiana Legislative Session of 1890

Indeed, Governor Nicholls made no mention of separate cars in his opening address on May 12, 1890. He devoted more time to the denunciation of the Louisiana Lottery Company than to any other subject. Calling it "gambling of the very worst description," Governor Nicholls stated: "That institution ought to be destroyed on both political and moral grounds. . . . I think it was an outrage on other states and a disgrace to ours to make Louisiana the acknowledged headquarters of gambling, and to legalize an institution avowedly based upon certain losses and certain impoverishments to others, and a still greater disgrace for the commonwealth to be a partner in such a transaction. Nothing better could be expected of the legislature of 1868."[19]

With its lease running out, the lottery company wanted to be rechartered by a vote of the people as a constitutional amendment.[20] It appeared unthreateningly in the stack of bills

filed during that session as House Bill #214: "An article on levees, schools, charities, pensions, and drainage."[21] Despite this
pleasant wording, the fate of the Louisiana Lottery Company
produced a firestorm and split Louisiana's Republican and
Democratic parties into pro- and antilottery factions. Proponents and antagonists ran the gamut. The white-separatist *New
Orleans Times* supported the lottery.[22] The *Daily Advocate,* the
state's official journal, carried lottery ads everyday. While the
wife of the president of Tulane University headed a woman's
pro-lottery group, the New Orleans archbishop stepped forward and prohibited a longstanding custom of priest's blessing
parishioner's lottery tickets in New Orleans churches. Lottery
proponents brought forth Thomas Jefferson's 1826 "Thoughts
On Lotteries" essay to buttress their position.[23]

The Louisiana Lottery Company painted a picture of benig-
nity and magnanimity. When torrential flooding in the state
between March and May of 1890 caused breeches in over fifty levees, the company provided a boat to help and offered a $100,000
gift to the state to rebuild the levee system.[24] Governor Nicholls
rebuffed their offer, but the unhesitant mayor of New Orleans
gleefully accepted $50,000, only to be lambasted by an antilottery
Methodist minister. Louis A. Martinet's Republican *Crusader*
newspaper mused, "The lottery holds the strings of an unlimited
purse. The Governor is obstinate and controls the ballot boxes.
It will be a contest of giants—boodle against votes. . . . the fight
will soon open. The situation is interesting."[25]

The Separate Car Act

As the state's attention focused on the upcoming bitter lottery fight, it was May 14 when the seemingly unrelated Separate Car Act began its journey through the byzantine world of
Louisiana politics. Introduced as House Bill #42, the measure
was presented by Rep. Joseph Saint Amant of Ascension Parish
as "an act to promote the comfort of passengers in railway
trains." With the exception of city streetcars, the law forced
railway companies to divide the races into separate coaches.

Section 2 established a punishment of twenty-five dollars or twenty days in the Orleans Parish Prison for violators and ordered the railroads to physically stop anyone who tried to enter the wrong coach. Section 3 fined noncomplying railroads up to $500 and their employees up to fifty dollars for each offense and mandated posting copies of the law in every railroad coach and ticket office. Section 4 gave railroad companies sixty days to comply.[26]

Representative Saint Amant's bill was meanspirited. The Separate Car Act denied people of different races the right to travel together. In the case of interracial couples, the law physically separated husbands, wives, and children. Additionally, it mandated that railroad companies provide an additional coach even if only few black passengers purchased tickets. Like the black codes of old, the law classified people by ancestry. Indeed, for Louisiana legislators of African heritage, the law prohibited them from traveling with their fellow government officials or many of their constituents. To those who remembered days before the Civil War, the Separate Car Act was reminiscent of the *Dred Scott Decision* and the limiting caste system before the war. On May 24, 1890, a delegation from the American Citizens' Equal Rights Association traveled to Baton Rouge to speak out against the bill. Led by former lieutenant governor P. B. S. Pinchback, former Unification Movement members James Lewis and Laurent Auguste; the *Crusader*'s publisher, Louis A. Martinet; writers Paul Trevigne and Rodolphe Desdunes, and thirteen others, the American Citizens' Equal Rights Association delivered what Louis A. Martinet called a "manly protest" against state-mandated segregation of its citizens:

> We, the undersigned American citizens, and citizens of the State of Louisiana, do most respectfully but earnestly protest against the passage of any class legislation now pending before the General Assembly, . . . for the following reasons: That such legislation is unconstitutional, un-American, unjust, dangerous and against sound public policy.
>
> We say that it is unjust, unchristian, to inflict upon any portion

of the people the gratuitous indignities which take their motive and their bitterness from the dictates of an unreasonable prejudice. The people against whom such legislation is directed are respectable, useful and law-abiding; they represent, it should be remembered, a considerable percentage of the capital and almost all the labor of the State; they share the burdens of a common responsibility with their fellow-citizens and contribute by their special qualities and temperament to the honor, peace and dignity of the commonwealth.

We do not think that citizens of a darker hue should be treated by law on different lines than those of a lighter complexion. Citizenship is national and has no color. We hold that any attempt to abridge it on account of color is simply a surrender of wisdom to the appeals of passion."[27]

In addition to ACERA's sentiments, members of Louisiana's House of Representatives expressed their views for and against the bill. When, on June 3, an amendment was added to exempt personal servants from the act, Rep. Victor Rochon of St. Martin Parish remarked: "Why, Mr. Speaker, the idea that you and family would not be offended in traveling hundreds of miles with a dozen or perhaps more negro servants. But would be insulted to travel any distance with me and my family on account of our color." Another representative, Mr. C. F. Brown of Jefferson Parish, observed that "if a number of colored men meet to discuss any question betwixt the races, they are charged with drawing the color line, but here we find the Democratic party drawing the color line and legalizing it into laws."[28]

White representative W. C. Harris of Desoto Parish doubted the need for the bill but added, "I think its failure to pass would provoke in some instances race conflicts, which an enlightened public ought to endeavor to provide against. I do not approve of some of the provisions of the bill and especially those which refer to Chinamen and Dagoes, which classes I consider not as desirable citizens as the colored people. I vote yes." Orleans Parish representative S. S. Patten voted no: "I vote no, because I am opposed to all caste legislation. Also, because I believe there is no necessity for the passage of this act, as the railroads already have full power and control in designating the car that any and all passengers may ride in."[29]

However, on the Separate Car Act's third reading, the House of Representatives approved it by a vote of fifty-six to twenty-three, with fifteen absences sending it to the Senate for action.[30] Conventional wisdom expected the lottery issue to occupy the Senate's time and opponents hoped that the Separate Car Act would bottleneck in the upper chamber. Indeed, the Separate Car Act moved to the Senate just as the lottery battle was beginning to boil. On June 4, the Senate received the Separate Car Act and, two days later, dispatched it to the Committee on Railroads, where its opponents hoped it would languish until the session's end. The lottery issue greatly consumed the energies of the powerful president pro tem Murphy Foster, who was also the vice president of the Anti-Lottery League of Louisiana. Sen. Murphy Foster had arrived at the session from his plantation in St. Mary's Parish, suffering from grippe.[31] Like many other legislators arriving for the 1890 session, he had to wade through flooded roads and byways to get to Baton Rouge. An ally of Governor Nicholls, Senator Foster headed both the Judiciary Committee and the Rules Committee.

The white-supremacist contingent of the state's Democratic Party saw the lottery battle as a conduit for white supremacy. They pressured Senator Foster to back their call for a white-people-only primary to decide the lottery's fate. Foster initially resisted the overtures, scribbling on one correspondence "I decline to receive this proposition."[32] However, his battles for votes against the lottery were bearing little fruit and his efforts were rebuffed each time a roll call vote was taken. On July 1, 1890, the lottery won big as the Senate voted twenty-four to twelve in their favor and handed Foster and Nicholls a stinging defeat. But with Nicholls' veto power, the battle still waged.

As the session plunged into its last ten days, the Separate Car Act began its deadly embrace with the lottery amendments. Debate took an ugly racial turn when Sen. Murphy Foster resurrected the Separate Car Act as punishment to only the black legislators who supported the lottery.[33] After the pro-lottery vote on July 1, the Separate Car Act bolted out of committee and fast-tracked to the Senate calendar. By July 3, the Separate Car Act was read on the floor of the Senate and was made a special order of business for Tuesday, July 8 at 3 P.M., only two days before the session was scheduled to end!

So now, debate over the Separate Car Act received priority in the state Senate. Senator Soniat expressed his opposition to the Separate Car Act, stating that if one wanted to promote the comfort of decent white people "it falls short of that purpose, as it fails to exclude low white people of the worst possible stamp, and the Chinese, both more obnoxious than most colored persons." Senator Henry's opposition reflected the railroads' reluctance to undertake the expenses of adding extra cars. "They have spent $300,000 in the last four months in struggling with the waters of the Mississippi to protect their property," Senator Henry told his colleagues. "This bill would compel the alteration of about 250 coaches, at an average expense of $75 per coach, and if two extra coaches are put on each passenger train it would entail an additional expense of fifteen cents per mile for hauling same, or in the aggregate for all roads of $1450 per day."[34]

The Separate Car Act required nineteen votes to pass—half of the Senate plus one. However, the black pro-lottery Republican senators retained confidence in their alliance with the white Democratic pro-lottery senators. On July 8, 1890, at 3 P.M., on the Senate floor, the Separate Car Act was read in full and the roll call taken. It received only fifteen yeas, including Senator Foster's, and twelve nays, with eight senators skipping the vote altogether. All but three of the pro-lottery senators voted "no" or were absent.[35] A motion to reconsider was a perceived formality but allowed a recast of the vote at a later time. It seemed that the Separate Car Act business had ended. In its editorial the following day, the *New Orleans Times* lamented the vote:

> The bill providing separate cars for white and colored failed to pass the Senate yesterday in consequence of . . . three votes.

This is greatly to be regretted because it places Louisiana in opposition to the other Southern States; and because failure will be misunderstood by the negroes and produce unpleasant results. Neighboring States have passed a law of this kind. It has, in the case of Mississippi, been pronounced legal; it is in actual operation and wherever it has been tried, it has given satisfaction. The Southern whites, in no spirit of hostility to the negroes, have insisted that the two races shall live separate and distinct from each other in all things, with separate schools, separate hotels and separate cars.

They give the Negroes schools; but these must be separate; and the cars also should be separate, in order to keep the races as far apart as ever. We cannot afford to surrender anything in this case. The law—private not public—which prohibits the negroes from occupying the same place in a hotel, restaurant or theatre as the whites, should prevail as to cars also. Whites and blacks may there be crowded together, squeezed close to each other in the same seats, using the same conveniences, and to all intents and purposes in social intercourse.

A man that would be horrified at the idea of his wife or daughter seated by the side of a burly negro in the parlor of a hotel or at a restaurant cannot see her occupying a crowded seat in a car next to a negro without the same feeling of disgust. The Louisiana Senate ought to step in and prevent this indignity to the white women of Louisiana, as the Legislatures of other Southern States have done."[36]

Early on July 9, the seesaw legislative drama once again switched back to the lottery as the session roared to a close. That morning, the House of Representatives sent the Senate a message that Governor Nicholls had vetoed the lottery bill. However, the message continued, the House had overturned his veto by a vote of sixty-six to thirty-one. They requested the Senate to do the same. The Senate would need twenty-four votes to overturn Nicholls' veto, but they previously received that number of votes on their initial passage of the lottery bill. But then, panic struck the pro-lottery camp in the Senate. A pro-lottery supporter from Sabine Parish, Sen. J. Fisher Smith fell deadly ill to the point of his family being summoned to the Capitol.[37] Without Senator Smith's vote, the lottery senators were surely one vote short of the two-thirds needed to override. In a desperately insensitive move, Sen. Lloyd Posey took the floor and presented as a deathbed request from Senator Smith that the Senate adjourn and reconvene in Senator Smith's hotel room where he lay dying: "I move . . . that the Senate with the consent of the house, shall proceed at 12:00 on July 10, 1890, to the Mayer Hotel, where Our brother Senator J. Fisher Smith lies physically ill, but sound in mind, and, in accordance with his request, that the Senate do then and there do sit to vote upon his Excellency's veto message on the Lottery amendments."[38]

After a recess, a calmer Senator Posey unsuccessfully sought to withdraw his motion. Still, without the vote of Senator Smith, the pro-lottery forces lacked the votes necessary to overturn the veto. Meantime, a bevy of unfinished regular business swamped the senators. They put off the lottery question until 7:00 P.M. When they reconvened, the pro-lottery forces had regrouped. Senator Goldwaithe moved that the bill be given to the Judiciary Committee to decide "whether House Bill 214 is of such a matter to require the Governor's approval or disapproval." Sen. Murphy Foster objected, since the Judiciary Committee contained a majority of pro-lottery senators. Once again, his objection was voted down. So, at a quarter to nine, Senator Foster and the rest of the Judiciary Committee retreated to chambers to start their deliberations. At 10:00 P.M., they emerged, as a glum Senator Foster reported back to the full Senate. Predictably, the eight pro-lottery senators on the Judiciary Committee voted that the governor *did not* have the right to veto a constitutional amendment. The five antilottery senators voted that he *did* have the right to veto constitutional amendments. As chairman of the committee, Senator Foster faced the humbling task of submitting the majority report that accused the governor of having "usurped to himself a pretended power to veto the House Bill #214." At the end of the long and fitful legislative day of July 9, it was the Louisiana Lottery Company that exhaled. Its fate would be submitted to the voters

in 1892 as a constitutional amendment that would guarantee
the company twenty-five more years. It was just what the lottery
company wanted. For Foster, the lottery still breathed and the
Separate Car Act had been pushed aside. A tired and defeated
Senator Foster retired to his quarters at Mrs. Blum's boarding
house, where he spent the legislative sessions. But there was
still one day left in the 1890 Louisiana legislature. There was
still one last spin of the wheel.

On July 10, the final day of the session, treachery and pay-
back were on the agenda as the Separate Car Act breathed
anew. Senator Hampton, who voted against the Separate Car
Act, brought it up again on a motion to reconsider. Black senators were stunned as three pro-lottery White senators who earlier voted against the Separate Car Act switched their nays to
yeas. In addition, five senators who had previously absented
themselves from voting now returned to vote in favor of the
Separate Car Act.[39] Sen. Henry Demas, in his last session as a
senator, verbalized his anger to his legislative fellows on the
floor of the Louisiana senate:

> Like the Jews we have been driven from our homes and fire-
> sides, from our churches and school houses, from our civil and
> political liberties, and from the elevated avenues of livelihood,
> and now in order to reach the lowest depth of infamy, in order
> to surpass all other indignities heaped upon us, you are willing
> to forget you are men and vote for the passage of this bill.
>
> Mr. President, when this bill shall have passed it is the last
> indignity left for you to heap upon us. You have exhausted every
> indignity, you have inflicted upon us every oppression known to
> your race, and we have born it with a patience unknown to other
> races without a single word of resentment; because we desired
> the security of peace, prosperity, and happiness for all. But the
> time will and must come in our case, as it has in the history of
> other races, when we will rise and strike, for our liberties, let the
> chips fall where they may or consequences be what they will.
>
> It is an undeserved stigma upon the Negro. The prosperity of
> Louisiana depends in a great measure upon his industry and toil.
> It is to him we owe our vast fields of waving cane; it is to him we
> are indebted for our broad expanse of fleecy cotton; and to him

must be credited our far-reaching acres of wholesome rice. He is the bone and sinew of the agricultural interests of our state; It is by his persistent efforts that our forests have been cleared.

The Negro in his own humble capacity has been a factor in the progress of this state, and while contending against almost insurmountable obstacles, has steadily elevated himself above the plane of twenty-five years ago. His advancement challenges the admiration of even those who are prejudiced against him, and the highest honors of today being accorded him in the educational institutions of this country.

Mr. President, I have met with the response that as the colored man had sided with the Lottery Bill, the passage of the separate car measure would be urgently pushed by way of retaliation.

In voting for the Lottery amendment myself and my colored colleagues on this senate floor were actuated by the purest of motives, and were moved by necessity in the present depleted condition of the state treasury; The measure recommended itself to us, was sanctioned and endorsed by the bulk of the people, both white and colored, and received the unqualified approval of the press of this state.

Consult your consciences and if the answer returned is not in keeping with the tenor of my remarks, then prejudice must have so warped your natures that you are not qualified to calmly and deliberately pass upon this matter."[40]

The Senate voted anyway, and the Separate Car Act passed with a vote of twenty-three to six, with seven absent. If Governor Nicholls were to sign the bill, within two months, Louisiana's citizenry would be sorted by race into segregated cars, irrespective of their wealth, position, or behavior. Black legislators and activists could now only hope that Governor Nicholls would remember his Reconstruction-ending pledge to consolidate the races as equals.

The *Crusader*

The *Crusader* newspaper emerged as the most vocal opponent of the Separate Car Act. Founded in 1889 by attorney Louis Martinet, the *Crusader* provided an alternative to the coarse racial commentary in some of the city's daily newspapers. From his offices at 411 Exchange Alley in the French Quarter, Martinet's paper billed itself as "newsy, spicy, progressive, liberal, stalwart, and fearless." Published every Saturday morning, the *Crusader* cost a nickel and contained news, "base ball" scores, opinions, and literature in French and English, along with social and political tidbits. It recalled Civil War military episodes, documented racial attacks, and reported on news at the city's political and educational institutions. For the *Crusader,* the Separate Car Act was a line in the sand. It was the star-cars separation of the 1860s all over again. Martinet, who briefly served in a Nicholls legislature in the 1870s, telegraphed the governor on the last day of the session: "Governor, thousands good and true men urge you to veto Separate Car Act."[41] Despite Martinet's entreaty, Governor Nicholls signed the act into law on July 10, 1890.

In addition to its reportage on the Separate Car Act, the pages of the *Crusader* presented a written and illustrated portrait of everyday life, occupations, and interests in the African-descent communities of New Orleans in the 1890s. The paper listed the graduation classes for the Catholic Saint Mary's Academy and printed news from the Louisiana Freedmen's Baptist Association. Its advertisements hawked pianos, sails, cotton scales, violin lessons, first-communion wreaths, and blanket-cleaning devices. Prof. J. A. Moret advertised violin and vocal lessons from his home on Bourbon Street. Mrs. W. A. Halston of Valence Street sold "flags, banners, badges, regailia and rosettes," while J. St. Aurin, at the corner of North Rampart and Saint Phillip Streets, sold "Havanna & Domestic" cigars. There were clothiers, hatters, and furnishers. Joseph Giardelle's Veau Gras veal butchers operated at the Tremé outdoor market at stall numbers 102 and 103. There were ads for New Orleans University's Medical College and School of Theology. There was a raffle for a "Splendid New Bowlby Church Organ" and a silver-handled umbrella.

Martinet's *Crusader* was also a bulletin board for social events. There were grand-dancing festivals for the benefit of the "widow V. Marchand at Economy Hall" and another by a "committee of gentlemen for their library fund." The Ladies of Moses

Benevolent Association held a festival to benefit their relief fund. The Knights of Pleasure entertained at a masquerade ball at the Masonic Hall in Tremé, while the Mount Olive Baptist Church hosted "Christian entertainment." The Co-operators Companions Debating Social Circle admonished that "no lady will be admitted without an invitation" at their picnic.

The *Crusader* also told of the doings of the many benevolent associations dating back to before the Civil War, such as the "Ladies and Gentlemen Friendship M. A. B. A. picnic at Spanish Fort for the benefit of their tomb fund." The paper posted job

Crusader, 1890

opportunities. One ad sought women to market "Monesia, a South American Hair Invigorator and Magic Balm." The paper informed of marriages and deaths such as that of Edmond Dede, the black New Orleans musician who left New Orleans and conducted the orchestra at Bourdeaux. It also noted the death of John C. Frémont at age seventy-seven as "the first Republican candidate for President, in 1856, and his death removes another of the old landmarks of Abolition agitation days." The *Crusader* published the schedules of the Queen and Crescent train routes and excursions from the Press Street Depot to "Little Woods, a Garden of Eden on the Northeastern Road." Their ads also featured balms and ointments that were all the rage in a pre-Food and Drug Administration era. J. Grossman's "'CAPALINE" made from a "reliable vegetable compound" cured "baldness, dandruff, and scalp disease." Try "Mexican Mustang Liniment for Man and Beast." Clean your blankets "by a new sulphur process." Don't forget "the Great Malarial Microbe Killer: Dr. C. Delery's Indian Vegetable Ferbifuge."

But the *Crusader* was first and foremost a Republican journal. Its creed called for "A Free Vote and Fair Count, Free Schools, Fair Wages, Justice and Equal Rights." It was in many ways the philosophical successor to the Reconstruction-era *New Orleans Tribune*. Indeed, the *Tribune*'s former editor, Paul Trevigne, wrote for the *Crusader*. Visitors of political and religious importance would drop by Martinet's offices to give their spin on current events. Sen. Henry Demas dropped in after the Separate Car Act passed to chat with Martinet.

The paper was militant about the rights of blacks as American citizens. They reported on acts of racial violence and kept them before the public eye. One story told of "Robert J. Moncrieff, who was arrested here Monday for killing a White man near Port Hudson in 1883. Nothing has been heard from in since he was taken back to the parish." Another told of the Bethlehem Lutheran Church on Washington and Dryades Streets, where "a gang of hoodlums terrorized the congregation by bombarding with brickbats the house of worship. The pastor of this church is a young German, Rev. August Bourgdorf, but the congregation is colored." Another item told of harassment "near Oakridge, La., [when] a party of 36 Negro laborers, who were moving from the State into Arkansas, were cruelly shot upon by a mob in pursuit. Seven were killed and six wounded. Are we in slavery times?" the paper queried. Still, another item spoke of other outbreaks of violence in the countryside: "Last week in Fayette County, Ga., in an affray between colored and whites, provoked by the latter, eight Negroes were killed and six wounded. Eight whites were shot, but only one fatally. However deplorable these affrays, it is refreshing to see the Negro defending himself, but he must learn to shoot straight."

As the Separate Car Act made its way through the legislature, the *Crusader* followed its every move. The paper published articles, reported on protests, criticized politicians, and dispatched members of its board of directors to the state capitol. Its most prolific writer, Rodolphe Lucien Desdunes, fiercely attacked the Separate Car Act and issued point-by-point refutations of the supremacist views of other local papers. The *Crusader* also criticized some black legislators for being seduced by the lottery. In an article entitled "Was it a matter of revenge", Desdunes called for a boycott of the railroads: "The issue is made and we must meet it. . . . . [T]he colored people have largely patronized the railroads heretofore; they can withdraw that patronage from these corporations and travel only by necessity."[42]

In an editorial written after the Separate Car Act became law, Martinet chronicled the Separate Car Act and what should be done to fight it:

> The separate car bill is now a law. The *Crusader* was the first to raise its voice against the enactment of this iniquitous piece of legislation. The American Citizens' Equal Rights Association took up the cudgel in defense of the right at the first opportunity.
>
> A manly protest, which has been published in this paper, was prepared against the enactment of this unjust law, and, with the assistance of public spirited citizens, a delegation was sent to Baton Rouge to present it to the Legislature.
>
> The actions of these delegates are known to the public. They secured a recommitment of the bill, which had been reported

favorably to the House, to the Committee on Railroads and had hearing before that committee. A majority was apparently disinclined to make a favorable report, but had not the courage to make an adverse one. The House forced a report and accepted the report of the minority as that of the majority. The bill was put through the house and sent to the Senate. There after considerable delay, it was brought to a vote and failed to pass. A motion was made to reconsider this vote, pending which we sent a telegram to Senator Demas, that it was the wish of the colored population that the colored Senators withhold their vote on the passage of the Lottery bill over the Governor's veto until the car bill was killed. Senator H. Demas has since told us that if he had the opportunity he would have done so. But the death of Senator Smith prevented the vote over the veto, and the car bill passed the Senate with a slight amendment.

Crusader

Before the House had time to concur we wired the Chief Executive of the State. . . . Gov. Nicholls paid no heed to this telegram. That night, before adjournment . . . he returned the bill to the House with his approval. There are good reasons for believing that had the colored members divided on the Lottery question his course would have been different. It is unfair to punish a people because of the act of a few. We have made this statement to place all the facts connected with this iniquitous law before our readers. . . . They had the power to pass or not pass the law and they passed it. . . . The Lottery's official organ, the *Times-Democrat*, was the most loud-mouthed advocate of the measure.

Senator Murphy J. Foster is reported as having said that if the colored senators had stood with his side as firmly against the Lottery as they stood by it, he would have suffered his body to be cut in pieces before he allowed the infamous car bill to go through. If Senator Foster said it, he meant it. But the Senator has no right to inflict a grievous wrong on the colored population of the State because a few colored Senators voted with a majority of the white Senators, even if, in imitations of their white colleagues, they did so for a "consideration." The colored people of St. Mary have been especially kind to Senator Foster, and if his sense of justice is not developed sufficiently to induce him to do the right thing for justice's sake, he ought at least to have been grateful to those who have been so kind to him.

The next step is for the American Citizens' Equal Rights Association to begin to gather funds to test the constitutionality of the law. We'll make a case, a test case, and bring it before the Federal Courts on the ground of the invasion of the right of a person to travel through the State unmolested. No such case has been fairly made or presented. The American Citizens' Equal Rights Association will make it, if it understands its duty.[43]

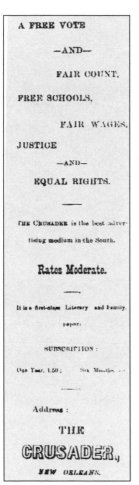

Crusader

CHAPTER 6

Who Will Bell the Cat?

> Liberty has always had a hard road to travel, whenever preju-
> dice was the consulted oracle. The United States will not be an
> exception to the rule, as long as race antipathy will be allowed to
> overshadow every other within our territory. But the obligation
> of the people is resistance to oppression.
> —*Crusader*, August 1891

The atmosphere in early 1890s New Orleans did not bode well
for civil rights. On March 14, 1891, an organized group of men
gathered at Canal Street in front of the Clay Statue—the same
rallying point used by the White League in the 1870s. Chant-
ing "Yes, yes, hang the dagoes," they marched to Orleans
Parish Prison, rammed the door down, then hunted and shot
eleven Italians who were acquitted by a jury in the assassination
of city police chief David Hennesy. Many of the victimized Italians spoke sparse or no English. Evidence linked them only
marginally to the crime. The mob took their bodies outside
the prison and then lynched them on nearby light posts in
Faubourg Tremé and from oak trees in Congo Square. As they
dangled lifelessly, they shot them again. Disturbingly, the
mob's headmen encompassed some of the city's prominent
civic leaders, including a newspaper editor and two prominent
attorneys. Viewing the phalanx of men armed with Winchester
rifles and shotguns, an elderly black woman in Tremé gasped,
"Thank God it wasn't a nigger who killed the chief."[1]

An ominous wind was blowing across the landscape of American democracy in 1891. Alabama, Kentucky, Arkansas, and

Georgia passed railroad-segregation laws that year. At the same time, Mississippi established literacy and "understanding" tests as a requirement to vote. That year, the Fifty-second Congress contained only one black Congressman, down from the nineteenth-century high of eight who served in the 1875-77 Congress. Indicative of the growing political strength of the Southern states, Congress abandoned a bill that authorized federal supervision of elections, after Southern Congressmen successfully filibustered. Nationwide, one hundred thirteen blacks died from lynching that year.[2] And in Louisiana, the Separate Car Act was in full effect.

From his offices at the *Crusader* in New Orleans, Louis Martinet held out hope that the fledgling American Citizens' Equal Rights Association would challenge the hostile climate across the South. Early in his political life, Martinet seemed an idealistic sort. Back in 1876, in his twenties and fresh out of Straight College Law School, Martinet joined the Democratic Party in the hope that a black presence would stave the formation of an all-white political party dominated ideologically by white supremacy. And in that light, he found Governor Nicholls to be a moderating influence on the state Democratic Party's actions and philosophies. Nicholls appointed blacks to offices and voted against efforts to turn Democratic primaries into whites-only primaries. But Martinet became dismayed by "the reactionists in the Democratic party [who] kept up a constant warfare. Their cry was 'white supremacy' all along the line," he wrote. "During the campaign and after the elections, they forced the more liberal & conservative whites to take a stand on their ground—they kept this up until they brought about a series of outrages that exceeded in atrocity anything that had ever taken place in this state."[3]

Martinet's experience with the Democrats shook his idealism. It also made him realize that the ascendancy of white supremacy required national containment. In the 1880s, writer George W. Cable asked Martinet to detail the antiblack violence in the South for Cable to publicize. Martinet enthusiastically responded, but Cable never followed up, and Martinet marshaled his own resources and started the *Crusader* in 1889. Martinet watched as white supremacists in the South whittled black rights away. He saw a paramount need for a national newspaper based in Washington. He wanted to "disseminate information of happenings, events & outrages gathered all over the South by our own trusty correspondents with no color line about it, but colored men as writers would be powerful. . . . in educating the North as to conditions & affairs in the South & creating a public sentiment that might ultimately manifest itself by. . . . national legislation or otherwise." While Martinet's *Crusader* published the constitution of ACERA and reported on its proceedings, he did not sense the proper amount of urgency from ACERA and other organizations, despite the gravity of the moment. Yes, with regard to the Separate Car Act, ACERA successfully convinced the state republican convention to approve a resolution of condemnation. And, yes, they also garnered support from Reconstruction figure Judge Tourgee and Congressman William Kellogg, a former Louisiana governor who lost his office in 1876 during the congressional Hayes-Tilden Compromise.[4] But while ACERA's information campaign elicited support and contributions, Martinet saw no concrete steps to defeat the Separate Car Act in the courts. Meanwhile, white supremacy seemed to be moving at lightning speed in states surrounding Louisiana.

Martinet privately complained of ACERA's lack of direction. "The proper men were not at the head," he wrote. "Its last national convention was turned into a purely political resolution machine." His hope for the organization's effectiveness dwindled precipitously amidst members who, he said, cared little except for "the moment it gave them by their connection with it."[5] As a delegate by proxy to the founding convention of the Afro-American League in 1890, Martinet also found disappointment. He could not obtain assurances that the group would not exclude other races. Martinet felt that blacks-only organizations fell short of what was needed—a broad-based multiracial campaign against segregation and racial violence.

The *Crusader* Speaks

Despite the racial climate, and perhaps in an effort to change it, in the summer of 1891, the *Crusader* stepped up calls for a test case against the Separate Car Act. Columnist Rodolphe Desdunes went on record calling the fight against Jim Crow a *guerre a mort* (battle to the death).[6] The *Crusader* never wavered in that view, even as the cards stacked against their mission as months turned into years. P. B. S. Pinchback moved North, promising financial support that never arrived. When Rev. A. E. P. Albert aligned his Methodist newspaper with the *Crusader* and called upon Methodist churches to oppose segregation laws, church officials removed him as editor of the *Southwestern Christian Advocate*.[7] From his home in Washington, DC, Frederick Douglass expressed the opinion that a court loss would set a bad precedent. But, from the *Crusader*'s viewpoint, precedents already existed in state houses across the South, and only direct action could stop those precedents from becoming commonly accepted principles.

For its part, the *Crusader* continued telling its readership to boycott railroads. It repeated the need for a test case and offered use of its offices for those willing to work against the Separate Car Act. Rodolphe Desdunes felt that passivity enabled white supremacy rather than tempered it. In an article entitled "Forlorn Hope And Noble Despair," Desdunes responded passionately to a letter writer who cautioned against fighting segregation. Desdunes related the examples of scientist Galileo Galilei, American patriot Patrick Henry, Haitian revolutionary Toussaint L'Ouverture, and French abolitionist Cardinal Lavigerie of France—all voices for seemingly futile causes. Desdunes told a parable about the old Roman who became angered when his son fled a confrontation by three enemies. The old man's companion asked him, "What would you that he should have done alone against three?" The old Roman replied, "He should have died," or "trust to a noble despair to save him." Desdunes concluded, "Defeat is more honorable than flight or surrender."[8]

Rodolphe L. Desdunes (From *Nos Hommes et Notre Histoire,* courtesy of the University of New Orleans Louisiana Division)

But in the early 1890s, their cause against separate cars did not seem as forlorn as that of the Roman son. The 1890-91 United States Supreme Court represented an inverse demographic and political alignment from the tribunal that issued the *Dred Scott Decision*. Republicans held seven of the nine court seats. Only two of the justices heralded from Confederate states.[9] Additionally, Republican Benjamin Harrison occupied the White House. And even though the Court had previously ruled in favor of separate cars, the decision in that case centered on arguments related to interstate travel rather than to Fourteenth Amendment issues. There also existed a level of comfort with the city administration in New Orleans. Mayor Shakespeare appointed fourteen blacks to the police department and recommended two blacks for federal offices, much to the consternation of white-supremacist journals such as the *Mascot*.[10] Even in state government, Governor Nicholls proved more moderate than many in the state Democratic Party or his fellow Deep South governors. And to many, considering the way the Separate Car Act passed the legislature, the law seemed more of a cruel joke than a definable trend in Louisiana.

Still, the law grated. How would a black person living in the twenty-first century react if a state legislature passed a Separate Car Act? After all the sacrifices pursuant to the right for black families to travel without legal molestation, being herded into separate cars would be a bitter pill to swallow for anyone. And indeed, in the 1890s, integrated city streetcars had not resulted in social chaos. Rodolphe Desdunes asserted, "Every honorable person knows that the law was passed to discriminate against the colored people so as to degrade them." Still the question remained, according to Desdunes: "Who will bell the cat?" In the 1891 Fourth of July issue of the *Crusader*, Desdunes called upon the Republicans to step forward against the Separate Car Act, which he characterized as "that 'badge' of Negro inferiority, that menace to society, that breeder of discord":

> Among the many schemes devised by the Southern statesmen to divide the races, none is so insulting as the one which

provides separate cars for black and white people on the railroads running through the State. It is like a slap in the face of
every member of the black race, whether he has the full measure
or only one-eighth of that blood.

We should not be surprised to see Louisiana return . . . to the
system of star cars in our city . . . [But] if the people most
affected by race separation will present a united front against
that barbarous measure, such an attitude may have a salutary
effect.

We are American citizens and it is our duty to defend our
constitutional rights against the encroachments and attacks of
prejudice. The courts are open for that purpose, and it is our
fault if we do not seek the redress they alone can afford in cases
of injustice done or of wrongs endured.

If such officials as Gov. C. C. Antoine, Hon. H. F. Patty, and
the Rev. A. S. Jackson were to take the initiative in the case, we
feel sure that they would succeed in raising a very large amount
of funds. Their influence, their position, and their character as
gentlemen and representatives would surround the question
with an earnest that could not fail to have a most decided effect
upon the general public.

We need leaders in the present emergency, and it is natural
for us to look for them among those who occupy public stations
. . . The Republican officials at this point could not render a
greater service to Republican preamble than by being instru-
mental in blotting out of our statute books the separate car law
. . . Appoint your committee, gentlemen, and go to work . . . Are
we less patriotic than we were in 1870? Is it impossible to find
men of nerve in our times? That is to be tried, and we must try
it. By way of encouragement we are authorized to state that
many loyal hearts are waiting, ready to put their shoulders to the
wheel just as soon as the car of liberty is put in motion. In fact
they are anxious that the first steps should be taken toward the
vindication of American citizenship.[11]

The Comité des Citoyens

But the leadership that Rodolphe Desdunes sought from
the Republican hierarchy or civil-rights groups would not be
forthcoming. In the end, in his late sixties, the rapidly aging
Reconstruction stalwart Aristide Mary stepped forward to lend
his influence as he had done as a radical Republican in the
1870s, as cofounder of the Unification Movement in 1873 and

leader of protests against segregated schools in 1877.[12] While some dismissed the Separate Car Act as patently unconstitutional or pragmatically unenforceable, Mary assessed its passage as a test of the waters to return to a caste system that existed before the Civil War. He too felt that inaction and fear bred more injustices. He also felt that even in benign manifestations, such as the all-black Southern University, the precedent of racial separation could be later used for nefarious purposes. Separating the races for educational or transportation purposes would lead to segregated depots, entertainment, jobs, or marriages, Mary surmised. As his final political act, he employed his political reputation and stature to urge community leaders to stand alone, if necessary, and show the Separate Car Act the good fight.

On September 1, 1891, eighteen prominent New Orleanians responded to Aristide Mary's call and made their way through the rain to Martinet's *Crusader* offices. They included an assortment of professionals: educators, businessmen, lawyers, social activists, ex-Union soldiers, government workers, and writers. Many heralded from the free-people-of-color caste that existed in Louisiana before the Civil War. Some of the older attendees were Aristide Mary's comrades during Louisiana's Reconstruction battles, when he cochaired the Unification Movement. Laurent Auguste actively worked in the Radical Republican Club with Aristide Mary. Relatively younger members like Rodolphe Desdunes, Martinet, and L. J. Joubert came of age in the 1870s and 1880s. Desdunes was a member of the Metropolitan Police Force during the period that the White League attacked in 1874, killing eleven of city policemen. Martinet served on the Orleans Parish School Board in 1877 and unsuccessfully opposed efforts to resegregate public schools. Martinet, Desdunes, Eugene Luscy, and C. C. Antoine all graduated from Straight College Law School.[13]

Most of the men lived within walking distance from each other in Faubourg Tremé, Faubourg Marigny, New Marigny, and the French Quarter. Cigar maker and writer Numa E.

Laurent Auguste (From *Nos Hommes et Notre Histoire,* courtesy of the University of New Orleans Louisiana Division)

Mansion lived on Marais Street in Tremé, a block away from Desdunes.[14] Committee member A. J. Giuranovich made a living as a "jeweler and diamond setter," also selling eyeglasses, antiques, "old gold," and silver from his shop on Royal Street, around the corner from the *Crusader* office. Reserved, gentlemanly funeral-home director Alcee Labat lent his support, as did undertaker Myrthil J. Piron, whose ads offered "coffins of all kinds" and "carriages to hire" from his funeral parlor on North Rampart Street in Faubourg Marigny. Piron passed away shortly after the committee formed.

ADVERTISEMENTS.

Nine Years with
R. I. C. LEVY,
New Orleans.

Three Years with
MR VERAX,
Paris, France.

A. J. GIURANOVICH,
JEWELER AND DIAMOND SETTER,
ESTABLISHED 1875,
126 ROYAL STREET,
NEW ORLEANS, LA.
– DEALER IN –

Watches,
Clocks,
Diamonds,
Jewelry,
Spectacles
and Eye Glasses.

Antiques, Old Gold, Silver and Precious Stones Bought.

REPAIRS OF ALL KINDS NEATLY EXECUTED.

The *Crusader* office's nooks and crannies provided familiar surroundings as the committee bantered their options and ideas. Louis Joubert worked as the paper's business manager. The names Arthur Esteves, Alcee Labat, Louis Martinet, and Rodolphe Desdunes all appeared on its masthead. In addition, the *Crusader* listed attorney Eugene Luscy as the president of its board of directors. Also, Joubert, Piron, Giuranovich, Esteves, and Labat all advertised their business interests with the paper. With Republican Benjamin Harrison as president in 1890, some of the men also worked in government-patronage jobs at the custom house. City directories list G.

Jeweler A. J. Giuranovich was a member of the Comité des Citoyens who operated in the French Quarter.

G. Johnson and E. A. Williams as clerks at the custom house. Another notable, Rudolph Baquie was a former sergeant major in the Union army and served as adjutant general of the Grand Army of the Republic for Louisiana and Mississippi. Baquie also directed construction of "the reservoir on Canal Street and the Galvez Canal culvert," according to his obituary and research by his descendant Diane Baquet.[15] Another attendee, Alexander B. Kennedy, worked for the post office as a carrier. The night of September 1, 1891, they put aside their work-a-day concerns and listened to Aristide Mary's plea to organize and fight.

They unanimously chose fifty-six-year-old sailmaker Arthur Esteves as president. Esteves was a round, light-brown-skinned, balding man with crinkled hair and a goatee that fanned out from his chin. A businessman, financial administrator, signatory to the Unification Movement, and president of the board of the Couvent School, Esteves had a reputation as one who could get things done. His firm, Fauria and Esteves, was a leading sailmaking firm in the city and also manufactured "awnings, tarpaulins, and flags" with "prices to suit the times." He operated outlets on Carondelet Walk and on North Peters Street, near the old U.S. Mint. As a member of the board of directors of the Couvent School, he served from 1884 to 1908 and became president of the board in 1890. He received the credit for rescuing the Couvent School from financial ruin in the 1880s and placing it on a sound financial footing. Esteves affiliated with other members of the committee through his work with the Couvent School. Rodolphe Desdunes taught there, and Martinet functioned as the institute's legal advisor, while L. J. Joubert served on the school's board of directors for thirty years. Esteves also belonged to the Justice, Protective, Educational, and Social Club and served as its treasurer. Founded September 25, 1886, that group called for "uniting and protecting ourselves, both socially and morally . . . inculcating a true sense of the importance of education, and uniting ourselves politically that our support and influence may be

Arthur Esteves (From *Nos Hommes et Notre Histoire,* courtesy of the University of New Orleans Louisiana Division)

brought to bear where our interest . . . can be advanced as citizens of this state and of the United States protected and respected."[16]

For vice president, they looked to Caesar Carpentier "C. C." Antoine. Born in New Orleans in September 1836, Antoine was the grandson of an African woman on his father's side, his mother hailed from the West Indies, and his father fought with the Corps d'Afrique under Andrew Jackson in the War of 1812. In July 1863, Antoine joined the Union army and became a captain in Company I of the Seventh Louisiana Colored Infantry. In 1865, the *New Orleans Tribune* listed him as chairman of the Resolutions Committee for the Lincoln-memorial congregation in Congo Square. After the war, he became an associate editor of the *Black Republican* newspaper and served as delegate to the Louisiana Constitutional Convention from Caddo Parish. Political violence hit home when his son, Joseph Antoine, was killed in racial attacks that preceded the 1868 national elections. One person described C. C. Antoine as being "thoroughly African in color and physiognomy," and being "of pure African descent, small stature." Someone else described him as a "short, slender, active Negro,

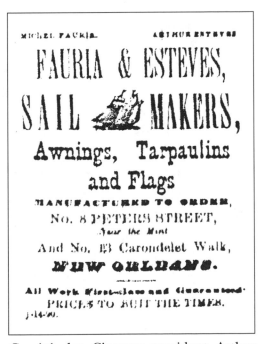

Comité des Citoyens president Arthur Esteves advertised his sail-making business in the *Crusader*. (Courtesy Amistad Research Center at Tulane University)

C. C. Antoine

as black as coal. He has a very intelligent face, with a moderate beard and mustache, worn English fashion."[17] During Reconstruction, Antoine was elected lieutenant governor in 1872 and cofounded the Unification Movement with Aristide Mary and others in 1873. The 1876 congressional Hayes-Tilden Compromise, which granted Francis Nicholls the Louisiana governor's chair, also denied Antoine his second term as lieutenant governor.

Tailor and horseman Paul Bonseigneur became the group's treasurer. His father fought under Andrew Jackson in the Battle of New Orleans.[18] Like committee members C. C. Antoine, Aristide Mary, and Laurent Auguste, Bonseigneur also served on the Committee of One Hundred during the Unification Movement. He would serve as point man in fund-raising efforts to fight the Separate Car Act and agreed to provide surety bonds for the test cases. Other officers included teacher Firmin Christophe, who became secretary, and G. G. Johnson, who became assistant secretary. Another prominent member, L. J. Joubert worked with Esteves as president of the Justice, Protective, Educational, and Social Club. Joubert was also business manager of the *Crusader,* president of a benevolent association named the Societe des Jeunes Amis, and held various positions in U.S. government jobs.

This Comité des Citoyens hardly represented a random sample of the South's black population. With many of mixed-race heritage, fluent in French and English, Roman Catholic, professional rather than laboring, they seemed more in tune with European pursuits than rural black life. The majority had French surnames and represented a sort of "talented tenth" coalition of New Orleans. They realized from their pre-Civil War experiences in New Orleans that even one drop of African heritage could instantly place one in a permanent and irrevocable state of second-class citizenship. In a landscape moving rapidly to only black or white America, they envisioned a third America without any color line. They possessed the wherewithal, education, and political space to mount the campaign, and they stepped forward to do it. Indeed, judging by the pigmentation and portfolios of some of the committee members, they could have easily disappeared into white society, emigrated to other states or countries, or retreated to the security of their personal wealth and been done with it.

Forged by their opposition, the Comité des Citoyens sought a strategy to impugn the Separate Car Act's constitutionality. A United States Supreme Court ruling in their favor would annul the statute in Louisiana while uprooting similar measures that sprouted throughout the South. In addition, pursuing a legal course seemed more efficient than lengthy, costly, and uncertain legislative remedies. Much valuable time had already been lost in that arena. Further, the Comité des Citoyens viewed the Separate Car Act as a direct violation of the equal-protection clause of the Fourteenth Amendment. Sensing that events were moving quickly, they emerged on September 5, 1891, and issued an urgent statement entitled "An Appeal":

> No further time should be lost. We should make a definite effort to resist legally the operation of the Separate Car Act. This obnoxious measure is the concern of all our citizens who are opposed to caste legislation [an]d its consequent injustices and crimes.
>
> We therefore appeal to the citizens of New Orleans, of Louisiana, and of the whole union to give their moral sanction and financial aid in our endeavors to have that oppressive law annulled by the courts.
>
> We call for such a demonstration as will plainly show the temper of the people against that infamous contrivance known as the 'Jim Crow Car'.
>
> We invite a popular subscription whereby the mite of the poor may equal in merit the liberality of the rich; for we want this fund to constitute not only an indispensable agency to defray judicial expenses, but also a proof of public sentiment and determination.
>
> At all events, it is the imperative duty of oppressed citizens to seek redress before the judicial tribunals of the country. In our case, we find it is the only means left us. We must have recourse to it, or sink into a state of hopeless inferiority.
>
> The necessity for the annulment of this separate car law

becomes still more apparent when we consider the many serious annoyances and wrongs which have ensued by the existence of the supreme evil.

It is unnecessary to recapitulate. Occurrences are fresh in the minds of all. Every manner of outrage, up to murder, without redress, has followed the operation of this obnoxious law.

With such revelations, we cannot but be apprehensive of worse results in the future. We feel that unless promptly checked by the strong power of the courts, the effects of that unconstitutional and malicious measure will to encourage open persecution and increase to a frightful degree, opportunities for crimes and other hardships.[19]

Arthur Esteves, President
C. C. Antoine, Vice-President
Firmin Christophe, Secretary
G. G. Johnson, Secretary
Paul Bonseigneur, Treasurer

One by one, they affixed their names and reputations to that document: Laurent Auguste, R. B. Baquie, R. L. Desdunes, A. J. Giuranovich, Alcee Labat, E. A. Williams, Pierre Chevalier, L. A. Martinet, N. E. Mansion, L. J. Joubert, A. B. Kennedy, M. J. Piron, and Eugene Luscy. They publicly committed themselves to stand as a unit and fight the separation of citizens based on race or skin color. They would meet on Thursday nights and monitor the progress. They called themselves the Citizens' Committee for the Annulment of Act No. 111 Commonly Known as the Separate Car Law. The next three months and the next five years would take their measure.

The Mite of the Poor—The Liberality of the Rich

Thus activated, the newly formed Comité des Citoyens and their supporters filled the autumn and winter of 1891 with urgent appeals. They turned to the tightly knit networks of benevolent and religious societies, labor clubs, lodges, and church groups in 1890s' New Orleans as their core constituency.

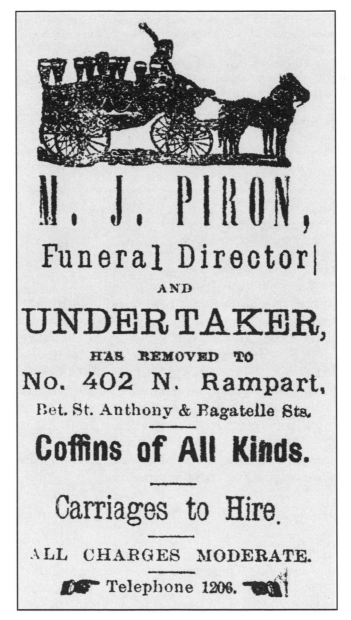

M. J. PIRON,

Funeral Director

AND

UNDERTAKER,

HAS REMOVED TO

No. 402 N. Rampart,

Bet. St. Anthony & Bagatelle Sts.

Coffins of All Kinds.

Carriages to Hire.

ALL CHARGES MODERATE.

☞ Telephone 1206. ☜

Undertaker M. J. Piron was another member of the Comité des Citoyens who advertised in the *Crusader*.

Alcee Labat (From *Nos Hommes et Notre Histoire,* courtesy of the University of New Orleans Louisiana Division)

Individuals walked the streets with subscription lists, asking their friends and neighbors to contribute. Their supporters held concerts and wrote letters. In their appeal, the Comité des Citoyens asked for financial support "whereby the mite of the poor may equal in merit the liberality of the rich." They wanted to raise funds and consciousness. In the short three months after "An Appeal" was published, nearly three thousand dollars rolled in from the neighborhoods of New Orleans and from cities as far away as Chicago and San Francisco. In total, over one hundred and fifty donors contributed to the effort. They reflected a wide divergence of city, religious, athletic, union, literary, Masonic, political, governmental, and individual sources.[20]

The bulk of support came from the many New Orleans religious and social benevolent societies, which also served as insurance organizations by providing health and burial benefits. The *Crusader* often published notices of their festivals and outings. Indeed, Louis Martinet notarized many of their articles of incorporation, and during the fund-raising drive, many reciprocated with contributions. Le Silence Benevolent Association raised $103. The Societe Economie, Societe des Artisans, and Societe des Jeunes Amis also participated. Literary salons, such as the Ida Club, Baton Rouge's Australia Literary Society, and Straight University's Sumner Literary Debating Club, responded enthusiastically, as did labor groups such as the Cigar Makers N. C. R. Club, the Bricklayers and Masons Union, and the Mechanics Social Club. Reverend Hunter of the Outpost African Methodist Episcopal Church forwarded $43. By October 11, 1891, they had raised $1,500.[21]

While the Comité des Citoyens consisted of all males, the support of women was key to their fund-raising. The Ladies Societe des Francs Amis led the fund-raising with a concert and other activities that brought in $140. Also contributing were the female religious societies, such as Ladies of St. Joseph, Dames et Demoiselles Jeunes Amis, Les Dames Saint Clothide, and the Ladies of Liberty League. From across the state, citizen groups collected monies from small Louisiana towns of Shriever, Cheneyville, Smoke Bend, Morgan City, Shreveport, and Mandeville, while the Louisiana parishes of St. John, Plaquemines, Point Coupee, and St. Bernard pooled their resources and sent them to the Comité des Citoyens. From Mississippi, the citizens of Scranton, Wilkinson County, and Round Lake sent money, and the Young People of Vicksburg, Mississippi, chipped in $3. From outside of the South, Mrs. E. K. Tourgee and J. H. Durfee from Woodstock, Illinois, donated, as did a group of four men from Chicago who collected $113.75. Other donations came from Kansas, San Francisco, California, and San Antonio, Texas. A group called the Benjamin Harrison Social Club contributed $10, as did "Friends in the 6th Auditor's office, Washington D. C." At the end of the fund-raising, the Comité des Citoyens tallied $2,982.55. As important as the fund-raising was the message that people were voicing their opposition to segregation with their dollars and cents.

Hon. A. W. Tourgee, My Very Dear Sir

As the rallies and fund-raising took place, Louis Martinet worked feverishly on planning a test case. Early in the campaign, the Comité des Citoyens accepted the offer of writer, jurist, and Civil War officer Albion Tourgee as their lead counsel and gave him the authority to choose his cocounsels. In the battle against the Separate Car Act, Tourgee found Martinet to be a tactical and philosophical complement. He followed Martinet's writings in the *Crusader*. Martinet possessed the brashness about citizenship that Tourgee admired. Martinet likewise read Tourgee's "A Bystander's Notes" in the *Chicago Inter-Ocean*. Martinet told Tourgee, "You are fighting a great battle, Judge. You are, if not the only one, the foremost militant apostle of liberty in the whole land."[22]

To support the efforts of the Comité des Citoyens and encourage similar efforts, Albion Tourgee used his Bystander column to issue his nationwide call for the National Citizens' Rights Association. According to Otto H. Olsen: "The initial response to Tourgee's announcement was impressive, as from throughout the nation thousands enrolled in the N. C. R. A., whites and Negroes, southerners and northerners, individuals and organizations, the educated and the illiterate, the self-seeking and the selfless, the famous and the unknown." Letters of support from ex-Confederates and Union veterans, blacks in the South, everyday people, a bookkeeper, and cashiers came into Thorheim. Clubs formed in Mississippi and Chicago. Between two hundred and three hundred names would sometimes arrive on a single day. Antilynching crusader Ida B. Wells joined the National Citizens' Rights Association. A meeting of 800 black men in Topeka, Kansas, endorsed it. In Cambridge, Massachusetts, there was a move to convert the Afro-American League into National Citizens' Rights Association chapters.[23] Frederick Douglass and a group of others invited Tourgee to speak on race relations to the Howard University alumni.

Albion Tourgee told his reading audience of the fight of the Comité des Citoyens and their need for support, while the Comité des Citoyens ordered 1,000 copies of Tourgee's *Is Liberty Worth Preserving?* Comité des Citoyens members Numa E. Mansion, Eugene Luscy, and Alcee Labat even formed an Albion W. Tourgee Citizens' Union and raised $30 to defray the costs of defending a National Citizens' Rights Association member in Mississippi—a widow arrested for holding meetings of blacks organizing to leave Mississippi.[24]

Tourgee hoped the National Citizens' Rights Association could raise 2 million members and represent a righteous reckoning army of the masses at the 1892 Republican convention. The National Citizens' Rights Association prepared circulars supporting their candidate—Thomas B. "Tom" Reed, Speaker of the House—and called for more commitment to civil rights, stating, "Wealth and prosperity are noble but human liberty is magnificent." Still, Reed lost the next election to Grover Cleveland.

In an intriguing series of intimate letters that spanned the life of the efforts of the Comité des Citoyens, Martinet and Tourgee discussed civil rights, the Republican Party, the execution of the test case, and the complexion and gender qualities of the test riders. They also vented their deep feelings concerning America's future and the role of black people in it. Tourgee, who lived in relative security in Mayville, New York, considered Martinet a hero for taking up such a weighty cause from inside the Deep South. Martinet responded, "I am a plain, ordinary man. I prefer that. In that way I'll not disappoint you."[25] In a December 7, 1891, letter, Martinet related the strategy discussions that had taken place to put the test cases in motion:

> We hope to bring this matter up before the court by writ of habeas corpus. We hope to make a test case by understanding with some of the railroads. We have waited thus far at the suggestion of some of them. With the first road tried, the officers finally told us that their road did not enforce the law. They had a coach for colored persons, and the sign required by law hooked up, and the conductors were instructed to show them the car, and if they refused to go into it, they were not to be violent in any way—a victory already as you can see. The other road . . . saw the law as bad; they would like to get rid of it, and asked us to wait a few days so they could consult their attorneys, and we have been waiting and here we are. The plan is for us to put a colored passenger on board and the conductor to direct him or her, for we may have a lady, to the Jim Crow car and any refusal to go into it to enforce the law by legal means, that is to make the proper affidavit against the passenger under their act.[26]

As they wrote back and forth on their legal options, they considered a light-skinned female to show the lack of chivalry in it all, while making the point that a person's racial makeup could not necessarily be visually determined. Martinet pointed out that some black people in New Orleans had lighter skin than members of the city's immigrant population. Also, since their ultimate goal required a United States Supreme Court action, the arrest needed to happen in a precise fashion. If the railroad refused to sell the test rider a ticket, stopped the person from boarding the train in the first place, or charged him or her with disturbing the peace rather than a violation of the Separate Car Act, their efforts would be meaningless. For a while they tinkered with having a person get into the Jim-Crow car, cross over into a white car while the train was in motion, and then be subsequently ejected. Martinet worked desperately at getting a railroad to cooperate with them. Without their assistance in the endeavor, it would be difficult to initiate a test case or have the proper charges levied. "The roads are not in favor of the separate car law, I find, owing to the expenses involved," Martinet told Tourgee, "but they fear to array themselves against it."[27]

Railroads had become a key aspect of New Orleans' port economy. Engineers constructed jetties at the mouth of the Mississippi in the 1870s and made New Orleans a deepwater port. Railroads flocked to the city to get their share of the booty in a profitable confluence of New Orleans' port and transportation industries. In the years between 1887 and 1892, tons of freight forwarded from the city by rail nearly doubled from 720,840 to 1,403,538 tons, and New Orleans became the final stop for five of the largest railway systems in America.[28] From the railroads' standpoint, the Separate Car Act made no business sense. It forced private railroad companies into the expensive task of providing extra cars that might only be half-used. Also troubling, it saddled their employees with the burden of becoming the state's race policemen. Some railroads vigorously enforced the new law. In an October 5, 1891, letter to Tourgee, Martinet stated, "I know of one case, 3 or 4 months old, where two colored ladies were actually forced out of the 'white' coach into the 'colored' while the train was going at the usual rate of speed." Others in the industry saw it as government interference. They posted the mandatory copies of the act but did not demand compliance. In December 1891, the committee tallied the last of the donations. Happily, their supporters had given them enough funds to proceed with the test cases. A pleased Martinet reported more good news to Tourgee in a December 28, 1891, letter. "My very dear Sir,"

Martinet wrote, "I talked to people of the Louisville & Nashville R. R. today. They are willing that we shall make the case in their road."[29]

The Comité des Citoyens Acts

In 1892, with a new year, a full war chest, a clear position, and lawyers at the ready, the Comité des Citoyens prepared to challenge the interstate aspects of the Separate Car Act. Could the state regulate people traveling from, say, Florida to Texas, passing through Louisiana? Or could they regulate someone departing in Louisiana to a state outside of the state's jurisdiction? Homer Plessy would not be the first to test the law.

On February 24, 1892, the Comité des Citoyens acted. Its operatives provided the musician son of Rodolphe Desdunes, Daniel Desdunes, with a first-class ticket. At 8 A.M. that morning, the younger Desdunes made his way to the L&N Depot on Canal Street and took a seat in a whites-only car bound for Mobile, Alabama. But he got no further than the two miles it took to get to the corner of Elysian Fields and North Claiborne Avenues. Here, the conductor stopped the train. Private detectives hired by the Comité des Citoyens got on board and arrested Daniel Desdunes. They booked him with violating the Separate Car Act.[30] Comité des Citoyens treasurer Paul Bonseigneur arrived at the precinct station to have the thirty-year-old younger Desdunes released on a surety bond. A Comité des Citoyens statement detailed this first strike against the Separate Car Act:

> The public having generously responded to our appeal, The Citizens' Committee decided to make a test of the law, and to that end Daniel F. Desdunes offered his services to the Committee. He was provided with a first class ticked to Mobile, Ala; on the 24th of Feb. 1892, he boarded the Louisville & Nashville Railroad at Canal Street, entered and took a seat in a first class coach. An employee of the road came to him and informed Mr. Desdunes that he would have to go into the coach reserved for

Daniel Desdunes was a musician and a member of the Creole Onward Brass Band. He later taught music at Boys Town in Nebraska. (From *Nos Hommes et Notre Histoire,* courtesy of the University of New Orleans Louisiana Division)

colored people. Mr. Desdunes politely refused to comply. The conductor being called, he threatened to stop the train and put him off. Mr. Desdunes quietly replied that he would not move unless force was used. The conductor then stopped the train at the corner of Elysian Fields and Claiborne streets, when Capt. Ed. Flood of the City Secret Service, who was on the train signaled to Detectives Flotte and Dale, who stepped and placed Mr. Desdunes under arrest. He was taken to the Second Recorder's Court, where Capt. Flood swore out an affidavit against him for violating Act No. 111 of 1890 . . . Mr. Desdunes waived the preliminary examination, and was remanded to the Criminal District Court, under a bond of $500 Mr. Paul Bonseigneur becoming the surety.

The Citizens' Committee had retained as local counsel Judge James C. Walker, one of the leading lawyers of our criminal bar.[31]

As the Comité des Citoyens awaited Desdunes' hearing, Separate Car Act proponent Murphy Foster won the governor's race. Inauguration day was May 16, 1892. Shortly thereafter, he appointed departing governor and ally Francis T. Nicholls as chief justice of the state supreme court. By June 1892, the Comité des Citoyens readied themselves to move forward on the intrastate portion of the act, knowing this could be the toughest legal nut to crack. Now came Homer Plessy's turn to ride the train.

CHAPTER 7

Are You a Colored Man?

> The law will never make men free; it is the men who have got to make the law free.
>
> —Henry David Thoreau, July 4, 1856
> Framingham, Massachusetts

> We have now to fight the Plessy case for our right to travel in the State.
>
> —Louis A. Martinet, July 4, 1892
> New Orleans, Louisiana

> And the said Homer Adolph Plessy in his own proper person cometh into Court here, and having heard the said information read, says: That this Honorable Court ought not to entertain further cognizance of this cause, because protesting that he is not guilty as in the said information above specified.
>
> —Defendant's Plea, Exhibit D
> *State of Louisiana v. Homer Adolph Plessy*
> Criminal District Court, Section A, Judge Ferguson presiding
> Parish of Orleans, October 1892

In the weeks leading up to Homer Plessy's fateful railroad ride, the details of his test case took form. Working behind the scenes, Martinet obtained the cooperation of a railroad, just as they had done with the Louisville & Nashville Railroad in the Daniel Desdunes test case. They also secretly hired Christopher C. Cain—a former captain of the guard at the Orleans Parish Prison who ran a detective agency on St. Charles Street—to make the arrest.[1] Plessy's arrest also played on the national political scene. Martinet and Tourgee timed the action to coincide with the National Republican Convention in Minneapolis, as a prod for the party of Lincoln to focus more on civil liberties in the South.

Plessy's Moment

Homer Plessy was younger than most members of the Comité des Citoyens, but at the time of his train trip, the world of his youth was rapidly fading. There were deaths in his family that year. In February 1892, Plessy's half brother, Charles Dupart, died at nineteen of acute cerebral congestion. His uncle Gustave Plessy also died that month.[2] Professionally, the intimate shoemaking concerns that flourished in the preindustrial South gave way to large factories. The New Orleans Keiffer Brothers factory boasted shoe outputs exceeding 350 pairs a day.[3] Indeed, in 1891, Homer had taken to selling shoes near St. Bernard Circle. Culturally, the city was more Anglicized and less tolerant, as tales of the heady westward expansion supplanted Civil War and Reconstruction lore. For all this so-called progress, from Homer's perspective, the Separate Car Act was a step backward from the South in which his parents lived. It unfairly set him apart from his neighbors, no matter what his education, industry, or roots were in the city. Plessy fit the committee's criterion: his fair complexion would challenge a conductor's ability to do racial classifications. With the 1892 election of Murphy Foster as Louisiana's governor, and Foster's appointment of Nicholls as chief justice of the state supreme court, Plessy's act had become all the more crystallizing and dramatic. The Separate Car Act's floor leader and the governor who signed it into law now held the two highest offices in Louisiana.

Get the ticket. Get on the train. Get arrested. Get booked. On June 7, 1892, Homer Plessy traveled the nearly two miles from his residence in Faubourg Tremé to the train station at the hustling Press Street railroad yards at the edge of Faubourg Marigny. The Press Street Depot was only a stone's throw away from the Mississippi River. One could hear the horns of steamboats as scores of dockworkers unloaded bales, barrels, and sacks from the many ships and barges that docked along the river.[4] With a coal yard and freight sheds on either side of the depot, the complex housed the combined offices of the East Louisiana Railroad and also the New Orleans Northeastern Railroad.[5] There was also a restaurant, company offices, a baggage platform, and three train sheds. A combination waiting room and ticket office remained open to Plessy, but the freshly posted copies of the Separate Car Act made the office less than hospitable. Still, he purchased a first-class ticket on the East Louisiana Railroad's number eight train. It was scheduled to depart at 4:15 P.M. for a two-hour run to Covington, Lousiana.

The East Louisiana Railroad was the targeted train for his exercise in civil disobedience. Since it never left Louisiana, it provided the stage for a test of whether the Separate Car Act could apply to cars traveling solely within the state. With great fanfare earlier that year, the East Louisiana Railroad laid tracks that extended its service to the beaches at Mandeville, then to Covington, which the East Louisiana Railroad advertised as the

East Louisiana Railroad ticket

"healthiest spot in America." On a preliminary ride, the press raved at its sumptuous new cars with mahogany interiors, brass lamps, adjustable seats of the "richest plush and comfortable form," and "toilet rooms and tiled mirrors at each end."[6] Homer Plessy prepared for a different reception than those who rode on the exhibitory trip. As boarding time neared, Homer walked toward the first-class coach, ignoring the cars with the Colored Only designations. He likewise disregarded the edicts of the prominently posted Separate Car Act and took a seat in the well-adorned first-class accommodation. The whistle blew, the doors shut, the steam blasted from the engine, and the East Louisiana train's wheels creaked forward.

As the train inched away, the conductor, J. J. Dowling, collected tickets. He paused when he got to Plessy—then, the question: "Are you a colored man?"[7]

"Yes," said Homer Plessy.

"Then you will have to retire to the colored car," Dowling responded.

Homer asserted that he was an American citizen who paid for his ticket and intended to ride to Covington. Others in the car began to stir.

Once again, Conductor Dowling asked him to leave. Again, he refused.

Dowling then signaled the engineer, who brought the number eight train to a dead stop. Dowling disembarked, walked back to the depot, and returned to the coach with Detective Cain to find Plessy still sitting there.

Detective Cain then took over and cautioned Plessy: "If you are colored you should go into the car set apart for your race. The law is plain and must be obeyed."

Again Plessy refused to budge and said he would rather go to jail than abandon the coach.

At 4:35 P.M., twenty minutes after the train's scheduled departure, Detective Cain and others forcibly dragged the neatly dressed Plessy from the whites-only coach and executed his arrest at Royal and Press Streets. The East Louisiana number eight train resumed its otherwise uneventful trip to Covington sans Homer Plessy. Detective Cain was conducting him to the Fifth Precinct station on Elysian Fields—a block away from where his father lived on Burgundy Street and two blocks from where Joseph Guillaume protested segregated star cars in 1867. At the station house, Plessy submitted to the same booking procedure applied to the array of drunks, petty larcenists, and foul-mouthed New Orleanians arrested that day on the city's streets.[8] But his charge of "Violating Section 111 of the Separate Car Act" was anything but a typical Tuesday-evening New Orleans petty crime. Members of the Comité des Citoyens—Eugene Luscy, treasurer Paul Bonseigneur, Rodolphe Desdunes, L. J. Joubert, and Louis Martinet—all converged at the Fifth Precinct station, perhaps somewhat giddy over the success of Plessy's ticket purchase, train boarding, arrest, and being booked with a charge they could scrutinize with the Fourteenth Amendment. Now, they had a case to take before the courts. Furthermore, they convinced Judge Moulin to release a disheveled Plessy on temporary bail, sparing him a night in parish prison.[9] Homer still held his first-class ticket as he and his compatriots walked from the Fifth Precinct station and made their way across Elysian Fields and back toward Tremé.[10] They had just purposefully, intentionally, and openly defied Gov. Murphy Foster; Francis Nicholls, chief justice of the state supreme court; and the 1890 Louisiana legislature.

The next day, on June 8, 1892, at 10 A.M., Homer Plessy reported to Judge Moulin's Second Recorder's court, located in the Cabildo next to St. Louis Cathedral. Detective Cain, Conductor Dowling, and another witness, J. L. Mott, also showed up to swear affidavits giving their versions of events. At the same time, the Comité des Citoyens' treasurer, Paul Bonseigneur, arrived at the court. Bonseigneur plunked down a $500 surety on his North Claiborne Street residence to ensure Plessy's appearance for trial. Meanwhile, the press got wind of the story.

Daily Crescent:

IN THE WRONG COACH
A Snuff-Colored Descendant of
Ham Kicks Against the "Jim

State of Louisiana v. Homer Plessy bond document

Crow" Law,
And Takes the Jail End of It Rather
Than Comply With Its Distinctive Provisions

Yesterday afternoon at 4:15 o'clook private detective C. C. Cain arrested from the East Louisiana train Adolph Plessy, [a light mulatto], and locked him up in the Fifth Precinct station, on a charge of violating section 2 of act 111 of the statute of 1890 relative to separate coaches. Detective Cain made an affidavit this morning against Plessy in the Second Recorder's Court.

Capt. Cain, speaking of the circumstances of the arrest, stated that he and the conductor both ordered the man from the white coach into the one set apart for colored people. The negro refused to leave the coach, saying that he had bought his ticket and was going to ride to Convington . . . Plessy was arraigned before Judge Moulin this morning. He was represented by J. C. Walker, Esq, who waived examination on the part of his client, and the judge committed Plessy to the Criminal District Court under a bond of $500, which was signed and Plessy released.[11]

Daily Picayune:

ANOTHER JIM CROW
CAR CASE

Arrest of a Negro Traveler
Who Persisted
In Riding With the White People

It appears that Plessy purchased a ticket to Covington and shortly before his arrest, the Conductor asked him if he was a colored man. On the latter replying that he was, the conductor informed him that he would have to go into the car set aside for colored people. This he refused to do, and Mr. Cain then stepped up and requested him to go into the other coach but he still refused. Mr. Cain thereupon informed him that he would either have to

James C. Walker, Plessy's local attorney

go or go to jail. He replied that he would sooner go to jail then leave the coach and was thereupon arrested.

He waived examination yesterday before Recorder Moulin and was sent before the criminal court under $500.00 bond.[12]

Crusader:

Homer A. Plessy boarded the East Louisiana Railroad, at the foot of Press Street, for Covington. He held a first-class ticket and naturally took his seat in a first-class coach. As the train was moving out of the station, the conductor came up and asked if he was a white man. Plessy, who is as white as the average white Southerner, replied that he was a colored man. Then, said the conductor, "you must go in the coach reserved for colored people.

Plessy replied that he had a first-class ticket and would remain in the first-class coach.

The conductor insisted that he retire to the Jim Crow coach. Plessy determinedly told him that he was an American citizen and proposed to enjoy his rights as such and to ride for the value of his money.

The conductor seeing his own powers of persuasion unavailing, invoked the aid of the police. Capt. C. C. Cain, who was at the station, entered the car and told Plessy, that if he was a colored man, he would have to go to the colored coach.

Plessy again refused. The officer told him he would have to go into the coach or to jail. Plessy said he would go to jail first before relinquishing his right as a citizen.

The conductor signaled the engineer, and the train, which was moving slowly, came to a stand still at the intersection of Rampart Street, and the officer alighted with Plessy and a couple of citizens, who apparently had volunteered their aid to make the arrest.

The Citizens' Committee has volunteered its aid and has retained Jas. C. Walker, Esq., the leading attorney of the criminal bar, to defend Plessy, and will fight the case to the finish.[13]

In year one of the Plessy saga, 1890 witnessed the passage of the Separate Car Act. In year two, 1891 saw the respondent organization of the Comité des Citoyens. In year three, 1892 assembled the players and set the stage. Perhaps in leaner-news years, Plessy's act of civil disobedience would have received more national attention. But in 1892, racial separation on railroad cars represented only one in a myriad of conflicts and events that swirled across America in the last decade of the 1800s. In 1892, a wide variety of interests, ideologies, economic classes, and regions clashed. Lines of demarcation were drawn. Those with radically opposing visions of America's future relentlessly jockeyed to position themselves for control of the coming twentieth century. Quite the year was 1892. So many dramatic events unfolded in its first semester. And what was yet to come?

In addition to racial conflicts, the first half of 1892 witnessed pitched battles as militant labor unions and intransigent capitalists locked horns in their own bloody guerre a mort. In Pennsylvania, strikers and strikebreakers engaged each other in the no-holds-barred Homestead strike, a watershed event in labor-union history. In New Orleans in 1892, white and black unions united in a general strike. Though many capitalists employed race in dividing unions, and some union leaders employed racial separatism to attract members, national Populist Party leader Tom Watson told farmers "You are kept apart that you may be separately fleeced of your earnings. You are made to hate each other because upon that hatred is rested the keystone of the arch of financial despotism which enslaves you both."[14]

The first half of 1892 also launched presidential conventions. National politics produced a rematch between the two opponents of the nation's 1888 presidential contest with incumbent Republican Benjamin Harrison facing off against former Democratic president Grover Cleveland. The year also witnessed the Populist Party as the first third-party ticket in American history to garner more than a million votes.

The year 1892 also marked thirty years since the Union occupation of New Orleans and Abraham Lincoln's drafting of the Emancipation Proclamation. The country had survived the Civil War with the Union intact and America moved closer to its Bill of Rights ideals by abolishing slavery. On the other hand, its commitment to the Reconstruction ideals of equality regardless of race faced increased battery. The year had the highest number of lynchings in American history, with blacks being killed at an average of two to three a week. That year, Frederick Douglass led a group of New Yorkers to the White House to request that Pres. Benjamin Harrison address the growing problem. The group even used the 1891 massacre of Italian immigrants in New Orleans as a glaring example. Harrison responded by establishing a commission to study the situation and report back in a year—well after the election. In addition, calls for disenfranchisement and segregation laws in many Southern legislatures cascaded at an alarming rate. In that context, Plessy's attempts to ride in a first-class coach across Lake Pontchartrain to Covington did not seem to many to be the issue most worthy of attention. Yet Louis A. Martinet and the Comité des Citoyens continued to view the Plessy matter as bedrock to the maintenance of the spirit of the Reconstruction amendments. Through their eyes, if the law allowed the use of race to determine seating assignments, it could also undermine other aspects of an individual's political, legal, educational, and social life.

In the spring of 1892, political victory came to the opponents of the Louisiana Lottery Company as the state voted against the company's attempt to renew its charter. Additionally, Separate Car Act proponent Murphy Foster won Louisiana's gubernatorial election with a plurality of forty-four percent as the antilottery Democratic candidate. He defeated a pro-lottery Democrat, a pro-lottery Republican, an antilottery Republican, and the People's party (Populist) candidate.[15] Shortly after Murphy Foster became governor, he nominated his predecessor and former governor, Francis T. Nicholls, as chief justice of the Louisiana Supreme Court. Foster also appointed John Ferguson as senior judge of the Orleans Parish Criminal Court.

For Martinet, Homer Plessy, and the Comité des Citoyens, the first half of 1892 brought court and legislative ups and downs. Their test cases went off smoothly. They secured local lawyer James C. Walker to represent Daniel Desdunes and Homer Plessy. The *Crusader* continued to publish. Still, political brush fires seemed unending, as white separatists stepped up their legislative and political march toward legal segregation. Martinet had spent the good part of the spring season traveling to Baton Rouge in a successful but time-consuming effort to turn back an antimiscegenation bill that found its way to the Senate.

Martinet to Tourgee

Less than a month after Plessy's arrest, 1892's Fourth of July fell on a typically hot New Orleans summer day—muggy with no appreciable breeze. Even the iceman suffered a heatstroke while making deliveries near the French Quarter and had to be taken by ambulance to a local hospital. That unfortunate incident aside, the heat and humidity did not dampen this celebratory Independence Day. The now-segregated East Louisiana Railroad brought Orleanians on dollar excursions to enjoy red-white-and-blue festivities across the lake in Mandeville. Over three thousand "base ball" fans gathered to see New Orleans beat Mobile five to four in "one of the best games of the season." At the fairgrounds, John Fitzpatrick, mayor, presided over St. Mary's orphan asylum benefit picnic and festival. In the West End area, on Lake Pontchartrain, "fireworks specially designed" lit up the air over the lake. And what a difference thirty years made! In a New Orleans that once was a part of the Confederate States of America, businessmen at the city's elitist Commercial Club toasted the red, white, and blue, sang "Hail Columbia," and talked of patriotism and the "equal rights to all" espoused by the founding fathers.[16] On this 1892 Fourth of July, the Civil War that once rented the nation in two now seemed like the fading memory of a bad dream.

While the city and the rest of the nation reveled in the nation's one hundred sixteenth birthday, Louis Martinet found himself in a pensive, restless mood alternating between high hopes and low despair. The Fourth of July held meaning for him precisely because of the Union victory in the Civil War and the Reconstruction amendments. Those events engendered a political climate that allowed him to attend law school in his own state, be admitted to practice law, vote, and seek elected office. Unlike free people of color in New Orleans before the war, Martinet did not have to journey overseas to pursue his education. Nor did he need passes and permits to walk down the city streets. And until passage of the Separate Car Act of 1890, he felt free to travel on public conveyances.

Events unfolding on the national political scene also troubled Martinet. Pres. Benjamin Harrison received the nomination instead of the Tourgee-Martinet-backed candidacy of Tom Reed, leaving the National Citizens' Rights Association without a political lever and, thus, politically ineffectual. Even worse, Harrison appointed Howell E. Jackson, a Southern Democrat, to the Supreme Court as an overture to Southern Democrats.

Where was it all headed? Perhaps, writing would give Martinet perspective. He pulled out some *Crusader* stationary, took pen in hand, and began writing a long encompassing letter to his confidant and fellow attorney, Albion W. Tourgee, ostensibly to inform him of the progress of the two test cases. But it took a week to complete the letter that evolved into a twenty-eight-page expository message exploring a wide range of moods and topics. More so than other correspondences, Martinet's Fourth of July letter to Tourgee provided history, with a peek into this early attempt at igniting a civil-rights movement against segregation. It looked into the political and social machinations of this pivotal year as seen through his eyes—as a lawyer, activist, and civil-rights advocate in the South. Though Martinet's public articles brimmed with confidence and righteous indignation, that summer's letter revealed the anxiety, hopes, fears, and anger behind the scenes of the Plessy matter.

Louis Martinet was described as a "very neat man who always wore a black suit, with a black bow string tie and a black felt wide brim hat."[17] He stoked numerous irons in the fire as a notary, a member of the board of directors of Southern University, a demonstrator of anatomy at a medical school, an editor of a newspaper, and a key member of the Comité des Citoyens. The oldest of five children born to Belgium native— Hippolite Martinet—and Louisiana-born Marie Benoit, Louis

Martinet was born a free person of color in St. Martin's Parish in the southwestern part of Louisiana. He received a law degree in 1876 from Straight College in New Orleans. At the time of the case, Martinet kept residency right outside the French Quarter on Burgundy Street. Martinet's notary and *Crusader* office was at 412-14 Exchange Alley between Royal and Chartres Streets in the heart of the downtown commercial area. His wife, Lenora, served as principal of the high school at Southern University, which was then located on Magazine Street in uptown New Orleans. The couple had two children: Devonne, who died in childhood, and Leslie Louise.[18]

It had been months since Martinet corresponded with Reconstruction figure Albion Tourgee. But 1892's events happened so rapidly, he explained to Tourgee, that every time he collected his thoughts on one topic, something else would

Plessy's signature on notary document signed by Louis Martinet (Courtesy University of New Orleans Louisiana and Special Collections)

come along to supplant it. And even though Tourgee was eleven years his senior, the two men had much in common. They both combined the careers of writers, lawyers, and activists. As idealists, they envisioned an America where the color line did not exist and they felt a shared despondency about whether they would obtain that vision. Martinet saw Tourgee as a soul mate in a quest for equal treatment regardless of race. Theirs was at once a legal, political, and moral crusade for civil rights. Corresponding at least twenty-four times over the eight-year span of their fight against segregation, they found each other's writings a place to float ideals, vent their innermost feelings, exhilarate in their victories and successes, comfort each other, and plan theie next moves.

But while Tourgee offered commentary from the relative peace and quiet of western New York, Martinet toiled in the post-Reconstruction South. Tourgee is credited as the legal architect of the Plessy case, but Martinet labored in the trenches. He worked the legal system, obtained the local lawyer to defend Plessy at the state level, planned the mechanics of the test cases, and engaged railroads to cooperate in their efforts. He recruited test riders, notarized affidavits, and hired detectives. He published the *Crusader* once a week and kept abreast of national politics and developments. Living in the South, Martinet had a close-up view of the evils and horrors around him. His *Crusader* offices functioned as something of a clearinghouse for reporting abuse. He related a wrenching account to Tourgee of a garment brought to his office—a "tattered, torn and blood-stained shirt of a half-witted Negro, who tended his mother's farm, murdered a few days previously in my native parish."[19] Someone showed him a souvenir postcard that was being sold—a picture of a black man burned alive in Texarkana. Even Martinet's brother, who ventured into their home parish of St. Martin, was told to leave for reasons unclear. "Things do not change much in this State," Martinet told Tourgee. "My oldest brother, who has been away from his home for a year and a half, ventured to go back two or three weeks ago; being in bad health. He was at once notified to

leave again; he returned here, there being absolutely no protection in the parishes & no means of defense. I was very sorry
& even mad at this. He had gone without my knowledge, & I
don't believe he ought to have done so unless he was ready &
willing to insist on his right to live in the parish even at the risk
of his life."[20]

Martinet told Tourgee of his family concerns and his anxiety
for their future in a race-driven South. "My wife is compelled
to work—she teaches—to enable me to get along," Martinet
explained to Tourgee. "It is thus that I am enabled to make sacrifices of labor, time, and even money in the cause we are fighting for . . . And besides our child is getting to an age where we
must begin to think seriously of her education. I cannot, I
would not—unless I could not do otherwise—rear her in this
prejudiced southern atmosphere."

As one who spent his adult life pursuing intellectual, political, and journalistic goals, Martinet saw himself as second to no
man. He had just two months prior completed an unsuccessful
run for state superintendent of education on the Republican
ticket. Martinet did not accept or pretend to engage in the
inferior stature that white supremacy required. He did not
aspire to be treated as an American citizen as much as he
assumed to be a citizen and carried himself as such. "In days
gone by," he wrote, "when I was actively in politics as a Republican leader—a beardless youth I was then—I never permitted
myself to be driven away . . . Gangs and regiments of men
(Democrats) used to go about armed; but I never was influenced by threats or inimical public demonstrations, & I believe
I remain the only active politician who was not, at one time or
another, driven from the parish through fear and intimidation.
I was often threatened & several times saw guns leveled at me.
But I never flinched & always maintained my ground & used to
carry openly an arsenal about me."[21]

Though they shared the same goals, Tourgee held to a
Christian view of politics while Martinet could not humble
himself before what he considered an uncaring God. "I am
sorry that I did not meet your expectation in regard to the day

of prayer," Martinet wrote. "But I am not a hypocrite. I did not then, & I don't now, feel like praying for the injustices & outrages heaped upon us in this country. No just God should permit such abominations." He elaborated that he did not oppose religion for others. "I was not criticizing its observance so much as the readiness of certain 'national leaders' to affix their names to public documents for buncombe, but never make the slightest sacrifice, or do anything to help unless it benefits them." While Martinet's *Crusader* articles invariably predicted victory, his letter to Tourgee sounded a darker and more somber tone. Martinet realized the magnitude of the task and the consequences of segregation. But while the Comité des Citoyens had spent much time organizing and raising funds, victory was anything but a forgone conclusion, and the window of opportunity was closing. Letters and fund-raising ledgers produced a goodly amount of everyday public support but seemingly natural allies such as Frederick Douglass and P. B. S. Pinchback did not support them; Booker T. Washington preached accommodation with segregation. Martinet found state and national Republicans likewise impotent when it came to organizing support against bills that banned interracial marriages or limited suffrage. The 1892 Louisiana legislature attempted to pass such laws, but Martinet armed himself with petitions and a letter from the archbishop of New Orleans. With the help of a sympathetic white Democratic senator from downtown New Orleans, he was able to have the measures defeated. "We had not the help of the Republican 'leaders' or politicians & fought the battle without them . . . We must unload & stand on our manhood & dignity & rely on our own efforts," Martinet wrote to Tourgee. Despite the victory against the antimiscegenation bill and antisuffrage measures, Martinet sobered, "We must not rejoice too much. It is only a breeding spell . . . We must brace up for the fight two years hence."[22]

Martinet felt that, like the state Republican Party, the national Republican Party had also become politically quiescent on the matter of racial injustice in the South. From his perspective, the wrong Republican received the presidential nomination. Martinet told Tourgee that Benjamin Harrison was "a shrewd man, but narrow minded, selfish, & unscrupulous in his own interest." He added, "Harrison's conduct toward us in this state has been positively shameful. Under the pretext of assisting to crush the Lottery, he has helped the Bourbons to put their heels on our necks more effectively than ever. The Democratic element in power are the real Bourbons." Just as he felt the wrong Republican received the party's nomination, he also felt the wrong Democrat had been elected governor. He expressed disappointment in Murphy Foster's victory over a more down-to-earth Democrat—Samuel McEnery, who Foster defeated in a five-way contest. "With the Lottery out of the way it were better for the State & for us that the McEnery wing had succeeded," Martinet stated. "Foster & his clique represent the aristocrats, the 'oldest & best;' the McEnery side, the riffraff, the poor whites & the hoodlums. The latter are more in touch with the 'common herd'; on occasions you can elbow them; the former never. They (the Foster clique) are your 'superior' by divine ordinance," he sarcastically noted. And as great his dissatisfaction with the political situation grew, there was no other place to turn. "Unfortunately for us in the South there is no other party that we can affiliate with but the Republicans," Martinet told Tourgee. "The Third party (Populist or People's party) here is but little more liberal than the Democratic & not strong enough yet."

Martinet told Tourgee of his growing sense of despair and burden as he tried to focus on the goal of the Supreme Court case. "You wrote sometime ago that I was despondent. I don't know how you knew it, but you spoke right," he confided. "The fight we are making is an uphill one under the best circumstances . . . And then again one is surrounded by so much petty jealousy & envy that it's quite disgusting. Those about you, that is too many of them—think that you have some ulterior object in view; that you are seeking prestige, influence or advancement, & too often instead of upholding you they are apt to do the contrary in some covert, hypocritical way. All this is disgusting to me."

"What have I to gain in fighting this battle?" Martinet rhetorically asked Tourgee. "Like you, I have asked myself this question a thousand times. Certainly I gain nothing, but spend time, labor & money in it. There is no doubt that if I turn my attention to, or put my energies in professional or some private pursuits I would get along much better in this world. Yes, why do I do it? I want no political influence, no prestige, no office. Like you, I believe I do it because I am built that way."

Martinet put away his pen on that Fourth of July with the letter uncompleted.

On the Bench in Section A

With the letter to Tourgee still unsent by the next weekend, irony had it that one of newly appointed Judge Ferguson's first rulings would lift Martinet's spirits. On July 9, 1892, Comité des Citoyens lawyer James C. Walker informed Martinet that Judge Ferguson had thrown out the charges against Daniel Desdunes—the test case for interstate travel. In this case, Ferguson cited the case of *Abbot v. Hicks,* a Louisiana case that ruled interstate commerce as a federal prerogative. To say the least, the decision elated Martinet, and perhaps—just maybe— the committee could achieve victory at a state level and have a strong precedent for challenges in other states. He sounded a considerably more ebullient and confident mood than he showed in the beginnings of his Fourth of July letter as he relished victory in the *Crusader:*

> The Jim Crow car is ditched and will remain in the ditch. Reactionists may foam at the mouth and Bourbon organs may squirm, but Jim Crow is as dead as a doornail.
> Monday, the case of Prof. D. F. Desdunes, arrested sometime ago on the L. & N.R.R. and charged with violating the separate car law, which Judge Marr had under advisement on a plea attacking the constitutionality of the law at the time of his disappearance in April last, was called up before his successor. After argument by Counsel, Judge Ferguson overruled the State's demurrer to defendant's plea, holding the law, as applying

to interstate passengers, unconstitutional. . . . It is well to remark here that the report of a morning paper that Desdunes had been incarcerated at the time of his arrest is totally incorrect. Mr. Desdunes was never in jail. He was bailed out as soon as arrested.

Judge Ferguson's decision is an application of the principle declared by our State Supreme Court recently in the Pullman Palace Car Company case from Shreveport, that Congress alone has the power to regulate commerce or travel between the States; and thus one's right to travel unmolested on railroads through Louisiana is ingrained in our jurisprudence, and the railroad hereafter denying it will render itself liable in damages.

The young Professor Desdunes is to be congratulated on the manly assertion of his right, and his refusal to ride in the Jim Crow coach. The people should cherish the performance of such patriotic acts and honor the patriots.

The result is also a triumph for the Citizens' Committee, which undertook the defense of the case. When The Crusader, for a whole year, pleaded for organized resistance to the infamous Jim Crow car law, it was regarded as cranky. When as a result of its agitation the Citizens' Committee was formed a few months ago, it has sought to swerve that hand of patriots from their purpose. Democratic journals cited decisions of the United States Supreme Court to prove the law constitutional, and Negro leaders— National leaders—refused aid or encouragement.[23]

Now with Desdunes cleared, the Plessy matter moved forward. Reenergized, Martinet continued his letter to Tourgee. Rising above the doldrums, Martinet once again filled with ideas and renewed confidence. "We have now to fight the Plessy case for our right to travel in the State," Martinet affirmed. "We need to reach a larger audience that can be reached in a few churches at one time—and then our agitation must be continued thereafter & not sporadic . . . The people of the North must be educated to conditions in the South, & this can only be done through the press—and through our own press. . . . We must expose continually to the people of the North the hideous sores of the South & the ever-recurring outrages to which we are subjected & the lurking therein to the Nation." Martinet, who could be inspired out of depression by a rousing battle against injustice, lent some of his new surge of optimism to Tourgee. "We must not lose heart," he wrote. "I notice you are as low spirited as I am sometimes. Your last letter to me showed a depth of discouragement that was painful. But I was in the same mood and only aroused by the anti-miscegenation bill in the legislature."

In closing, Martinet stated "I ought to rewrite this letter, and shorten it by one-half or two-thirds, but really I can't." He tried to brighten Tourgee's spirits and enclosed articles about the victory over the antimiscegenation bill along with a list of new people who had signed up as members of Tourgee's National Citizens' Rights Association. He requested copies of Tourgee's pamphlet *Is Liberty Worth Preserving?* to distribute. "But life has its pleasant incidents after all," he shared as he told Tourgee that a group of friends had presented him with a watch in appreciation of his years working for equal rights. The victory in the Desdunes case pumped new life into Martinet and the Comité des Citoyens. The first half of 1892 thus far did not seem that bad after all. Martinet signed and sealed the letter to Tourgee and mailed it. With Daniel Desdunes set free, Plessy's day in court lie on the horizon. It was time to get back to work.

When Plessy Met Ferguson

As important as Homer Plessy's case was to Louis Martinet and Albion Tourgee, the shoemaker's predicament did not top Judge Ferguson's agenda. In the days leading to Plessy's court date, for John Ferguson, case number 19117—albeit unique—counted as just one of many criminal cases that came before his bench. The docket in Section A bulged with charges of aggravated assault, petty larceny (six months in parish prison), embezzlement (one year in the penitentiary), stabbing and wounding, concealed weapons, severing growing crops (six months in the penitentiary), horse-stealing, entering at night, violation of the Sunday laws, and detaining a woman without her consent.[24]

It was October 11, 1892, when Homer Plessy received his

notice of arraignment to appear in Judge Ferguson's court the following Thursday.[25] The charge was that Plessy had violated the Separate Car Act, the charge that the Comité des Citoyens wanted. The time had come. On the morning of October 13, 1892, the principals began arriving at St. Patrick's Hall in Lafayette Square as Homer Plessy and John Ferguson moved closer to their crossroad. Judge Ferguson had taken his routine four-mile journey from Henry Clay Street to Section A to digest New Orleans' daily crime menu. Homer Plessy and Rodolphe Desdunes arrived from their domiciles in Tremé. Committee lawyer James C. Walker's office was but two blocks away on Camp Street. Walker carried the petition that he and Tourgee had produced, asking Judge Ferguson to dismiss the charges against Plessy. It took Martinet less than a half-hour to walk from the *Crusader* offices on Exchange Alley to Royal Street, cross Canal Street onto St. Charles, and then walk another few blocks to Lafayette Square.

The weather on October 13, 1892, was showery and cool, with the temperature hovering between seventy and eighty degrees as summer turned to autumn.[26] In contrast, the racial climate along these streets had heated considerably. Indeed, the day after Judge Ferguson ruled with the Comité des Citoyens in the Daniel F. Desdunes case, a newspaper pointedly detailed a Missouri Supreme Court decision that supported segregation. Under the title "Oklahoma's Race War," another newspaper talked with derision of a group of Oklahoma blacks who sat in to protest segregated schools.[27] Meanwhile, the *Times-Democrat* continued to clamor for segregation at every level of society, as newspapers in New Orleans openly encouraged and applauded vigilantism. Front-page stories told of "Black Brutes" who were "Shot, Lynched, and Cremated for their Crimes."[28] In an anti-intermarriage article, a paper stated that "the negro type occupies the lowest position, physically, mentally, and morally," and has never "produced a man of science, a poet or an artist."[29] And over in Section B of Orleans Parish Criminal Court, district attorney Charles A. Butler engaged in a high-profile prosecution of the Comité des Citoyens' vice president and former Louisiana lieutenant governor, C. C. Antoine, for failing to inform a property buyer about a lien—charges that subsequently escalated to bribery.[30]

Inside Section A, the respective parties took their places. Other accused criminals on Judge Ferguson's October 13, 1892, docket included Henry Kelso, standing trial for petty larceny, and M. Daley, convicted of assault and battery.[31] At 10:30 A.M., all rose as court opened for business. Judge Ferguson entered the courtroom and called forth the parties in *Case No. 19117 The State of Louisiana v. Homer Adolph Plessy.*

Assistant district attorney Lionel Adams represented the State of Louisiana against Homer Plessy. Described as a "crack trial lawyer," Adams served as New Orleans' district attorney from 1884 to 1888. The bespectacled Adams had taken the assistant-district-attorney's position in 1892 only on a temporary basis to give newcomer district attorney Charles A. Butler a chance to get his feet wet. No stranger to high-profile cases, Lionel Adams served as defense attorney for the Italians charged in the assassination of police chief David Hennessy in 1891. A citizens group that investigated the trial accused Adams and subordinates of jury-tampering and stated that Adams' detective had bribed "a man working at the electric company who was paid to dim the lights when the jurors visited the murder scene." Despite these charges, the grand jury took no legal action against Adams.[32]

Lionel Adams, assistant district attorney who prosecuted Homer Plessy (Courtesy *New Orleans Times-Democrat,* April 2, 1893)

Across from Adams, at the defense table, sat Plessy's local

attorney, fifty-five-year-old James Campbell Walker. Born on January 24, 1837, Walker was of Albion W. Tourgee's generation. Like Tourgee, Walker also fought in the Civil War, albeit on the other side of the conflict. Walker served as private in the Confederate army, never seeking a promotion from 1862 until he surrendered in 1865 with the last remnants of the Confederate army.[33] After the war, he became active in Republican Party politics and represented the Republicans "free of charge" before the federal board that certified the votes in the election of 1876 during the Hayes-Tilden Compromise. Martinet called Walker, who had a wife and seven children, a "good, upright, and conscientious man" in describing him to Tourgee. Martinet further related that the Republican managers in Louisiana "did him (Walker) dirt, as they did, & still do, to all honest men in the party," which caused Walker to get "disgusted and quit politics."[34] Through letter or telegraph, the full-bearded Walker was quite judicious about informing Tourgee of case developments. He often called on Martinet to hurry Tourgee along when Walker needed information or guidance. Martinet had initially negotiated with another lawyer—"aristocratic" T. J. Semmes, who requested $2,500— but Walker agreed to do the case for $1,000.[35]

Next to Walker at the defense table sat citizen Plessy. Plessy had become something of an afterthought amidst the legalese and lawyers, with their briefs, motions, and writs. As his test case had been hastily arranged by Walker, Tourgee, and Martinet, Plessy had not even know at the end of May 1892, that he would be riding that fateful train ride on the seventh of June. Since that time, his name had appeared in arrest books, legal documents, newspapers, and notices of arraignment. Five months ago, he was shoemaker Plessy and now he was arrested Plessy, defendant Plessy, "snuff-colored," a "descendant of Ham," "a light mulatto," "the negro," "silly negro," and "colored." This would be one of four court appearances for Homer Plessy in 1892.

Presiding over all of this from the bench, of course, was Judge Ferguson. Ironically, given the circumstances and nature of the case, Plessy and Ferguson had the same skin color. Ferguson faced a moral conundrum similar to that which his mentor, Benjamin Hallet, faced in the 1856 Anthony Burns case—a process that sent an escaped slave back to slavery. While Plessy's case was not as grave as Anthony Burns' situation, the politics of Ferguson's sponsors and the magnifying glass of the local press brought intense pressure for a ruling against Homer Plessy.

But instead of a plea or a trial, Walker sought an outright dismissal of the charges on the grounds that the law was unconstitutional. As Plessy sat facing Judge Ferguson, Walker laid out his brief stating why Homer Plessy should be set free. His client was "orderly, well-dressed, and not intoxicated" at the time of his arrest and "uttered no profane or vulgar language." His client had purchased a first-class ticket and no passenger objected to his behavior aboard the train. The problem, as Walker laid it out, was not his client but the Separate Car Act, which sought to "confer upon a conductor the power to determine the question of race and to assort the passengers on his train" and to label passengers "criminal" for not complying. Walker asserted the Separate Car Act established an "invidious distinction and discrimination based on race, which is obnoxious to the fundamental principles of national citizenship." He further stated, "Race is a legal and scientific question of great difficulty and the state has no power to authorize any person to determine the same without testimony, or to make the rights and privileges of any citizen of the United States dependent on the fact of race. The State has no right to distinguish between citizens, any reason, privilege or immunity they may possess."[36]

Walker filed a motion to delay the proceedings so they could argue the constitutionality of the Separate Car Act. Judge Ferguson agreed and set a date. The clerk of court dutifully summarized Homer's meeting with Judge Ferguson:

> The defendant in person was placed at the bar of the Court in custody of the Sheriff attended by his counsel Jas. C. Walker Esq. to be arraigned on the charge preferred against him in the

said information. After reading the said information by the Clerk, the defendant was called upon to plead thereto. Now comes counsel for the defendant and presents to the Court a plea in bar to prosecution on the aforementioned information. The Court ordered said information filed. The defendant was discharged on his bond to await further proceedings.[37]

Plessy's second appearance in Section A came on October 28, 1892. Attorney Walker continued to press his argument that Plessy should go free, while Lionel Adams supported the rights of states to establish their own guidelines of racial association. Ferguson congratulated Plessy's counsel for "great research, learning, and ability" and adjourned court while he considered the two arguments.[38] In coming days, Grover Cleveland won the presidential election, giving Democrats control of the White House, the governor's house, and Supreme Court appointments. And even though the Separate Car Act argued the inability of blacks and whites to function together, an interracial general strike that hit New Orleans on November 8 seemed to refute segregation as a priority among everyday citizens. According to Bernard A. Cook: "Thousands of workers in the deep South had shown that they could unite in common struggle. Negro and white, skilled and unskilled, and . . . stay united despite the efforts of the employers and their agents to divide them by appeals to anti-Negro prejudice. From November 8 until November 11, 20,000 to 25,000 unionists refused to work."[39] The strike ended only with a threat by Governor Foster to dispatch the militia.

Ferguson's Decision

On November 18, 1892, the week after the general strike ended, Ferguson rendered his decision. His ruling supported state-mandated racial separation: "There is no pretense that he was not provided with equal accommodations with the white passengers. He was simply deprived of the liberty of doing as he pleased, and of violating a penal statute with impunity . . .

Criminal District Court for the Parish of Orleans.

LIONEL ADAMS, Asst District Attorney for the Parish of Orleans, who, in the name and by the authority of the said State, prosecutes in this behalf, in proper person comes into the Criminal District Court for the Parish of Orleans, in the Parish of Orleans, and gives the said Court here to understand and be informed that one

Homer Adolph Plessy

late of the Parish of Orleans, on the Seventh day of June in the year of our Lord one thousand eight hundred and ninety two, with force and arms in the Parish of Orleans aforesaid and within the jurisdiction of the Criminal District Court for the Parish of Orleans being then a passenger travelling wholly within the limits of the state of Louisiana on a passenger train to the East Louisiana Railroad Company, a railway company carrying passengers in their coaches within the state of Louisiana and on which the officers of the said East Louisiana Railroad Company had power and were required to assign, and did then assign the said Homer Adolph Plessy to the coach used for the race to which he, the said Homer Adolph Plessy belonged — unlawfully did then and there insist on going into a coach to which by race he did not belong;

contrary to the form of the Statute of the State of Louisiana in such case made and provided, and against the peace and dignity of the same.

Signed Lionel Adams
Asst District Attorney for the Parish of Orleans.

As assistant district attorney, Lionel Adams charged Homer Plessy with violating the Separate Car Act. (Courtesy University of New Orleans Louisiana and Special Collections)

The railway company was blameless in the matter. The ticket purchased by the defendant was not used simply because the defendant refused to ride in the car, or compartment, to which he was assigned by the conductor, without a valid reason for said refusal, and insisted on going into a coach in which by race he did not belong."[40]

The *Crusader* put its best spin on the ruling:

> As was expected Judge Ferguson of the Criminal Court overruled the plea to the unconstitutionality of the separate car law in the well-known Plessy case on a motion to quash information. We have no favors to ask of the Judge or of the Assistant District Attorney and consequently . . . we will exhaust all remedies which the laws of our country allow to its citizens for a redress of grievances.
>
> This of itself is a great stride out of oppression. Everyone knows that notwithstanding the constitution and statutory enactments, due process of law is absolutely denied to men of the black and mixed races in many parts of the United States, notably in the South.
>
> Judge Taney's decision has more force upon the minds and consciences of Southern jurists than any portion of the Federal Constitution. In consequence of that perverted spirit it is impossible for the colored people to obtain a fair trial if [it] appears to be a well-grounded complaint by a colored man against a white man. Justice is out of the question if the Judge must decide that a colored man has any rights which the white man is bound to respect.[41]

The war of words between the *Crusader* and the *Times-Democrat* became more contentious in subsequent days as the *Times-Democrat* heartily applauded Judge Ferguson's ruling, belittled the efforts of Plessy and the Comité des Citoyens, and called for an outright ban on interracial marriages:

> We are glad to see that Judge Ferguson has decided the separate car act constitutional, and thus put a quietus to the efforts of some negro agitators to disobey it and sweep it aside.
>
> The Times-Democrat earnestly urged the Legislature to pass

that act at the time it first came up, and congratulated the people of the State on its passage. Indeed, we should have liked even more far-reaching legislation that would tend to separate the two races in the South thoroughly. The law, however, was a move in the right direction, framed in the interest of the traveling public and intended to show the negroes that while they lived side by side with the whites the line of distinction and separation between the races was to be forever kept up.

Some negro agitators did not like the statute, and ever since its passage have sought to excite and arouse the colored people against it. There were no complaints that they did not receive the same accommodation as the whites in the cars, but they insisted on occupying the same car and sitting side by side with them.

Quite a campaign against the law was begun, and the political clubs and negro societies raised subscriptions to attack it in the court. A large sum was collected in this way, and every negro who desired to gain a little notoriety was anxious to rush forward and offer himself as a victim, to try and force his way into the white car, to be expelled from there: and on that basis attack the law in the Courts.

One of the cases came before Judge Ferguson, who has completely disposed of the African claim, and shown how little there is in it . . . Judge Ferguson has added his decision to those already given on this point, and presents some additional strong reasons in favor of the law. It is to be hoped that what he says will have some effect on the silly negroes who are trying to fight this law. The sooner they drop their so-called "crusade" against "the Jim Crow Car," and stop wasting their money in combating so well-established a principle—the right to separate the races in cars and elsewhere—the better for them.

What the Times-Democrat would like to see, and what it hopes to see, is the extension of this principle of keeping the races apart, and the Legislature at its next session could make a good beginning by passing the law pigeon-holed this year—prohibiting intermarriage between the races.[42]

The tirade by the *Times-Democrat* elicited a point-by-point refutation by Rodolphe Desdunes in the *Crusader:*

The Times-Democrat has a perfect right to be happy over the decision of Judge Ferguson. But when it says that decision will put a quietus to the efforts of most Negro agitators it is entirely in the dark.

In the first place the colored people are not alone in this agitation. There are people of different races connected with the movement to set aside a law intended to nullify the Fourteenth Amendment to the Federal Constitution, and to subordinate the dignity of the citizen to the malice and caprice of a few tyrant and demagogues.

Now as to the term agitators, we will mildly suggest that the Times-Democrat take heed of what people may think of the varied kinds. We are agitating for liberty, for justice, for life, for property by peaceful and constitutional methods . . . Every honorable person knows that the law was passed to discriminate against the colored people so as to degrade them. The "silly Negroes" to which allusion is made most audaciously, represent a group of people who would reflect honor on any community . . . We will state for the edification of the Times-Democrat that these "silly Negroes" represent from the doctor down to the laborer without whom the fields of Louisiana would probably become a howling wilderness. These "silly Negroes" are neither foreigners nor parvenus, nor are they marked by the seal of Cain. They pay taxes . . . in support of the government and feel keenly the oppression which is saddled upon them for purposes of gain and power by individuals who have no better claim than brute force at their command. These 'silly Negroes' and their ancestors have built up this country from its incipiency, and have defended its soil at the cost of their blood and treasures.[43]

On November 22, 1892, Plessy appealed to the Louisiana Supreme Court in case number 11134. Now headed by ex-governor Francis Nicholls, the court swiftly upheld Ferguson's ruling and provided the *Times-Democrat* with the last word in 1892:[44]

Yesterday the Supreme Court of Louisiana rendered a decision in favor of the constitutionality of the separate car act on practically the same grounds as led Judge Ferguson, of the Criminal Court, to, the same conclusion.

Homer A. Plessy, colored, was ejected from a train, because in defiance of the company's regulations and the conductor's order, he persisted in occupying a seat in a car reserved for white people, although there was a car on the train with equal accommodations for the use of colored passengers. In a suit in the Criminal District Court, Judge Ferguson, in an able and elaborate decision, justified the ejection.

> The community at large will be glad to hear that this race question is settled by the supreme tribunal of the state; and that it is settled on grounds which must commend themselves to the enlightened sentiment as well of the colored as of the white citizens. The two races will not mix, any more than oil and water; and it is better that the fact should be recognized at once, and made binding on both races by a law which will render all deliberate attempts at mixing penal.[45]

Year three of the Plessy saga drew lines and heightened tensions. The Comité des Citoyens looked northward toward the United States Supreme Court in year four of their battle with segregation. Tragedy lay in their path.

CHAPTER 8

My Dear Martinet

"Don't you hear the knocks? There are three men outside the door who have come to assassinate me." With such words Aristide Mary startled his family at the dinner table. He told his wife to hurry to the house door and shouted to his servant to follow her.[1]
— *Times-Democrat,* May 1893

It is of the utmost importance that we should not have a decision against us as the court has never reversed itself on a constitutional question.
—Tourgee to Martinet, October 1893

"Three Deadly Shots"—The Death of Aristide Mary

On January 5, 1893, Tourgee and Walker filed for a hearing before the United States Supreme Court. But in May, the Comité des Citoyens absorbed an emotional tragedy. It was 6:00 P.M. on the warm rainy evening of May 14, 1893. The committee's founding father, Aristide Mary, had just eaten dinner at his Ursulines Street mansion when he dispatched his wife and servant to fend off imagined assassins. As the two women walked down the hall to comply, three shots rang out from the room where Mary had just taken dinner. Mary's wife returned to find the curdling sight of her husband in a chair with his clothes ablaze from gunpowder. His blood poured from a stomach wound near his navel. His head leaned lifelessly against a window sill. His hand clenched a .38 Smith and Wesson. An eerie blue haze engulfed the room. Aristide Mary was dead—shot by his own hand.

The gunshots reverberated through the Ursulines Street neighborhood where Mary lived. Within moments, Policeman Evans of the Fourth Precinct arrived at the scene, removed the pistol from Mary's clenched hand, and blocked entrance to the house. Soon thereafter, acting coroner A. G. Maylie arrived and pronounced the cause of death as a "G.S.W. (gunshot wound) of abdomen."[2] The coroner determined that Mary had "fired three shots in such rapid succession that each bullet went through the one bullet hole," according to a newspaper report. Mary's family intimated that age had brought a decrease in faculties—a dementia. Friends and neighbors began gathering in front of the house. A newspaper reported: "Last night the Mary residence was besieged by friends of all nationalities who went there to condole with the family in their affliction. The deceased was unusually popular in his neighborhood, and great sorrow was publicly expressed."[3]

Aristide Mary's death delivered an emotional blow to the Comité des Citoyens. His influence brought them together in 1891. He embodied a generational link between antebellum New Orleans and the New Orleans of the 1890s and was an influential voice in each consecutive decade. Born in the late 1830s, the son of a white father and a black mother, he inherited a block of Canal Street, New Orleans' principal thoroughfare. At the time of his death, his estate was estimated to be a quarter of a million dollars.[4] Educated for law in Paris, Mary emerged as a key player in post-Civil War Republican politics in the 1860s and was once nominated for governor. In the 1870s, Mary publicly opposed caste legislation and financed suits against segregated establishments. As a cofounder of the Unification Movement in 1873, Mary was among the earliest in the Reconstruction period to call for an integrated society. He was on the board of trustees of Straight College in 1871 and organized protests against segregated schools as early as 1877. He also helped out personally and even signed a $5,000 bond so Martinet could secure his notary license.[5] In his will, he left money that went toward the construction of a new building for the Couvent School. Using his influence to bring the Comité des Citoyens into being was his last political act.

Aristide Mary's funeral was held at the home of his brother, on St. Ann Street. In an eighteen-page brochure written in French, entitled *Hommage Rendu a la Memoire de Alexandre Aristide Mary*, Rodolph Desdunes eulogized the committee's founder as one who "never failed to wage combat against all of the attacks which injustice continued to inspire against the rights and dignity of the citizen . . . Without thinking of himself," Desdunes stated, "he helped all those who made appeals upon his generosity. He was a philanthropist without bounds."[6] Martinet called Mary's death a "blow to us and our community."[7]

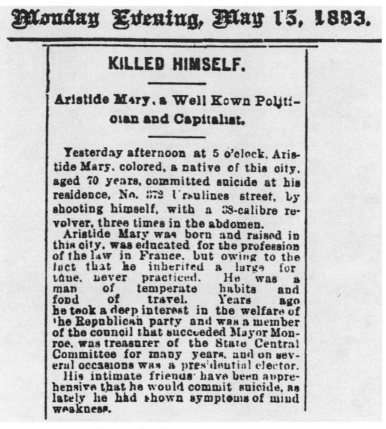

Aristide Mary's death was reported in several newspapers.

Aristide Mary's tomb in St. Louis Cemetery #3

1893—Economic Panic

Mary's death foreshadowed an increasingly difficult economic and political future. In 1893, there was a Democratic president, Grover Cleveland, and a Supreme Court in flux. An economic atmosphere that Benjamin Harrison described as never "a time in our history when work was so abundant, or when wages were as high" had now been hit by the Panic of 1893 and embarked on a tailspin rivaled only by the Depression of the 1930s.[8] To get the Plessy case moving along, Plessy's local attorney, James C. Walker, asked Judge Ferguson to meet with the state attorney to obtain a status. Judge Ferguson met with the attorney general of Louisiana to get him to advance the Plessy case but reported that the attorney general told him "the case seems to be getting along well enough."[9] It seemed that the state was stalling. If 1892 had been the year of high moments, 1893 would be a year of sober reflection and soul-searching, a year of death, a year of self-doubt, a year of difficult choices, a year of national economic catastrophe, and a year of fading hope. The quest of the Comité des Citoyens would become all the more uncertain.

Springtime in Mayville

As New Orleans pondered the death of Aristide Mary, springtime settled into the village of Mayville. Albion Tourgee had celebrated his fifty-fifth birthday on May 2, 1893, and his thirtieth anniversary of marriage on the fourteenth—the day Aristide Mary died. He was preparing to travel to Chicago for the 1893 antitrust conference when he received a letter at Thorheim from Louis Martinet informing him of Mary's traumatic end. Martinet, as it happened, was in Chicago as a medical student at Policlinic, residing at the second flat at 119 Wells Street. He heard that Tourgee would be in town for the antitrust convention. He suggested maybe the two could meet, which they did. Tourgee was staying at the Grand Pacific Hotel.

Martinet wanted Tourgee to grant an audience to Sarah A.

Farley, a woman from New Iberia, Louisiana. Miss Farley—a white lady—apparently taught black children and occasionally attended a black church with her father. For this, according to Martinet, a militia group called the Regulators burned down the church and forced the pastor out of town, while Miss Farley was "ostracized and traduced" in her community. After the harassment intensified, Miss Farley and her elderly father moved to Chicago, where Martinet hoped Tourgee could help her gain employment. Cases like that of Miss Farley and others gave pause to Martinet.[10]

Tourgee's files likewise bulged with stories of injustice from throughout the South, which arrived in a daily stream at Thorheim. The antilynching-crusading journalist Ida B. Wells reported that there were 118 lynches of blacks that year— eighteen in Louisiana, ranking it third in the nation.[11] One sobering commentary to Tourgee dated the Fourth of July 1892, came from one S. R. Kendrick of Duncan, Mississippi. Commenting on Tourgee's attempts to sensitize Northerners to rights violations in the South, Kendrick asserted, "We are a little tired of having to show our Corpse to prove to the world that the Laws of this Country is not sufficient to protect the Black man." Mr. Kendrick's reality showed that violence rivaled the days when Tourgee wrote The Invisible Empire. From Kendrick's perspective, Tourgee's calls for Southern blacks to organize could be a death sentence for the organizers:

> There is no Law in this State to protect a Black man who makes any attempt to enlighten his Race on any political question; Surely you do not realize the situation as we do, who lives here, the man or Woman who attempts to strike a Blow here for Freedom must be killed out right—or he must be Exiled from all he possesses.
>
> In a word he must be made such an example of, until no other Negro will attempt to do such a thing again . . . Our liberty have been taken from us so long until we have almost got use to it, In a word we see no possible chance of ever being Free under The Flag of Liberty and christian civilization.
>
> Do you know my Dear Sir, that there are standing armies in every county in every Southern State called Malitia, and are at

the command of the Governers of the different States, who are
Negro haters and who are willing to sacrifice everything even
Life in order to give the negro to know that he must obey the
white man, These armies are always ready to go to any scene
where a negro resist a White man no matter how small the case
may be, or however wrong the white man may be.

The Negro must submit It is no use to try the Law . . . It is possible that something can be done, but how it is to be done, is as
fare out of our sight as the God who created the heavens & the
Eart.[12]

Foe Louis Martinet, widespread, violent, and unpunished
repression forced him to grapple with the strategy of encouraging people to assert their rights with no assurances that they
would not be killed. "Are we helping the race or advancing the
cause of justice by the method we are pursuing?" Martinet
rhetorically asked Tourgee and himself. "Miss Farley doubts it. I
have grave doubts myself. Whenever the colored people show
any spirit—manifest any appreciation of the labors and sacrifices
on their behalf . . . 'white supremacy' is sure to assert itself, rise
up and crush it. Our pleadings for justice make no impression on
the oppressors except if in the opposite direction."[13]

But besides writing, lecturing, distributing pamphlets, and
appealing to politics, what could the Comité des Citoyens or
the National Citizens' Rights Association do? Did acquiescence
and accommodation hold the answer? Was it not the *Crusader*'s
own Rodolphe Desdunes who wrote that submission "aug-
ments the oppressor's power?" Throughout their lives, Martinet and Tourgee had both used Republican activism, writing,
lecturing, and organizing to convey their observations and
visions. They had pursued legislative and political avenues for
redress to no avail. As a Christian Socialist, Tourgee tried
appealing to America's conscience. All of their best efforts
seemingly led to dead ends. For them, the nation's highest tribunal increasingly represented the court of last resort. There
was no backup plan.

"The question forces itself upon me," Martinet continued,
"are we not fighting a hopeless battle—a battle made doubly

L. A. MARTINET, EDITOR.

L. J. JOUBERT, Business Manager.

The Crusader,

No. 117 EXCHANGE ALLEY.

New Orleans, La., Aug. 4 1893

Hon. A. W. Tourgee –

My dear Judge :

It is really a shame that I have not addressed you a line since leaving Chicago – but what I found here on my return added so much to my discouragement - of ever accomplishing anything for this people, that I did not know myself whether I would not quit. Our friends had quarreled among themselves and some who had the least cause – who had been aided & benefited by or through the Crusader, or by me, were trying to pull down the paper & had done some injury. My heart bled at the falseness, deceit, hypocrisy, ingratitude of men; I was prepared for many disappointments from the

Martinet letter to Tourgee, August 4, 1893 (Courtesy Chautauqua County Historical Society, Westfield, NY)

hopeless by the tyranny and cruelty of the Southern white? Are the Negroes progressing, or are they not retrograding under the yoke of the Southern barbarians, and are not our efforts for their betterment put forth in a method & manner calculated to do little good, or perhaps harm?"

> The Booker Washingtons, the Prices & others have their uses & are doing a useful work. I don't know, but it is, that if these men preached true manhood to their pupils, if they sought to instill in the youthful minds committed to their training the spirit of true manhood, they would not be tolerated in the communities where they are.
>
> But if our fight is fruitless, or rather our own manner fighting . . . so what is to be done? . . . The colored man must plead his cause at the bar of American public opinion. He must show that his condition is a forced one & give lie to those who assert he is satisfied with it . . . The colored people must be given a chance to develop, to rise & the hand of oppression must be stayed from them . . . They must be taught not only to read & pray, but also that to combat wrong and injustice, to resist oppression and tyranny, is the highest virtue of the citizen . . . They must be taught at school, and in present conditions this is impossible. These conditions must therefore be changed. But how? This is the question.[14]

Chicago changed the graying Martinet. It made him that more acutely aware of the daily psychological battles that Louisiana forced on him. He had done everything a citizen could do, but the laws and the press daily tried to relegate him to a second-class citizen. In Chicago, Martinet met a number of black cigar makers from New Orleans who earned an impressive eight dollars a day and, in a short span of time, were able to buy homes. He also realized that while the *Crusader* had established a following, it was not a known quantity in Chicago or in most places. Martinet confessed to Tourgee:

> I return South with a heavy heart. I have lived here a new man—a freeman. Of course, I am a freeman in the South, and knowing it, to a great extent, I act as a free man . . . I ride in any car, and go in any public place I want, but I know too how often

I carry my life in my hands for doing so for I will not be ejected
without physical resistance.

You don't know what that feeling is, Judge. You may imagine
it, but you have never experienced it. Knowing that you are a
freeman, & yet not allowed to enjoy a freeman's liberty, rights,
and privileges unless you stake your life every time you try it. To
live always under the feeling of restraint is worse than living
behind prison bars. My heart is constricted at the very thought
of returning—it suffocates me.[15]

Perhaps, Martinet did not know about Tourgee's doubts and
pressures. Tourgee's wife, Emma, had her own recurring crises
of confidence in her husband's battles. "I have no faith in what
he is doing," Emma Tourgee wrote in her diary as Tourgee
meticulously answered letters from obscure correspondents in
remote locales such as Robinson, Kentucky. "Merely wasting
time which should be given to other work, whereby we could
have something to live on. My heart is very heavy."[16] Martinet
also expressed that Tourgee never experienced the feeling of
daily racial discrimination. True, but Tourgee had borne the
hatred in the South as a carpetbagger and had been mocked
for his personal associations with blacks. Tourgee's persever-
ance lay in the hundreds of correspondences from Southern
blacks who wrote to him over the years. And in the end, his
personal agonies could not obscure the admiration they
expressed, their hope, and their suffering. And, of course,
Martinet generally offered encouraging words to lift Tourgee's
spirit—sort of: "You may not live to see the fruit of your labors
and sacrifice, or to receive the gratitude of those benefited by
them," Martinet told Tourgee. "It will be reserved to future
generations to properly and justly estimate them."[17]

After the Chicago antitrust convention, Albion Tourgee
caught the train for Mayville, Emma, and Aimee. Likewise,
Louis Martinet returned to his "dear ones" in New Orleans to
find the *Crusader* staff in disarray and in need of his firm hand.
Martinet erroneously thought that since there was no legislative session in that odd-numbered year, he might be spared
those time-consuming protests against race-based legal

onslaughts. But Comité des Citoyens treasurer and bond-holder for Homer Plessy, Paul Bonseigneur, and his invalid wife had been forced to leave their home in Covington after threats by hostile white neighbors. In the case of the Bonseigneurs, Martinet noted, there was not even any suggestion that they committed any offense. Chicago seemed ever so far away as Martinet led the Comité des Citoyens into Hope Hall on Tremé Street and Economy Hall on Ursulines Street and spoke against continuing infringements to standing-room-only crowds. "Let Us Meet and Protest!" said their flyers. And instead of taking time off to pursue more commercially rewarding pursuits, Martinet spent his summer publishing a pamphlet entitled *The Violation of a Constitutional Right*.[18]

"My Dear Martinet"

Meanwhile, Tourgee grappled with the matters at hand—*Plessy v. Ferguson* and hard choices. Changes at the United States Supreme Court did not bode as well for fighting segregation as they had in the earlier part of the decade. Tourgee felt the chance of victory slipping away as he surveyed the new faces on the court. As Mayville settled into the autumn of 1893, the cool fall evenings with multicolored leaves taking their time falling to the ground were now replaced by the cold winds off Lake Erie and the accompanying blasts of wind and ice. And by the last weekend in October, like Tourgee and Martinet in their battle for equality, only the most stubborn

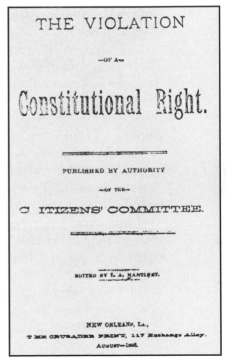

The Violation of a Constitutional Right (Courtesy Amistad Research Center at Tulane University)

and persistent leaves still clung to the trees, as snow and freez-
ing rain fell from the evening skies. October's final week in
Mayville had been particularly slushy—two inches of snow on
Monday and drizzly cold throughout the day on Tuesday.[19] On
October 31, 1893, a rainy freeze came. Tourgee took refuge in
his office, sitting at his desk close by a bay window that looked
out onto Chautauqua Lake. In the warmth of his study, surrounded by memorabilia, correspondences, and publications
from his lifetime, a now rotund Tourgee picked up a pen to
write to Martinet. He abandoned his customary ponderous letter style in favor of the matter-of-fact presentation of *The Invisible Empire*—laying out the hard cold case.

"My Dear Martinet," Tourgee began, "I have been having
some very serious thoughts in regard to Plessy's Case of late, as
my preparation for the hearing has extended." When Martinet, Desdunes, Tourgee, and the others began, an outside
chance of victory existed. But recent appointments to the
High Court cast grave doubts on a successful resolution.
Tourgee's assessment of the current Court's makeup proved as
dreary as the weather in Mayville that evening. He calculated
only one judge in their corner, three maybes, and five
opposed. He then added this foreboding postscript: "It is of
the utmost importance that we should not have a decision
against us as the court has never reversed itself on a constitutional question." Tourgee recommended that the committee
stall the case in the hope of a more favorable judiciary.

"I know you will be surprised to hear this from me, and I will
explain the reason of it," Tourgee stated. "When we started the
fight there was a fair show of favor with the Justices of the
Supreme Court. One, at least, had come to regret the "Civil
Rights Cases" who had been most strenuously for them. There are
now four men on the court who are not fully committed by participation in those cases. If Hornblower is confirmed there will be
five."

7438   1

Mayville=Au=Chautauqua
Oct-31-1893.

My dean Martinet:

I have been having some
very serious thoughts in regard to Plessy's
Case of late, as my preparation for the hear=
ing has extended.

Shall we press for an early hearing
or leave it to come up in its turn
or even encourage delay?

I know you will be surprised to hear
this from me, and I will explain the
reason of it. When we started the fight-
there was a fair show of favor with the
Justices of the Supreme Court. One, at least,
had come to regret the "Civil Rights decision"
who had been most strenuously
for them. There are now four men on the

Letter from Tourgee to Martinet, October 1893 (Courtesy Chautauqua County Historical Society, Westfield, NY)

Tourgee then painted an unpromising portrait of the current court: "Of the whole number of Justices there is but one who is known to favor the view we must stand upon. One is inclined to be with us legally but his political bias is strong the other way. There are two who may be brought over by the argument. There are five who are against us. Of these one may be reached, I think, if he 'hears from the country' soon enough. The others will probably stay where they are until Gabriel blows his horn."

Tourgee presented the options:

> Now, I do not wish to take the responsibility of deciding this matter without the knowledge of the committee. I wish you would call them or have them called together and lay this letter before them. My advice is
>
> 1—To leave the case to come up when it will and not attempt to advance it.
>
> 2—To bend every possible energy to secure the discussion of the principle in such a way as to reach and awaken public sentiment.
>
> Of course, we have nothing to hope, for in any change that may be made in the court; but if we can get the ear of the Country, and argue the matter fully before the people first, we may incline the wavering to fall on our side when the matter comes up.
>
> The prospects of the National Citizen are beginning to show so unexpectedly well that I am strongly inclined to say, let the case go over and in the meantime array the sentiment of the Country against Caste and against the Supreme Court as the ally of Slavery, Secession and Caste. The newspaper press worships the Supreme Court; the people do not. Such an attack would bring the press down upon the Citizen but would awake attention and reach the Court—at any rate it could do no harm in comparison with an adverse decision.

After discussing the case, Tourgee cautioned Martinet about a *Crusader* story that sanctioned emigration for Southern blacks. And now it was time for Tourgee to encourage Martinet to stay and fight:

> If they [the Negroes] should go to Africa, the white American would go with them, and at first as a superintendent of emigration; then, as a merchant, a factor, a trader, a planter, and very

soon the old contest would be renewed at a distance from the best influences among the American people, and with the power and flag of the Republic protecting and supporting the white man's wrong-doing.

There is but one way: the battle of liberty, justice and equal opportunity must be fought out here. The colored man and those white men who believe in liberty and justice—who do not think Christ's teachings a sham—must join hands and hearts and win with brain and patience and wisdom and courage.

There are millions of the white people of the United States who believe in justice and equal right for the colored man. Who desire for him all that they would wish and pray for were they in his conditions. You know this is true.

Now, the time has come when both must work on sound, practical lines, for the special good of your people and the general advancement of all that American liberty professes and all that Christianity proclaims as its earthly function. The will, the purpose, the means exist, and may he reached and united. The appeal, and, in some sense, the initiative, must come from your people. You must unite in making appeal to, and in demanding of the American people and of American Christians, Justice. Those of us who already believe must join with you and echo this appeal so that it shall be heard by all the world.

Without both united, there is no hope of success.[20]

And with that thought in mind, 1893 ended as it started, with *Plessy v. Ferguson* still stuck in a legal limbo between the state of Louisiana and the United States Supreme Court. Only now, it was the Comité des Citoyens that opted to leave *Plessy v. Ferguson* just where it lay.

CHAPTER 9

We as Freemen

> Separate as the fingers.
> —Booker T. Washington, September 1895

> The destinies of the two races, in this country, are indissolubly linked together.
> —Justice Harlan, May 1896

1894—The *Daily Crusader*

For the remainder of its existence, the Comité des Citoyens worked under arduous economic, racial, and political circumstances. Their devotion to this cause and this case can be measured against the surroundings in which they labored. By 1894, the depression of 1893 careened through the country's commercial life at full force and dampened the exuberance that marked the Gilded Age. Farm prices dropped; farms foreclosed. Wages decreased; layoffs became commonplace.[1] Nationwide, according to J. Kingston Pierce, "more than 15,000 assorted business ventures and 642 banks had gone belly up across the nation. Twenty percent of American workers (between two and three million men) lost their employment."[2] In New Orleans, British shippers replaced white screw men with lower-paid black screw men from Texas. Resulting racial violence on the docks sullied the solidarity of the 1892 general strike. According to Joy Jackson, author of *New Orleans in the Gilded Age:* "As always happened under economic stress, racial animosity erupted on the wharves. White screwmen boarded vessels, threw the tools of Negroes overboard, and several Negroes were drowned after jumping into the river to avoid being beaten. Governor Foster had to call out the militia in March to protect Negro screwmen."[3]

And while the Comité des Citoyens preached equality, black leaders such as Booker T. Washington called for accommodation with segregation. Whatever their anxieties about the outcome of *Plessy v. Ferguson,* the Comité des Citoyens and Tourgee did not go quietly into the night. Indeed, the adversity and maddeningly sudden turns of events pushed them to multiply their efforts. Martinet and Tourgee always agreed that the Supreme Court was a political body that "must hear from the country," as Tourgee put it. The Comité des Citoyens represented an 1890s New Orleans version of the 1950s civil-rights movements. But in the 1890s, there was no zeitgeist to spirit them along. Still, they marched forward, even as political options fell by the wayside one by one. In 1894, the Comité des Citoyens began its final charge.

For their part, Louis Martinet and friends hurled themselves into converting the *Crusader* into a daily newspaper. That would make it the only black daily paper in the country at that time and the only Republican daily in the South.[4] To accomplish this, the printers and laborers agreed to work for half pay while the paper's editors worked for free and rotated editorial duties.[5] Under the new structure, Rodolphe Desdunes became editor. Martinet became managing editor and treasurer while Comité des Citoyens president, Arthur Esteves, presided over the paper's board of directors. Other Comité des Citoyens members involved in the new *Daily Crusader* included L. J. Joubert, who served as secretary. Members Alcee Labat and Eugene Luscy sat on the board. Committee member Numa E. Mansion—son of antebellum poet and writer Lucien Mansion— contributed articles. A single copy still cost a nickel, a one-year subscription cost $5.50, and a year's subscription to the weekly *Saturday Crusader* cost $1.50. The *Daily Crusader* declared itself "Republican," "Pro Justitia," and "Liberal, Stalwart, True, and Fearless" and continued to publish in French and English. The masthead boasted of being the only Republican daily south of the Mason-Dixon line and the friend of honest politics, education, labor, and justice.

Like its weekly predecessor, the *Daily Crusader* wrote against state-mandated separation of the races. The paper's reporters and commentators challenged all-white juries, legislative attempts to ban interracial marriages, and segregated churches, in addition to separate railroad trains. Tourgée was a contributor to the *Daily Crusader*, extolling the National Citizens' Rights Association in the May 19, 1894, edition. Poems and letters from readers appeared along with notes on labor-union activity, national news, legislative doings, forthright and sometimes scowling commentary by Martinet, and the sarcasm and pointed presentations of Rodolphe Desdunes. Federal-budget battles in Washington

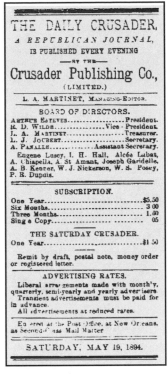

Daily Crusader

received notice, as well as serialized works of fiction, such as *Traced in Blood* by French detective novelist Émile Gaboriau. As a local newspaper, the *Daily Crusader* now included police and court reports, weather forecasts, real-estate transfers, ship arrivals, an amusement directory, and board-of-health reports.

As the *Daily Crusader* made a final stand against segregation, Louisiana enacted more restrictive measures. In its 1894 session, the Louisiana legislature altered the Revised Civil Code of Louisiana of 1870 to read "marriage between white persons and persons of color is prohibited, and the celebration of all such marriages is forbidden and such celebration carries with it no effect and is null and void."[6] Then, on July 12, 1894, the legislature amended and reenacted the 1890 Separate Car Act to mandate separate railroad waiting rooms as well as railroad cars. These additional racial restrictions on travel were passed in the Louisiana House of Representatives on June 28, 1894, by a vote of fifty-four to fourteen. They then passed the Senate by a vote of twenty-nine to zero. Governor Foster readily signed both measures into law.[7] Nationally, in South Carolina, a state constitutional convention passed measures to regulate voting. That same year, Congress ended funding for federal marshals and supervisors of elections, thus allowing Southern states broad latitude in counting votes and determining winners.[8] Also, in Washington, DC, that year, abolitionist Frederick Douglass died at age seventy-eight, leaving a national void of a predominant black leader. In New Orleans, at Martinet's offices on Exchange Alley in the French Quarter, by sweat and strain, the *Daily Crusader* rolled off the presses.

1895—Segregation Challenged

As Plessy's case remained in legal limbo, the Comité des Citoyens challenged segregation on multiple fronts. Their issues and views held much in common with the 1873 New Orleans-based Unification Movement as well as later civil- and human-rights movements. They believed in equal rights for all citizens and the humanity of all. They framed their fight as equal rights versus racial supremacy rather than black versus white. Their historical experiences taught them that separate would never be equal. Those who were consigned to caste before the Civil War remembered the liberating victories of Reconstruction and sought to infuse the sentiments of past generations into the generation of the 1890s. Committee member Numa E. Mansion wrote in the *Daily Crusader*:

> Those giants who then undertook to present their just claims to the nation, who organized and disseminated among the masses the great principles of human rights, who composed the First Convention of the Friends of Universal Suffrage that met in the State; those men did not believe that it was too soon for

them to enjoy their God-given rights, which were guaranteed to them by the Declaration of Independence, although not enjoyed on account of the injustice of men. Was it anything else than sentiment that guided them? Was it not from that source that they found that courage which helped them to struggle in those dark days when it was almost a hopeless fight? Why should it not be so now? Have those years passed on us and [entered] our head only to convince us that we are not worthy to enjoy the rights of man?

"We cannot admit such a doctrine," Numa Mansion concluded. "It is a heresy; we cannot willingly submit to it. Injustice can deprive us of our rights; we can be illegally disenfranchised by foul means, but we will fall with colors flying, believing in the immortal principles of the immortal John Brown and Charles Sumner, and for which they shed their blood."[9]

The Comité des Citoyens bristled at well-meaning establishments of segregated institutions. They voiced strong displeasure when Mother Katherine Drexel (now Saint Katherine Drexel), the founder of the Catholic order of the Sisters of the Blessed Sacrament, joined with the archdiocese and opened a separate church for blacks—a colored church as it were. The *Daily Crusader* deplored this so-called benevolence: "Separation in one form may bring separation in another. This is the reason why we enter our protest against such benevolence. The colored people were created by the same God who created other nations of men, and like others, they were born to live in society with their neighbors so as to contribute their share of responsibility on this planet. While Christ has established the Fatherhood of God and the Brotherhood of man, the great Mother's benevolence is being used by destination to destroy that fundamental principle of our religion. If men are divided by, or in, the Church, where can they be united in the bonds of faith and love of truth and justice?"[10]

The Comité des Citoyens also challenged whites-only juries. This put them in defense of an appeal by James "Greasy Jim" Murray, who was convicted of capital murder in the death of a prison guard by an all-white jury.[11] The irritant proved to be racially prejudicial remarks by Section B trial judge Robert Moise, according to the *Daily Crusader*.[12] The Comité des Citoyens took up the cause with the passion that they employed toward building the Plessy case. They issued a statement, gathered funds to assist Murray's lawyer, Thomas Maher, in the legal fight, appealed the jury-selection law to the circuit court, and then to the United States Supreme Court. "Let our friends come forward with their mite to swell the fund of opposition to the Moise Idea of justice in the formation of juries," a *Daily Crusader* article implored.

And from Mayville, Tourgee likewise increased his effort, despite diabetes, frequent bouts of depression, and recurring back pain from his Civil War injury. In March 1895, he roused himself to begin publication of the *Basis: A Journal of Citizenship* with a staff consisting mainly of wife, Emma, and daughter, Aimee. Then, in July, Martinet wrote Tourgee to inform him that the United States Supreme Court had docketed *Plessy v. Ferguson* for the fall 1895 term. Louis Martinet offered Tourgee words of encouragement as they approached the last leg of their legal journey. "I desire to thank you for all the kindness and generosity you have for us," Martinet wrote, "am sorry . . . that you have again been ill. We hope that you are now well & able to resume your work on The *Basis*. I pray The *Basis* shall live & prosper . . . Get well & don't be sick. Don't be despondent. It saddened me to receive your last letter . . . You must get well & live. We need you yet. This is selfish—but then we love you too."[13]

Activity and anticipation heightened as the Supreme Court lay on the horizon. Plessy's local attorney, James C. Walker, was anxious to appear before the Supreme Court and present the arguments he and Tourgee crafted. He also wrote to Tourgee:

> Dear Sir: Our friend Martinet informs me that the case of Homer Plessy vs. Judge Ferguson is docked for trial in the Supreme Court at Washington during the . . . October term. I would remind you that I have not yet been introduced to the Supreme Court of the United States, although I am enrolled in

the Circuit Court and in the Circuit Court of Appeals. Perhaps your friends Phillips & Mc Kinney will suggest someway to get over this inconvenience. If required, I can go on to the City of Washington two or three days in advance of the hearing . . . At the same time I beg to be put down on the record as anxious to do my full part whatever required.[14]

IN THE

SUPREME COURT OF THE UNITED STATES

OCTOBER TERM, 1895

No. 210.

HOMER A. PLESSY,
Plaintiff in Error,

— vs. —

J. H. FERGUSON, JUDGE OF SECTION "A," CRIMINAL DISTRICT
COURT, PARISH OF ORLEANS,
Defendant in Error.

WRIT OF ERROR TO THE SUPREME COURT OF LOUISIANA.

BRIEF ON BEHALF OF DEFENDANT IN ERROR.

M. J. CUNNINGHAM,
Attorney-General of Louisiana,

LIONAL ADAMS,
ALEXANDER PORTER MORSE,
Of Counsel.

U.S. Supreme Court Case #210 *Plessy v Ferguson*

Separate as the Fingers

If the Comité des Citoyens hoped that their United States Supreme Court appearance would bring a nationwide spotlight on their cause, a Booker T. Washington speech in Atlanta undercut and outshined them. At the Atlanta Exposition in September 1895, educator Washington moved to fill the void of a national black leader. Preaching accommodation and separation instead of militancy and equality, Washington's message found favor among Northern industrialists and Southern separatists. He presented a different vision of America from the one expressed by the Comité des Citoyens: "In all things that are purely social, we can be as separate as the fingers, yet one as the hand in all things essential to mutual progress . . . The wisest among my race understand that the agitation of questions of social equality is the extremest folly, and that progress in the enjoyment of all the privileges that will come to us must be the result of severe and constant struggle rather than of artificial forcing . . . The opportunity to earn a dollar in a factory just now is worth infinitely more than the opportunity to spend a dollar in an opera-house."[15]

The month following Booker T. Washington's speech, Albion Tourgee filed briefs in *United States #210 Homer A. Plessy v. J. H. Ferguson, Judge of Section A Criminal District Court, Parish of Orleans.* His brief maintained an opposite sentiment from that of Booker T. Washington:

> —Has It [the State] the power to require the officers of a railroad to assort its citizens by race?
> —Is the officer of a railroad competent to decide the question of race?
> —Has a State power to compel husband and wife, to ride in separate coaches, because they happen the one to be colored and the other white?
> —Has the State a right to declare a citizen of the United States guilty of a crime because he continues to occupy a seat in a car?
> —Is not a statutory assortment of the people of a state on the line of race, such a perpetuation of the essential features of slavery as to come within the inhibition of the XIII Amendment.
> —Is it not the establishment of a statutory difference

between the white and colored races in the enjoyment of chartered privileges, a badge of servitude which is prohibited by that amendment.

—Is not state citizenship made an essential incident of national citizenship, by the XIV Amendment, and if so are not the rights, privileges and immunities of the same within the scope of the national jurisdiction?

—Can the rights of a citizen of the United States be protected and secured by the general government without securing his personal rights against invasion by the State?[16]

With 1896 came uncertainty. Martinet thought it better to wait until the fall of 1896 to present the case. This would give them one more try at securing a Thomas B. Reed nomination at the 1896 Republican convention, scheduled for June in St. Louis. "Don't you think it better to have the Plessy case fixed for November after the election instead of October, if possible?" Martinet queried Tourgee. "If Reed were the Republican nominee elected by a large majority men & minds might be changed." In the same letter, Martinet correctly predicted that a Murphy Foster reelection as Louisiana governor would lead to a constitutional convention to limit suffrage. Also troubling Martinet, the deteriorated economy caught up with the *Daily Crusader*. "Crusader is on its last legs," Martinet wrote sideways in the margins of a March 4, 1896, letter. "May close any week or any day."[17] Indeed, Tourgee's paper, the *Basis*, had similar problems, as subscriptions did poorly for both journals. Still, Tourgee took time to write a personal letter to United States senator William E. Chandler on behalf of the *Daily Crusader* depicting his continuing admiration of Martinet and the Comité des Citoyens:

> I send you by this mail a marked copy of the New Orleans Crusader. I wish you would take the time to read the editorial I have marked and then look at the little subscription account entitled "Mr. Desdunes' stocking." You will see that
>
> 1—That the Crusader is about to suspend publication
> 2—That it has been struggling along for months, living on little subscriptions of this sort
> Now I wish to say first—one word in regard to this matter:

The effort of the men who have run The Crusader . . . They have kept the paper afloat by simply giving part of their life every day to its support . . . It was The Crusader which set on foot the movement to test the constitutionality of the Jim Crow car law which will be reached in the Supreme Court, either the last of this term or the first of next term. For this they raised in nickel subscriptions mostly, about 3500.00 for counsel fees and costs I have had.

Louis A. Martinet the Editor, who is the glowing part of the whole enterprise, is a wonderful man . . . When he graduated in the medical school, the Crusader was a weekly. Ex-president Hayes called me to name a colored man whom I thought it would be really profitable to send abroad to study either art or science offering to give such a one 1200.00 a year for either three or four years. I named Martinet . . . After considering it a month he replied that the proposition was a tempting one . . . but that his duty to his people whom he had encouraged in the Crusader required him to forego even such a tempting offer . . . You say he was a fool? No doubt, but it was a grand sort of folly, was it not?[18]

The Court

The Supreme Court era under Melville Fuller as chief justice represented quite a different citizens' committee than the one in New Orleans. The eight 1895-96 Court justices who ruled on Homer Plessy were all white men of high privilege. All were Northerners except for Kentucky's John Marshall Harlan. Four were born or raised in Judge Ferguson's Massachusetts and all save Harlan had resided in traditional Yankee enclaves, including Maine, New York, Pennsylvania, and Connecticut.[19] The Fuller Court had a reputation for following precedent, due process, and individualism. Protection of businesses from regulation was sacrosanct. In *A History of the Supreme Court*, historian Bernard Schwartz gave his assessment of the Fuller Court:

> The Court became a primary pillar of the dominant jurisprudence of the day—its overriding theme that of the individualism of the law applied with mechanical rigor, with abstract freedom of the individual will as the crucial factor in social progress. This

> was the time when the Court apparently believed in everything we
> now find it impossible to believe in: the danger of any govern-
> mental interference with the economy, the danger of subjecting
> corporate power to public control, the danger of any restriction
> upon the rights of private property, the danger of disrupting the
> social and economic status quo—in short, the danger of making
> anything more, the danger of making anything less.[20]

Pres. Grover Cleveland appointed sixty-six-year-old Melville
W. Fuller as chief justice in 1888. Jeffery B. Morris, in 1981,
described the chief justice as an "old time Democrat, friendly
to the doctrine of state rights, and as a sincere believer in indi-
vidualism."[21] A Chicago lawyer who never held a federal office,
Fuller was raised in large part by his grandfather, who was a
judge on the Maine Supreme Court. He read law in Bangor,
Maine, and subsequently passed the bar after six months in
Harvard Law School. He dabbled in politics in Augusta, Maine,
and wrote for a local Democratic paper. After moving to
Chicago in the 1850s, where he practiced commercial law,
Fuller married the daughter of the president of Chicago's
Union National Bank. He won his stripes with the Southern
wing of the Democratic Party when he managed Stephen Doug-
las's presidential campaign against Abraham Lincoln. Fuller
received the appointment from Grover Cleveland after a fellow
Illinois attorney declined.

President Cleveland's other nominee came in his second
term as president in 1895. Rufus Wheeler Peckham came from
a New York family known for producing lawyers and judges.
Influential in the upstate faction of the New York Democratic
Party, Peckham served as the district attorney for Albany
County from 1869 to 1872 and was a member of New York
State's highest court when Grover Cleveland picked him for
the United States Supreme Court.[22] "Peckham was one of the
court's most consistent advocates of laissez-fair constitutionalism,"
Paul Sens wrote in *The Oxford Companion to the Supreme Court of
the United States*. He called a law that regulated grain elevators
"vicious in its nature and communistic in its tendency."

Republican president Benjamin Harrison was responsible

for three appointments to the 1896 Supreme Court of Melville Fuller. His 1890 appointee was David J. Brewer. Brewer was born in Asia Minor in what is now Izmir, Turkey. His father was a New England clergyman who returned to the United States and became a prison chaplain. His uncle was fellow justice Stephen Field. Brewer was a former Supreme Court justice in Kansas and also a former federal judge. During his tenure, Brewer advocated female suffrage, residency rights for Chinese immigrants, and Philippine independence.[23] He wrote in *Atchinson v. Matthews* that the "very idea of classification is that of inequality." In *Hodges v. United States,* Brewer opined, "It [the Thirteenth Amendment] is the denunciation of a condition, and not a declaration in favor of a particular people. It reaches every race and every individual, and if in any respect it commits one race to the nation, it commits every race and every individual thereof. Slavery or involuntary servitude of the Chinese, of the Italian, of the Anglo-Saxon, are as much within its compass as slavery or involuntary servitude of the African."[24] Surely, Brewer was a vote that Tourgee thought he might be able to sway.

In 1892, Harrison appointed sixty-four-year-old Pittsburgh native George Shiras. Shiras had no judicial experience but was a very successful lawyer whose clients included "large steel corporations and the Baltimore and Ohio Railroad."[25] According to a Lerner Law Books profile, "he held no public offices until his Supreme Court appointment. In 1881 he refused the Pennsylvania state legislature's offer of the U.S. Senate nomination. A moderate Republican, he remained aloof from party politics and the state political machine, facts that favored his appointment to the High Court."[26] In *The Oxford Companion to the Supreme Court of the United States,* Alice Fleetwood Bartee wrote that Shiras "did not always agree with the bloc of ultra-conservative justices dedicated to the establishment of laissez-faire economics through strict judicial review of state and national progressive reform laws."[27]

President Harrison's final Supreme Court appointment was Henry Billings Brown. A native of South Lee, Massachusetts,

Brown's father was a prosperous merchant. Additionally, his father-in-law was a wealthy lumber trader and his inheritance assured Brown of independent wealth. Brown studied law at Yale and Harvard. In the early days of President Lincoln's administration, Brown was appointed deputy marshal in Detroit and subsequently elevated to a position as assistant U.S. attorney for eastern Michigan. Francis Helminski, in *The Oxford Companion to the Supreme Court,* describes Brown as a moderate but "highly protective of property rights and reluctant to extend criminal procedure protections and civil liberties." Like fellow justice Peckham, Brown recoiled at attempts to regulate businesses. During his tenure, he voted to invalidate a New York law that limited the hours employees could be made to work.

Pres. Chester Arthur appointed Boston native and Harvard graduate Horace Gray, who served on the court from 1882 to 1902. As a young man, Gray was the member of the Free Soil Party, which vehemently opposed the expansion of slavery. From 1853 to 1861, he served as reporter for the Supreme Judicial Court of Massachusetts. He joined the Republican Party shortly after its inception and, in 1864, became the youngest person appointed to the Massachusetts Supreme Court at age thirty-six. A decade later, he became the Commonwealth's chief justice.[28]

The longest-serving member on the Court at that time was Lincoln appointee Stephen J. Field, who was called "the leader of the Court movement toward laissez faire in the Constitution."[29] Born in Haddam, Connecticut, and raised in a strict Puritan household in Stockbridge, Massachusetts, Field moved to California during the gold-rush year of 1849. He served in the California legislature and was appointed a justice by Pres. Abraham Lincoln in the emancipation year of 1863. Justice Field was unsympathetic to the spirit of the Reconstruction amendments. In the 1880 case *Ex Parte Virginia,* Field stated that the Fourteenth Amendment did not give Blacks any rights to serve on juries.[30]

John Marshall Harlan, the court's maverick, dissented 119 times from the majority opinion during his tenure on the court. The only Southerner, Marshall supported Unionism during the

Civil War but considered abolition of slavery to be a violation of property rights. As a colonel during the Civil War, Harlan's Kentucky regiment helped put to rout a Confederate raiding operation. Harlan had a black half brother named Robert, whom, according to Charles Thompson, was "treated to some degree as a member of the family."[31] After joining the Republican Party, the six-foot-tall Harlan became an outspoken court member on equal rights. Like many others in the Plessy drama, his life's path connected to the Hayes-Tilden Compromise. According to *The Oxford Companion to the Supreme Court,* "After the contested presidential election and the ordeal of the scrutiny by the Electoral Commission, Hayes was declared the victor. The new president . . . named a commission of five, including Harlan, to report on which of two rival Louisiana state governments was legitimate. In keeping with the president's policy of ending Reconstruction, the commission advised in favor of the Democrats, despite the fact that the same returning board that had certified the Hayes electors had also certified the state Republican candidates. Consistent with his policy of reconciliation, Hayes was determined to name a Southerner."[32]

1896—"If the Court Please"

According to Otto H. Olsen, at the time of the case, Tourgee was financially, emotionally, and physically at a low point in his existence: "Life for the Tourgee family had reached its nadir. The huge debt of ten years ago was gone, but the fifty-eight year old Judge felt the more frightening burden of exhaustion and depression. Not even a livelihood remained to him. His books were lying unsold. Two additional volumes, one already written, would bring almost no return, and because of his involvement with The *Basis,* his lecturing had become sporadic. Even more frightening was that sign of literary sterility, the rejection of new manuscripts by one journal after another. As the bills mounted, Emma's hopes, confided to her diary, were at their lowest ebb."[33]

In April 1896, the Tourgees spent their days mailing what would be the last issues of the *Basis.*

On April 9, James Walker wrote Tourgee informing him that the attorney general of Louisiana was in the midst of an election and there was no way he would agree to move the Plessy case to the next term as Martinet had hoped. Walker also informed Tourgee that he would not be making the trip to Washington as planned. Walker, who had relished the opportunity to present his case to the High Court, was suffering coughing and cold attacks. In actuality, Walker was witnessing the onset of the disease that would take his life. Walker the former Confederate private and Tourgee the Union officer had developed a mutual respect and warmth for each other over the course of their work on the case. "I hope your success will be commensurate with the energy, skill, and earnestness which has marked everything you have said and done in the case," Walker told Tourgee. Meanwhile, Tourgee received word from Supreme Court clerk McKenney that their case would be the first case argued on the second Monday in April. On Friday, April 10, Albion Tourgee caught the 11:00 A.M. train for Washington to present his case on behalf of Homer Plessy and the Comité des Citoyens.

In 1896, the Supreme Court met in the old Senate chamber that senators had deserted after the Capitol building was enhanced with two new wings in the late 1850s. While the Court's new space was an improvement from the Capitol's basement, it still lacked the physical stature and grandeur of the executive and legislative branches of government. They lacked private chambers and entered and left the courtroom through public hallways.[34] The court's old basement courtroom now served as its law library.

Fuller's court now sat behind a long table with a row of marble columns at their backs. Spectators sat on benches with cushions of red velvet. An observer described the courtroom as "a small white-walled room . . . a long massive desk, behind which, seated in their massive chairs . . . side by side, sit eight figures . . . clothed to their feet in flowing robes of 'solemn black.'"[35] According to Willard L. King, "The Justices assembled for their daily sessions in the robing room. Then the Marshal of the Court led them in their robes across the corridor to the courtroom. This procession at twelve o'clock noon each court day was witnessed by a cluster of sightseers who were kept bay by silk ropes stretched across the corridor. Justice Holmes often told how, one day as this parade passed, he heard a country visitor whisper in awe: 'Ker-riist, what Dignity!'"[36]

It was April 13, 1896. Tourgee made his way to the Supreme Court in the Capitol to make his case. He took a seat on the plush red benches as the Court went through preliminary business.[37] The oral arguments in *Plessy v. Ferguson* were the only arguments scheduled for that day. Tourgee had with him note cards on which his arguments had been typed for what would be his final forum in his long and distinguished life. There were legitimate chances at victory—outside as they may be. Since this court held sacred the rights of property, he would try to present the right to catch a train as a form of property. And since the Court recoiled at business regulation, Tourgee emphasized the burden the Separate Car Act placed upon the railroads. If the Court could not sympathize with the rights of Homer Plessy as a citizen, perhaps he could get them to show compassion toward the burdens of a corporate entity. Wasn't forcing railroad companies to provide separate cars a violation of laissez-faire, a hallmark characteristic of the Fuller Court? But the heart of his matter would be the inanity of racial legislation and the fact that the Fourteenth Amendment proscribed discrimination.

"If the Court please," Tourgee began. He emphasized that Plessy's rights were a "federal question," not one to be dictated by the states. He pointed out that the Reconstruction amendments had fundamentally altered the nature of citizenship. Instead of it being a state function to decide citizenship, the Reconstruction amendments created a condition where national citizenship superseded state citizenship: "The old citizenship of the United States was determined by race or descent. The new citizenship of the United States had nothing to do with race or descent. Under the pre-existing law no man having a drop of colored blood in his veins, could become a citizen of the United States. It was in all literalness a 'white man's government'. In the new citizenship color is expressly ignored and the sole condition of citizenship, is birth in the United States."

He also pointed out the burden the Separate Car Act placed on railroads to the justices who, heretofore, abhorred governmental regulation of business. He lampooned the entire notion of regulatory laws based on race. "What is the purpose of the Act?" Tourgee queried. "Evidently to assort passengers . . . according to color. Tourgee argued that "the statute does not use the ordinary scientific terms, Caucasian, Mongolian, Indian, Negro, etc. Why? Evidently, because the legislature recognized the fact that by this act they were imposing a greatly added expense on the railroad companies of the state in requiring them to provide separate accommodations for each race. In the first place, they reduce the whole human family to two grand divisions which they term 'races', the 'white race' and the 'colored race.' It is a new ethnology but prejudice based on the lessons of slavery, does not stop at trifles."

Tourgee concluded that the purpose of the law was only "to keep Negroes out of one car for the gratification of the whites—not to keep whites out of another car for the comfort and satisfaction of the colored passenger. It is simply an attempt to evade the constitutional requirements of equality of right and legal privilege to all citizens and to avoid the decisions of this court in regard to legislation intended to discriminate against the colored citizen by professing to discriminate against both."

"Its only effect," Tourgee proffered, "is to perpetuate the stigma of color—to make the curse immortal, incurable, inevitable."[38] After Tourgee finished his presentation, Alexander Peter Morse, a Washington, DC, attorney, delivered arguments on behalf of the state of Louisiana. Then, Plessy's Washington attorney, S. F. Phillips, presented a property-based argument, after which the Court adjourned.

Tourgee spent two more days in Washington and then returned to Mayville on April 16, 1896, to wait for the Court's

May decision. May was Tourgee's natal month, the month he was admitted to the bar, the month he began his law career in Ohio, and the month he married Emma Kilbourne. In his youth, he considered it his lucky month—but not this May of 1896. He journeyed to Washington to get word of the case and returned disappointed on May 14, his wedding anniversary. Emma Tourgee wrote, "Albion came home on 5:00 train having had a very disappointing trip—losing his trunk—and not getting his way—33rd anniversary of our marriage! It is well that this day did not cast its shadow before in those idyllic times."[39] Then, the eighteenth brought burden on a national scale. In a seven-to-one vote, the Court allowed states the authority to forcibly segregate people of differing races. Writing for the majority, Henry Billings Brown dismissed Plessy's thirteenth-, fourteenth-, and fifteenth-amendment claims and pointed to the existence of separate schools and bans on interracial marriages as precedents. As far as determining race, this too was left to the discretion of Louisiana and other Southern states:

> Similar laws have been enacted by congress under its general power of legislation over the District of Columbia, as well as by the legislatures of many of the states, and have been generally, if not uniformly, sustained by the courts.
> Laws forbidding the intermarriage of the two races may be said in a technical sense to interfere with the freedom of contract, and yet have been universally recognized as within the police power of the state.
> We consider the underlying fallacy of the plaintiff's argument to consist in the assumption that the enforced separation of the two races stamps the colored race with a badge of inferiority. If this be so, it is not by reason of anything found in the act, but solely because the colored race chooses to put that construction upon it. . . . Legislation is powerless to eradicate racial instincts, or to abolish distinctions based upon physical differences, and the attempt to do so can only result in accentuating the difficulties of the present situation. If the civil and political rights of both races be equal, one cannot be inferior to the other civilly or politically. If one race be inferior to the other socially, the constitution of the United States cannot put them upon the same plane.[40]

Buried under precedents, arguments, and legalese lay Homer Plessy's freedom to catch the train of his choice. The majority decision intruded on individuals' rights of association, placed states' rights above the rights of citizens, and mocked the Fuller Court's reputation for individualism and nonregulation of commerce. In practice, it gave states the constitutional protection to shun entire groups of individuals based on their race. Unlike the *Dred Scott Decision,* the Court's decision in *Plessy v. Ferguson* did not send outraged protesting masses into the streets. There were no William Lloyd Garrisons, Fredrick Douglass's, or Abraham Lincolns who voiced eloquent protests in halls of power. And unlike the era following the 1954 *Brown v. Board of Education,* no great social movement erupted. By setting up a tiered citizenship, the majority opinion dampened the spirit of the Declaration of Independence and the Bill of Rights. In a crude compromise between the *Dred Scott Decision* and the Reconstruction amendments, instead of blacks being "beings of an inferior order," for all practical purposes, the majority opinion reduced blacks to citizens of an inferior order.

The Harlan Dissent

For Tourgee, Plessy, and the Comité des Citoyens, the majority opinion sounded a deafening, gavel-thumping finality that only a United States Supreme Court decision could render. But the majority opinion was not the only voice spoken from the Supreme Court on the Plessy matter that day. Reflecting the brief of Albion W. Tourgee and the philosophy of the Comité des Citoyens, John Harlan issued a powerfully eloquent dissent. So, while the majority of Supreme Court justices ruled against Plessy and the Comité des Citoyens, the Harlan dissent planted their flag eternally in the annals of United States jurisprudence:

> These notable additions [the three Reconstruction amendments] to the fundamental law were welcomed by the friends of liberty throughout the world. They removed the race line from our governmental systems. They had, as this court has said, a

common purpose, namely, to secure "to a race recently emancipated, a race that through many generations have been held in
slavery, all the civil rights that the superior race enjoy." They
declared, in legal effect, this court has further said, "that the law
in the states shall be the same for the black as for the white; that
all persons, whether colored or white, shall stand equal before
the laws of the states; and in regard to the colored race, for
whose protection the amendment was primarily designed, that
no discrimination shall be made against them by law because of
their color."

It is one thing for railroad carriers to furnish, or to be
required by law to furnish, equal accommodations for all whom
they are under a legal duty to carry. It is quite another thing for
government to forbid citizens of the white and black races from
traveling in the same public conveyance, and to punish officers
of railroad companies for permitting persons of the two races to
occupy the same passenger coach.

But in view of the constitution, in the eye of the law, there is
in this country no superior, dominant, ruling class of citizens.
There is no caste here. Our constitution is color-blind, and neither knows nor tolerates classes among citizens. In respect of
civil rights, all citizens are equal before the law. The humblest is
the peer of the most powerful. The law regards man as man, and
takes no account of his surroundings or of his color when his
civil rights as guarantied by the supreme law of the land are
involved . . . In my opinion, the judgment this day rendered will,
in time, prove to be quite as pernicious as the decision made by
this tribunal in the Dred Scott Case . . . The destinies of the two
races, in this country, are indissolubly linked together, and the
interests of both require that the common government of all
shall not permit the seeds of race hate to be planted under the
sanction of law. What can more certainly arouse race hate, what
more certainly create and perpetuate a feeling of distrust
between these races, than state enactments which, in fact, proceed on the ground that colored citizens are so inferior and
degraded that they cannot be allowed to sit in public coaches
occupied by white citizens? That, as all will admit, is the real
meaning of such legislation as was enacted in Louisiana. . . . If
evils will result from the commingling of the two races upon
public highways established for the benefit of all, they will be
infinitely less than those that will surely come from state legislation regulating the enjoyment of civil rights upon the basis of
race. We boast of the freedom enjoyed by our people above all

other peoples. But it is difficult to reconcile that boast with a state of the law which, practically, puts the brand of servitude and degradation upon a large class of our fellow citizens, our equals before the law. The thin disguise of "equal" accommodations for passengers in railroad coaches will not mislead any one, nor atone for the wrong this day done.[41]

Harlan's dissent has been a classic in Supreme Court history. It became a beacon for future civil-rights lawyers who would later challenge segregation. Charles Thompson wrote in 1996:

> Even a full century after its delivery in 1896, Harlan's eloquent defense of civil rights for black Americans retains its power. Indeed, it was a fount of inspiration for one of the great lawyers of the century, the late Supreme Court Justice Thurgood Marshall. At a 1993 ceremony in memory of Marshall, a colleague, Constance Baker Motley, recalled that when Marshall was the lead attorney in the NAACP's fight to end segregation, he picked himself up in low moments by reading aloud from Harlan's dissent. As quoted in *Judicial Enigma,* a new biography of Harlan, Judge Motley said: "Marshall admired the courage of Harlan more than any justice who has ever sat on the Supreme Court. Even Chief Justice Earl Warren's forthright and moving decision for the court in *Brown* did not affect Marshall in the same way. Earl Warren was writing for a unanimous Supreme Court. Harlan was a solitary and lonely figure writing for posterity."[42]

Defeat but Not Ignominy

On May 18, 1896, the same day of the decision, Governor Foster was inaugurated governor for his second term. Also, the United States Supreme Court dismissed the appeal of the other case supported by the Comité des Citoyens—that of James "Greasy Jim" Murray, who was hanged shortly thereafter. As a sign of the times, on June 9, 1896, at the Republican convention in St. Louis, not one of the city's hotels would rent rooms to black convention delegates. And in September, the United States Supreme Court remanded its decision to the Louisiana Supreme Court.

Despite the adversity and the sacrifices of time and money,

to their honor, the Comité des Citoyens remained true to their pledge to fight the Separate Car Act to the end. As a testament to their camaraderie, fourteen of the same names that appeared in 1891 when they issued "An Appeal" remained on the final roster. Along the way, five new members joined—Julius Hall, Frank Hall, Noel Bachus, George Geddes, and A. E. P. Albert. As part of their final statement, the Comité des Citoyens published their financial statement, detailing income and expenditures. They disbursed the $220 left in the treasury to the Eye, Ear, Nose and Throat Hospital, the then-forty-six-year-old Couvent School, the Phillis Wheatley sanitarium, drought sufferers, Lafon's Old Folks Home, an orphan's asylum, and a testimonial of $60 to Judge Tourgee, who handled their case pro bono.

With all the legal options closed and their honor intact, without a hint of misgivings or regret, in year seven of the Plessy saga, the Comité des Citoyens issued their last statement before disbanding:

> We come now, dear friends, to render an account of our stewardship . . . In the name of the people, the Citizens' Committee battled for equal rights, by maintaining the principle that the State was wrong in passing laws which discriminate between its citizens. As freemen we protested against such encroachments upon the liberties of the people, by applying to the courts of the country for redress.
>
> The majority of the judges of the highest tribunal of this American government have cast their voice against our just appeal, in demanding the nullification of a State law which is in direct conflict with the American Declaration of Independence, which declares that "all men are created free and equal."
>
> Notwithstanding this decision . . . we, as freemen, still believe that we were right and our cause is sacred. We are encouraged by the indomitable will and noble defense of Hon. Albion W. Tourgee, and supported by the courageous dissenting opinion of Justice John Harlan in behalf of justice and equal rights. In defending the cause of liberty, we met with defeat, but not with ignominy.[43]

And so the Comité des Citoyens closed shop. For Homer Plessy, there was still one final matter.

1897—Twenty-five Dollars or Twenty Days

In year eight of the fight against the Separate Car Act, on January 11, 1897, Homer Plessy returned to Section A for his final appearance in the court saga that bears his name. By his side were his attorney James C. Walker and Comité des Citoyens treasurer Paul Bonseigneur. Things had changed remarkably since his arrest and court appearances before Judge Ferguson in 1892. The Comité des Citoyens had disbanded; the *Daily Crusader* had ceased publication. The court buildings had since moved from St. Patrick's Hall in Lafayette Square to new digs at Tulane Avenue and South Saratoga Street. Judge Ferguson's term had expired and Joshua Baker was now the judge who presided over Section A. His shoemaking days over, Plessy now worked as a laborer. He had ceased to be Plessy the shoemaker or Plessy the challenger to segregation. Now he was Plessy the product of the Supreme Court decision in support of racial separation. Wrongly, his name became associated with the existence of Jim Crow laws rather than with an early legal, social, and moral movement to end them.

If Plessy lived long enough, he could witness his arguments receive a more favorable Supreme Court reception in 1954. He could read about Rosa Parks' act of defiance on a public conveyance and her subsequent elevation as an American icon for doing so. Interracial freedom rides would roll across America and Congress would pass civil-rights and voting-rights acts—all eerily similar to laws that availed themselves to Plessy during the Reconstruction period. And what would a new millennium bring into the courts of the country and the hearts of its citizens? Would it rise to the ideals of the Declaration of Independence and the Bill of Rights? Or would it compromise its vision on an altar of political expediency and racial supremacy? But the future of civil rights would be the province of later generations of Plessys, Fergusons, Martinets, and Fosters. For Homer, the year was 1897 and the state of Louisiana and the United States Supreme Court had already determined his fate. It would not be historians and biographers who wrote his legal epitaph; rather it was the clerk of Orleans Parish Criminal Court Section A:

> The defendant Homer Adolph Plessy in person being placed at the bar of the Court attended by his counsel J. C. Walker Esq. With consent of the Court withdrew his plea of Not Guilty herein recorded July 20th 1892 and instead thereof pleaded guilty . . . The accused waived all legal delay and asked to be sentenced immediately. Whereupon in consideration of said plea and the provisions of Section 2, of Act no, 111 of the General Assembly of the State of Louisiana approved July 10th 1890, the Court sentenced him the said Homer Adolph Plessy to pay a fine of Twenty Five dollars and in default of payment thereof to imprisonment in the Parish Prison for Twenty days.[44]

Plessy paid the fine. He, treasurer Bonseigneur, and James C. Walker then walked out of Section A and into the apparently permanent world of segregated America.

CHAPTER 10

The Battle of Freedom

Doesn't it let the white man vote, and doesn't it stop the
negro from voting, and isn't that what we came here for?
(Applause)[1]

—E. B. Kruttschnitt, president
1898 Louisiana Constitutional Convention

The White supremacy for which we have so long struggled . . .
is now crystallized into the constitution.

—Gov. Murphy Foster
1898 Louisiana legislative session

The Battle Of Freedom Must Be Won, And Liberty Transmitted
From Sire To Son.

—Rev. James Keelan
Loyal National League rally in New Orleans, July 4, 1863

In February 1898, Louisiana began a sixty-six-day constitutional convention in New Orleans. In what Perry H. Howard
called "the Great Disenfranchisement of 1898," the convention's
stated goal was to disenfranchise as many blacks as possible.
"Their scheme was to provide several alternative suffrage requirements," Howard wrote. "If the Negro could not be refused the
vote under one provision, then he could be banned under
another."[2] At that convention, there was not even a façade of
equality as in the separate-but-equal language of the Separate Car
Act of 1890. Judiciary Committee chairman Thomas Semmes
bluntly declared, "We met here to establish the supremacy of the

white race and the white race constitutes the Democratic Party of this State. Our mission was to establish the supremacy of the white race in this state to the extent to which it could be legally and constitutionally done . . . We have established throughout the State white manhood suffrage."[3] (Semmes, paradoxically, had agreed to represent Plessy in 1892 but wanted $2,500.) By the end of the 1898 convention, the state whittled voters down to people who could demonstrate literacy, tax-paying property owners and their sons, and people who voted prior to 1867 and their male descendants—the so-called grandfather clause. Section 5 of the article on suffrage and elections stated: "No male person who was on January 1st, 1867, or at any date prior thereto, entitled to vote under the Constitution or statutes of any State of the United States, wherein he then resided, and no son or grandson of any such person . . . shall be denied the right to register and vote in this State by reason of his failure to possess the educational or property qualifications pre-scribed by this Constitution."[4]

Since no black person could vote prior to 1868, it effectively scuttled the chances of any black person to qualify under this measure. "Now, why was this exception made?" Thomas Semmes rhetorically queried and answered: "Because and I am ashamed to say it, Louisiana is one of the most illiterate states in the Union, It is more illiterate than any other state except North Carolina. We, therefore, have in this State a large White population whose right to vote would have been stricken down but for the creation of section 5. And all of these men had aided the white people of the state to wrest from the hands of the Republican Party, composed almost exclusively of negroes, the power which, backed by Federal bayonets, they had exer-cised for many years."[5]

Eighty thousand dollars had been spent on the convention to disenfranchise Louisiana's black citizenry. One hundred twelve members of the constitutional convention signed their names to the constitution. Twenty were absent.[6] There were two dissents, including that of B. W. Bailey of Winn Parish, a Populist who stated:[7] "I decline and refuse to sign this document, called the

Constitution of the State of Louisiana, for the reason that it contains so many measures, that are utterly and irrevocably antagonistic to the immutable laws of justice and equity. Before I should so far forget the inherent rights of my people as to violate that right by signing this Constitution I hope my arm will fall palsied by my side."[8]

Even with the purposeful exclusion of so many loyal citizens of Louisiana, the convention's president was still not completely satisfied with the results. "We have not drafted the exact constitution that we should like to have drafted," E. B. Kruttschnitt proclaimed. "Otherwise we should have inscribed in it . . . white manhood suffrage, and the exclusion of suffrage of every man with a trace of African blood in his veins."[9]

At the 1898 Louisiana legislative session later that year, Governor Foster congratulated the convention on its invention of the grandfather clause. He estimated that 30,000 extra white voters would be accommodated. It was all the more callous since black Democrats voted for Foster. As part of the 1876 Hayes-Tilden Compromise, it was Francis T. Nicholls who vowed to "obliterate the color line in politics." But Governor Foster had made no such pledge. In his address to the legislature, Governor Foster derided Louisiana's black voters, praised the convention, and stated that the last six years had been a fight for white supremacy. While he viewed blacks as an ignorant mass of voters, whites were "illiterate but not ignorant":

> Regardless of the capacity or fitness of the negro to intelligently or patriotically exercise the franchise, the fifteenth amendment forbade the States to deny or abridge this right on account of race, color or previous condition of servitude, and the evils and woes of reconstruction quickly followed this ill-advised legislation.
>
> It is useless to recount here the long, constant and heroic struggle which has taken place in this State for the supremacy of our race and the perpetuation of our institutions, and which was made necessary present in our electorate of a large and irresponsible mass of negro voters, which demoralized our politics and constituted a standing menace to honest and peaceable elections. About six years ago our people, having grown weary of

this condition of affairs, determined as far as possible under the organic law of our State, to eliminate this disturbing factor from our politics . . . In the face of the fifteenth amendment, the elimination of the negro as a controlling factor in our politics, without at the same time excluding from the electorate a large number of worthy white citizens was, perhaps, most difficult in its accomplishment in Louisiana than in any other Southern State . . . The white men thus affected, and their ancestors, have been in the undisputed enjoyment of the franchise and cherish it as their right by birth and manhood. While illiterate they are not ignorant. While poor, they are not paupers.

The Constitutional Convention was never called to so adjust the franchise as to exclude this class of our fellow citizens [White males] from this privilege, or deny them of a right which they naturally regard as inherent . . . The white supremacy for which we have so long struggled, at the cost of so much precious blood and treasure, is now crystallized into the Constitution as a fundamental part and parcel of that organic instrument . . . The whole nation with one accord is gathering itself in a common brotherhood for the exercise of its united power. The section will be wielded together in the fire and blood of battle. Together they will present a serried front to the whole world, and thus, undivided and irrefragable, will together work out the magnificent destiny, which an Allwise Providence has assigned to them, in establishing the great principles of self-government, and the God-given rights of man.[10]

The 1898 Constitutional Convention pronounced a death sentence for black suffrage in Louisiana. It was more than electoral decimation and even more than an electoral holocaust. It amounted to electoral genocide. Between the years 1897 and 1900, the state of Louisiana purged over one hundred twenty thousand of its citizenry from the voting rolls. Black voting strength in Louisiana dropped from forty-four percent in 1897 to four percent at the turn of the century and obliterated the Republican Party. White registration skyrocketed from fifty-six to ninety-six percent of the total. By 1910, blacks' voter registration in Louisiana dropped to .6 percent of voters.[11] After his stint as the governor who restored white supremacy, Foster was elected as United States senator for Louisiana.

Unfortunately, for New Orleans who wanted their children

educated, E. B. Kruttschnitt, the same man who presided over the 1898 constitutional convention, also presided over the Orleans Parish School Board. And just as Democrats undermined education supervised by Democrats after the Hayes-Tilden Compromise, the Orleans Parish School Board acted to ensure that black public-school students would never have an opportunity for any education that prepared them beyond menial labor. According to Donald Devore and Joseph Logsdon, in *Crescent City Schools,* E. B. Kruttschnitt "and the New Orleans School Board, which remained under his direction, completely refashioned the city's black education, plunging it to its post-Civil War nadir." When a group of parents approached the board seeking kindergartens for the black schools (they were available in white schools), "to the delegation's utter dismay, the school board brushed aside their petition and . . . instead limited all black schooling to the first five grades, thereby effectively shutting off any publicly supported route to the city's private black colleges." There would be no public high school for blacks until 1917, when McDonough #35 opened in New Orleans. The board's educational committee jettisoned any pretensions to equality. The goal of education under the new regime would be "to fit him and her for that sphere of labor and social position and occupation to which they are best suited and seem ordained by the proper fitness of things."[12] This suppression of blacks' education was all the more unjust since the school system had received a large injection of funds from increased property assessments. Black parents were cruelly forced, through their taxes, to subsidize the education of whites with a system that sought the subjugation of only their children. Louisiana had become a scene from Tourgee's *Invisible Empire.* But now, the philosophy of white supremacy that once roamed the countryside found expression in the statehouse. Entire generations of American black citizens were denied educational avenues for their children, participation in free elections, constitutional rights to serve as jurors and officials, and chances for employment that reflected their qualifications.

In 1902, in a final blow to Reconstruction in New Orleans, the Louisiana legislature passed the Wilson Bill, which mandated that New Orleans resegregate its streetcars—a return to the star-cars policy of pre-1867 New Orleans. Ironically, Lionel Adams, the assistant district attorney who prosecuted Homer Plessy in 1892 for the state, argued the unconstitutionality of this state law in his defense of a noncomplying streetcar owner charged with sixty violations of the Wilson Bill. The case was appealed to the Louisiana Supreme Court, which found in favor of the law. The owner, H. H. Pearson, president of the New Orleans Railway Company, was fined $1,100. Upon paying, he left the city.[13] In 1908, the legislature enacted laws requiring separate water fountains for black and white citizens.

One by One

One by one, the civil-rights gains of Reconstruction faded into history. So too did the principals in the *Plessy v. Ferguson* case. Homer Plessy returned to obscurity, his shoemaking days long finished. So were his days as a civil disobedient. He worked alternately as a laborer, warehouseman, and clerk before becoming a collector for the black-owned People's Life Insurance Company in 1910. He lived in various places—all in the downtown neighborhoods: 1438 North Roman, 1930 Bayou Road, and, toward the end of his life, 2507 St. Phillip Street. He also served as vice president of the Societe des Francs Amis, one of the older Creole organizations in New Orleans that harked back to antebellum New Orleans. Additionally, he and L. J. Joubert were board members of the Cosmopolitan Mutual Aid Association, incorporated in 1895.

Plessy's local attorney, James C. Walker, became ill the same year of the United States Supreme Court decision. His illness prevented his anticipated trip to Washington, DC, for argument before the Court. James C. Walker died in July 1898. His obituary in the *Daily Picayune* incorrectly labeled him as having

Colored Service sign in New Orleans

Albion Tourgee's memorial in Mayville Cemetery

argued *in favor* of the Separate Car Law. Albion Tourgee died in Bordeaux, France, in 1905 after having been appointed consul to Bordeaux by President McKinley in 1897. "The sun shines brightly but it's a dark day for us," Emma Tourgee wrote in her diary on March 21, 1905. "Albion breathed his last at 12:15 this morning. My heart is wrung."

Comité des Citoyens president Arthur Estevcs passed away in 1908 at age seventy-one. Monsieur Esteves had faithfully served as president of the Couvent School until his death. He had steered that institution, founded by Marie C. Couvent in 1848, into a new century. Esteves had also presided over the building of a new school in the 1890s—a rebuilding financed in part by a bequest from the will of Aristide Mary. Like Marie C. Couvent, Rodolphc Dcsdunes, and a number of other members of the Comité des Citoyens, Esteves was buried in Square #3 in St. Louis Cemetery #2, right outside of the Storyville district of New Orleans. Rodolphe Desdunes continued to write, but in 1908, he was injured in an accident at the custom house in New Orleans and lived out his life in various degrees of blindness. Still, before the accident, he had completed a manuscript called *Nos Hommes et Notre Histoire,* detailing the history of New Orleans' free people of color. It was published in Montreal in 1911. An English translation by Sister Dorothea Olga McCants of the Daughters of the Cross appeared in 1973. Desdunes died on August 14, 1928, of cancer of the larynx while visiting his son, Daniel, in Omaha, Nebraska. For his part, Daniel Desdunes left New Orleans and taught music at Boys Town.[14] Committee treasurer Paul Bonseigneur died in 1916. Louis Martinet died at age sixty-seven on June 7, 1917, at his home at 1722 Columbus Street in New Orleans—twenty-five years to the day of Homer's train ride. Comité des Citoyens vice president C. C. Antoine died at home in Shreveport, Louisiana, in 1921 at age eighty-five.

Judge Ferguson died in 1915 at age seventy-seven. In that year, he fell down on Camp Street near Canal, struck his head, and died three weeks thereafter of a cerebral hemorrhage. In his obituary, a daily paper praised him as one who "allied himself with the Democratic reform element, took part in the struggles for white supremacy, and was elected a member of the Nicholls legislature . . . When the lottery issue assumed prominence, he espoused the cause of the opposition, stumped the state and spoke often in this city in behalf of the Foster candidacy."[15] Ferguson was buried in Lafayette Cemetery on Washington Avenue and was interred in the same grave as his wife, son, and his abolitionist father-in-law, T. J. Earhart.

Homer Plessy died in 1925. His obituary was simple: "Plessy—on Sunday, March 1, 1925, at 5:10 a.m. beloved husband of Louise Bordenave."[16] He was buried in the Debergue-Blanco family tomb in St. Louis Cemetery #1.

Homer Plessy's gravesite in St. Louis Cemetery #1

The Cause of the Next Generation

But even as white supremacists gained control of the South and it seemed that Plessy's efforts would be little more than a curious footnote in the pages of American history, the principles of equality that moved the Comité des Citoyens took root in the formation of other organizations. In 1905, a group of twenty-nine black activists from fourteen states formed the Niagara Movement, a convention that echoed the Comité des Citoyens' commitment to the Fourteenth Amendment's ideals of equality and citizenship. And as one of the Niagara Movement's first acts, a memorial service paid tribute to the three "friends of freedom": Frederick Douglass, William Lloyd Garrison, and Plessy's attorney before the United States Supreme Court, Albion Winegar Tourgee. Like the now disbanded Comité des Citoyens, the Niagara Movement denounced state-mandated separation of the races and Booker T. Washington's philosophy of accommodation. Its Harvard-educated leader, W. E. B. Du Bois, proclaimed, "We want full manhood suffrage and we want it now." In subsequent meetings at historically symbolic locations—such as Harpers Ferry, West Virginia, and Boston's Faneuil Hall—Du Bois echoed the request of the Comité des Citoyens-issued, similarly militant call for recognition of the rights of American citizens:

> We claim for ourselves every single right that belongs to a freeborn American, political, civil and social: and until we get these rights we will never cease to protest and assail the ears of America. The battle we wage is not for ourselves alone but for all true Americans.
> We want full manhood suffrage, and we want it now, henceforth and forever.
> We want discrimination in public accommodation to cease. Separation in railway and street cars, based simply on race and color, is unAmerican, undemocratic, and silly.
> We claim the right of freemen to walk, talk, and be with them that wish to be with us. No man has a right to choose another man's friends, and to attempt to do so is an impudent interference with the most fundamental human privilege.

> We want the law enforced against rich as well as poor; against capitalist as well as laborer; against white as well as black. We are not more lawless than the white race: we are more often arrested, convicted and mobbed.
>
> We want the Constitution of the country enforced . . . We want the Fourteenth Amendment carried out to the letter and every state disfranchised in Congress which attempts to disfranchise its rightful voters.
>
> We want the Fifteenth Amendment enforced and no state allowed to base its franchise simply on color.
>
> We want our children educated . . . Either the United States will destroy ignorance or ignorance will destroy the United States . . . We want our children trained as intelligent human beings should be, and we will fight for all time against any proposal to educate black boys and girls simply as servants and underlings, or simply for the use of other people. They have a right to know, to think, to aspire.[17]

In 1908, after anti-black riots erupted in Springfield, Illinois—the home of Lincoln—white civil-rights activists joined with Niagara militants in founding the National Association for the Advancement of Colored People on February 12, 1909—the 100th anniversary of the birth of Abraham Lincoln. It was the interracial movement in support of civil rights for all citizens that Martinet and Tourgee had envisioned. In one of the first statements of the NAACP, the new organization vowed resistance:

> If Mr. Lincoln could revisit this country in the flesh, he would be disheartened and discouraged. He would learn that on January 1, 1909, Georgia had rounded out a new confederacy by disfranchising the Negro, after the manner of all the other Southern States. He would learn that the Supreme Court of the United States, supposedly a bulwark of American liberties, had refused every opportunity to pass squarely upon this disfranchisement of millions, by laws avowedly discriminatory and openly enforced in such manner that the white men may vote and that black men be without a vote in their government; he would discover, therefore, that taxation without representation is the lot of millions of wealth-producing American citizens, in whose hands rests the economic progress and welfare of an entire section of the country.

He would learn that the Supreme Court, according to the official statement of one of its own judges in the Berea College case, has laid down the principle that if an individual State chooses, it may make it a crime for white and colored persons to frequent the same market place at the same time, or appear in an assemblage of citizens convened to consider questions of a public or political nature in which all citizens, without regard to race, are equally interested.

In many states Lincoln would find justice enforced, if at all, by judges elected by one element in a community to pass upon the liberties and lives of another. He would see the black men and women, for whose freedom a hundred thousand of soldiers gave their lives set apart in trains, in which they pay first-class fares for third-class service, and segregated in railway stations and in places of entertainment; he would observe that State after state declines to do its elementary duty in preparing the Negro through education for the best exercise of citizenship.[18]

The NAACP would dispatch hundreds of lawyers and establish citizens' committees throughout the nation. They would provide an avenue for the long line of those seeking access to the Constitution in the spirit of Quock Walker of Massachusetts, Dred Scott of Missouri, Homer Plessy of New Orleans, and countless others throughout American history. In New Orleans, NAACP attorney Alexander Pierre Tureaud took up the cause of equality. In the tradition of Martinet, Tureaud initiated a number of civic and voter leagues and urged blacks to register to vote despite poll taxes and discriminatory tests. In 1941, in defense of Joseph McKelpin in *McKelpin v. the Board of Education*, Tureaud successfully won a suit against the school board to pay black teachers the same salary as white teachers. In 1946, Tureaud won a voter-registration suit on behalf of residents of St. John the Baptist Parish. That same year he led an investigation into the lynching of World War II veteran John C. Jones in Minden, Louisiana, and turned over the names of the attackers to the U.S. government. As a scholarly man who relished documents of history, his collection at the Amistad Research Center contains old *Crusader* printings and reports of the Comité des Citoyens. Tureaud was quite familiar with the work of Louis A. Martinet and the committee. Indeed, finishing what they started became Tureaud's lifetime work. In 1949, in *Bush v. Board of Education,* Tureaud initiated legal action that eventually led to the desegregation of New Orleans' school system. When a group of civil-rights lawyers formed an organization in the 1950s, it was Tureaud who suggested it be named the Martinet Society. Other activists—such as labor leader Ernest Wright, Zachary Ramsey, Daniel Byrd, Avery Alexander, A. L. Davis, and countless others in New Orleans—led mass marches to Gallier Hall to register as many as possible to vote as federal rulings began to reverse the disenfranchisement that had lasted thus far into the twentieth century. Nationally, Thurgood Marshall and other NAACP attorneys continued to whittle away at the constitutional basis of *Plessy v. Ferguson.* Louis Martinet once told Tourgee in 1893, "You may not live to see the fruit of your labors and sacrifice, or to receive the gratitude of those benefited by them. It will be reserved to future generations to properly and justly estimate them." And in 1950, with the Comité des Citoyens totally forgotten by many, Robert H. Jackson, Supreme Court justice, wrote a letter to a friend who lived near Mayville: "The Plessy case arose in Louisiana and how Tourgee got into it I have not learned. In any event, I have gone to his old brief filed here, and there is no argument made today that he would not make to the Court. He says, 'Justice is pictured blind and her daughter, the Law, ought at least to be color-blind.' Whether this was original with him, it has been gotten off a number of times since as original wit. Tourgee's brief was filed April 6, 1896, and now, just fifty-four years after, the question is again being argued whether his position will be adopted and what was a defeat for him in '96 be a post-mortem victory."[19]

In 1954, NAACP attorney Thurgood Marshall once again pressed Fourteenth Amendment contentions to the door of the United States Supreme Court and asked that separate but equal be struck down in the case of *Brown v. Board of Education.* On May 31, 1954, sixty-three years after the Comité des

Citoyens began their saga to fight against separate but equal, the Supreme Court acted. That time, the Court overturned *Plessy v. Ferguson* and ruled separate but equal to be unconstitutional. That time, Homer Plessy won.

APPENDIX

Further Reading

BOOKS

Anderson, James D. *The Education of Blacks in the South*. Chapel Hill, NC: University of North Carolina Press, 1988.

Arnesen, Eric. *Waterfront Workers of New Orleans: Race, Class, and Politics, 1863-1923*. New York and Oxford: Oxford University Press, 1991.

Bennett, Lerone, Jr. *Before the Mayflower: A History of Black America*. New York: Penguin, 1988.

Blasingame, John W. *Black New Orleans: 1860-1880*. Chicago: University of Chicago Press, 1973.

Desdunes, Rodolphe Lucien. *Our People and Our History*. Translated by Sister Dorothea Olga McCants. 1911. Reprint, Baton Rouge, LA: Louisiana State University Press, 1973.

Dibble, Roy F. *Albion W. Tourgee*. 1921. Reprint, Port Washington, NY: Kennicat Press, 1968.

Devore, Donald E., and Joseph Logsdon. *Crescent City Schools: Public Education in New Orleans 1841-1991*. Lafayette, LA: Center for Louisiana Studies, 1991.

Dufour, Charles L. *Ten Flags in the Wind: The Story of Louisiana*. New York: Harper and Row, 1967.

Finkelman, Paul. *Dred Scott v. Sandford: A Brief History with Documents*. Euless, TX: Bedford Books, 1997.

Fischer, Roger A. *The Segregation Struggle in Louisiana, 1862-17*. Urbana, IL: University of Illinois, 1974.

Foner, Eric. *Free Soil, Free Labor, Free Men*. New York: Oxford University Press, 1995.

—. *Reconstruction: America's Unfinished Revolution 1863-1877*. New York: Harper and Row, 1988.

Franklin, John Hope. *From Slavery to Freedom: A History of Negro Americans, Fifth Edition*. New York: Alfred A. Knopf, 1980.

Fredrickson, George M. *Racism: A Short History*. Princeton, NJ: Princeton University Press, 2002.

Furer, Howard B. *The Fuller Court, 1888-1910*. Milwood, NY: Associated Faculty Press, 1986.

Gambino, Richard. *Vendetta: First Edition*. New York: Doubleday, 1977.

Garvey, Joan B. and Mary Lou Widmer. *Beautiful Crescent: A History of New Orleans*. New Orleans: Garner Press, 1982.

Gehman, Mary. *The Free People of Color of New Orleans*. New Orleans: Margaret Media, 1994.

Gross, Theodore L. *Albion W. Tourgee.* New York: Twayne Publishers, 1963.

Gunther, Gerald. *Cases and Materials on Constitutional Law: Ninth Edition.* Mineola, NY: Foundation Press, 1975.

Hall, Gwendolyn Midlo. *Africans in Colonial Louisiana: The Development of Afro-Creole Culture in the Eighteenth Century.* Baton Rouge, LA: Louisiana State University Press, 1992.

Heffner, Richard D. *A Documentary History of the United States.* New York: Mentor, 1985.

Herda, D. J. *The Dred Scott Case.* Springfield, NJ: Enslow Publishers, 1994.

Higginbotham, A. Leon, Jr. *In the Matter of Color: Race and the American Legal Process.* New York: Oxford University Press, 1978.

Howard, Perry H. *Political Tendencies in Louisiana.* Baton Rouge, LA: Louisiana State University Press, 1971.

Huber, Leonard V. *New Orleans: A Pictorial History.* Gretna, LA: Pelican Publishing Company, 1991.

Jackson, Joy L. *New Orleans in the Gilded Age: Progress and Urban Progress, 1880-1896.* Baton Rouge, LA: Louisiana State University Press, 1969.

Jaffa, Harry V. *Crisis of the House Divided.* Chicago: University of Chicago Press, 1982.

Kemp, John R., ed. *Martin Behrman of New Orleans: Memoirs of a City Boss.* Baton Rouge,LA: Louisiana State University Press, 1977.

King, Willard L. *Melville Weston Fuller: Chief Justice of the United States, 1888-1910.* New York, McMillan Company, 1950.

Loomis, Rosemarie Fay. *Negro Soldiers—Free Men of Color in the Battle of New Orleans—War of 1812.* New Orleans, Aux Quartres Vents Limited, 1991.

Malcolmson, Scott L. *One Drop of Blood: The American Misadventure of Race.* New York, Farrar Straus and Giroux, 2000.

Martin, James Kirby et al., eds. *America and Its People.* Glenview, IL: Scott, Foresman and Company, 1989.

Oates, Stephen B. *With Malice toward None: A Life of Abraham Lincoln.* New York: Harper Perennial, 1994.

O'Connor, Thomas H. *Civil War Boston.* Boston: Northeastern Uni-versity Press, 1997.

Olsen, Otto H. *Carpetbagger's Crusade: The Life of Albion Winegar Tourgee.* Baltimore, John Hopkins Press, 1965.

———. *The Thin Disguise: Turning Point in Negro History.* New York: Humanities Press, 1967.

Rightor, Henry, ed. *Standard History of New Orleans.* Chicago: Lewis Publishing Company, 1900.

Rousseve, Charles Barthelemy. *The Negro in Louisiana.* 1937. Reprint, New York: Johnson Reprint Company, 1970.

Schultz, Christian. *Travels on an Inland Voyage.* New York: I Riley, 1810.

Schwartz, Bernard. *A History of the Supreme Court.* New York: Oxford University Press, 1993.

Smith, Elbert B. *The Presidency of James Buchanan.* Lawrence, KS: University Press of Kansas, 1975.

Steeples, Douglas, and David O. Whitten. *Democracy in Desperation: The Depression of 1893.* Westport, CT: Greenwood Publishing Group, 1998.

Stewart, James Brewer. *Holy Warriors.* New York: Hill and Wang, 1997.

Swann, June. *Shoemaking*. Buckinghamshire, UK: Shire Publications, 1997.

Thomas, Brook. *Plessy v. Ferguson: A Brief History with Documents*. New York: Palgrave Macmillan, 1997.

Toledano, Roulhac, and Mary Lou Christovich. *New Orleans Architecture Volume VI: Faubourg Tremé and the Bayou Road*. Gretna, LA: Pelican Publishing Company, 1980.

Tourgee, Albion W. *An Appeal to Caesar*. New York: Fords, Howard and Hulbert, 1884.

——. *Bricks Without Straw*. 1880, Reprint, Baton Rouge, LA: Louisiana University Press, 1969.

——. *Murvale Eastman Christian Socialist*. New York: Fords, Howard and Hulbert, 1890.

Vass, Laslo, and Magda Molnar. *Handmade Shoes for Men*. Germany: Neue Stalling, Oldenburg, 1999.

Von Frank, Albert J. *The Trials of Anthony Burns*. Cambridge, MA: Harvard University Press, 1977.

Zarefsky, David. *Lincoln Douglas and Slavery: In the Crucible of Public Debate*. Chicago: University of Chicago Press, 1993.

PERIODICALS

Sullivan, Lester. "The Unknown Rodolphe Desdunes: Writings in the New Orleans Crusader." *Xavier Review* 10, nos. 1 and 2 (1990): 1-15.

Notes

Chapter 1

1. *New Orleans Daily City Item,* August 31, 1892, p. 8, col. 5.

2. Dr. Boake Plessy, interview by author, 1985.

3. Joan B. Garvey and Mary Lou Widmer, *Beautiful Crescent: A History of New Orleans* (New Orleans: Garmer Press, 1982), 23-25, 28, 32-34.

4. Gwendolyn Midlo Hall, *Africans in Colonial Louisiana: The Development of Afro-Creole Culture in the Eighteenth Century* (Baton Rouge and London: Louisiana State University Press, 1992), 6.

5. Ibid., 29-34, 60, 73; Charles L. Dufour, "The Spanish Regime," in *Ten Flags in the Wind: The Story of Louisiana* (New York: Harper and Row, 1967), 79-80.

6. Hall, *Africans in Colonial Louisiana,* 5-6.

7. Ibid., 29, 34-37, 127-128; Alcee Fortier, *Louisiana Vol. 1* (New Orleans: Century, 1914), 92-99; Thomas Marc Fiehrer, "The African Presence in Colonial Louisiana: An Essay on the Continuity of Caribbean Culture," in *Louisiana's Black Heritage,* eds. Robert R. Macdonald et al. (Baton Rouge: Louisiana State Museum, 1979), 13-14.

8. Hall, *Africans in Colonial Louisiana, 278.*

9. *James Kirby Martin et al., eds.,* America and Its People (Glenview, IL: Scott, Foresman and Company, 1989), 282.

10. Ibid., 282-83.

11. Rosemarie Fay Loomis, *Negro Soldiers—Free Men of Color in the Battle of New Orleans—War of 1812* (New Orleans: Aux Quartres Vents Limited, 1991).

12. Loomis, *Negro Soldiers,* 5.

13. Edward C. Carter et al., eds., *The Journals of Benjamin Henry Latrobe 1799-1820: From Philadelphia to New Orleans Vol. 3* (New Haven and London: Yale University Press, 1980), 211.

14. "Suit Records, 1813-1815," (Louisiana: First Judicial District Court [Orleans Parish] G), #870, #7629, #7711.

15. Calendar, "Diocese of Louisiana and the Floridas," (New Orleans, 1841); University of Notre Dame Archives, http://archives1.archives.nd.edu/calendar/cal1841.htm. Entry in journal of St. Louis Cathedral: "Nov 8 Dan Cascy

and Margaret Tehan (on the back of this license is written), daughter of Pierre Courotte and Elina Laporte born February 23, 1844; godfather, Germain Plessy and godmother, Josephine Hoa."

16. Bobby Duplissey, comp., Plessy family history.

17. Ibid.

18. "News from Port Hudson," *New Orleans Daily True Delta,* March 18, 1863.

19. *New Orleans Bee,* January 5, 1869.

20. Charles Barthelemy Rousseve, *The Negro in Louisiana* (1937; reprint, New York: Johnson Reprint Company, 1970), 107.

21. Charles Vincent, "Black Louisianans during the Civil War and Reconstruction: Aspects of Their Struggles and Achievements," in *Louisiana's Black Heritage,* eds. Robert R. Macdonald et al. (Baton Rouge: Louisiana State Museum, 1979), 101.

22. Germaine A. Reed, "Race Legislation in Louisiana, 1864-1920," in *Louisiana History XI,* no. 4 (1965): 381-89.

23. "Mrs. Victor M. Dupart—Age 35—nee Louise Felicie Demazillere 12-17-69," *New Orleans Bee,* December 17, 1869, p. 1, col. 6.

24. Straight College Records, Amistad Research Center; U.S. Census of 1870, 520-7w.

25. *Seccession of Josephine Blanco, vvd. Michel Debergue,* Louisiana Division, New Orleans Public Library

26. Loomis, *Negro Soldiers,* 13.

27. Orleans Parish Poll Tax Rolls 1869-1870 (Le Comite des Archives de la Louisiane, 1996), 66.

28. "Grand Unification," *New Orleans Times,* July 15, 1873, 1.

29. "Reconciliation: The Dawn of a New Era," *New Orleans Times,* June 17, 1873, 1; "Grand Unification," *New Orleans Times,* July 15, 1873, 1.

30. Joy J. Jackson, "Municipal Problems in New Orleans" (Diss. Tulane University, 1961), 134-36.

31. U.S. Census of 1880, vol. 9, ed. 50, sheet 17, line 13.

32. June Swann, *Shoemaking* (Buckinghamshire, UK: Shire Publications, 1997), 11.

33. Laslo Vass and Magda Molnar, *Handmade Shoes for Men* (Germany: Neue Stalling, Oldenburg, 1999), 123.

34. John W. Blasingame, *Black New Orleans: 1860-1880* (Chicago and London: University of Chicago Press, 1973), 235.

35. Vass and Molnar, *Handmade Shoes for Men* 118-19, 122.

36. Ibid., 33.

37. Ibid., 119.

38. Donald E. Devore and Joseph Logsdon, *Crescent City Schools: Public Education in New Orleans 1841-1991.* (Lafayette, LA: Center for Louisiana Studies, 1991), 115.

39. Ibid., 82.

40. Ibid., 89, 91, 102.

41. Ibid., 115.

42. Soards' city directory, 1888.

43. Register of Marriages, Louisiana Division, New Orleans Public Library, vol. 13, p. 258.

44. "Silver Jubilee," *New Orleans Daily Picayune,* March 22, 1892.

45. *Crusader,* 1892-1894.

46. Roulhac Toledano and Mary Lou Christovich, *New Orleans Architecture Volume VI: Faubourg Tremé and the Bayou Road* (Gretna, LA: Pelican Publishing Company, 1980), 105.

47. The numbering system for New Orleans streets changed in the 1890s. Therefore, Plessy's address may be seen in some documents as 244^1/$_2$ North Claiborne.

48. Soards' city directory, 1892, p. 998.

49. Sanborn Fire Insurance maps, 1888-1896, Louisiana Division, New Orleans Public Library, vol. 3.

50. Voter registration records, Parish of Orleans, Sixth Ward, Third and Fourth Precinct, Louisiana Division, New Orleans Public Library.

Chapter 2

1. Kermit L. Hall, ed., *The Oxford Companion to the Supreme Court of the United States* (New York and Oxford: Oxford University Press, 1992), 92, 289, 321, 345. Henry Billings Brown was born in South Lee, Massachusetts; Stephen Field moved to Stockbridge as a baby; Horace Gray was born in Boston; Melville Weston Fuller briefly attended Harvard.

2. William Francis Galvin, secretary of the Commonwealth of Massachusetts, Citizen Information Service, http://www.state.ma.us/sec/cis/cismaf/ mf1c.htm.

3. Albert J. Von Frank, *The Trials of Anthony Burns* (Cambridge, MA: Harvard University Press, 1977), xii.

4. "The Quock Walker Case: Instructions to the Jury," in *Africans in America (www.pbs.org/wgbh/aia/part2/2h38t.html); Albert P. Blaustein and Robert L. Zangrando, eds.,* Civil Rights and the Black American: A Documentary History (New York: Simon and Schuster, 1968).

5. W. Augusutus Low and Virgil A. Clift, eds., *Encyclopedia of Black America* (New York: Da Capo Press, 1987), 768.

6. "Judge Ferguson, Retired Lawyer, Dead at Age 77," *New Orleans Times-Picayune,* November 13, 1915.

7. "Temperance," *Vineyard Gazette,* January 1847.

8. Boston directory, 1861, 160; Sanborn Fire Insurance maps (Boston: 1867).

9. M. A. DeWolfe Howe, *Boston Landmarks* (New York: Hastings House, 1947), 34-37, 96-99.

10. Albert Bushnell Hart, ed., *Commonwealth History of Massachusetts (New York: Russell and Russell, 1966), 58, 59, 70, 82, 85, 87, 92, 96.*

11. *James Grant Wilson and John Fiske, eds.,* Appleton's Cylopedia of American Biography (New York: D. Appleton and Company, 1887-1889).

12. James Brewer Stewart, *Holy Warriors* (New York: Hill and Wang, 1997), 72-73.

13. Albert J. Von Frank, *The Trials of Anthony Burns,* 130.

14. Ibid., 129-30.

15. James Brewer Stewart, *Holy Warriors,* 161-62.

16. Henry David Thoreau, "Slavery in Massachusetts," http://www.framingham.com/history/profiles/thoreau.htm.

17. Thomas H. O'Connor, *Civil War Boston* (Boston: Northeastern University Press, 1997), 109-12.

18. Massachusetts Historical Society document.

19. O'Connor, *Civil War Boston,* 55.

20. Sanborn Fire Insurance maps (Boston: 1867).

21. Garvey and Widmer, *Beautiful Crescent,* 155.

22. Minutes of the Loyal National League of Louisiana, printed by H. P. Lathrop, 1863, Historic New Orleans Collection.

23. *New Orleans Times,* December 5, 1863.

24. *New Orleans Daily Crescent,* October 19, 1865.

25. Garvey and Widmer, *Beautiful Crescent,* 149.

26. Ibid., 140

27. Christian Schultz, *Travels on an Inland Voyage* (New York: I Riley, 1810), 196-98.

28. The Order of Knights of Pythias, http://www.pythias.org/pythstory/.

29. "Judge Ferguson, Retired Lawyer, Dead at Age 77," *New Orleans Times-Picayune,* November 13, 1915.

30. "First Day's Proceedings," in *Official Journal of the Proceedings of the House of Representatives* (Baton Rouge: Extra Session, 1877).

31. "Second Day's Proceedings," in *Official Journal of the Proceedings of the House of Representatives* (Baton Rouge: Extra Session, 1877): 8.

32. Ibid., 8.

33. "Third Day's Proceedings," in *Official Journal of the Proceedings of the House of Representatives* (Baton Rouge: Extra Session, 1877): 9.

34. "Hennessy Case," *New Orleans Times-Democrat,* February 17, 1891, p. 8.

35. "Hon. John H. Ferguson," *New Orleans Daily Picayune,* July 1, 1892, p. 6, col. 3; *New Orleans Daily Picayune,* July 6, 1892, p. 3, col. 4; *New Orleans Times-Democrat,* July 1, 1892, p. 2, col. 5.

36. "A History of the Courts in the Parish of Orleans," Historic New Orleans Collection, 11.

37. "Going for Gamblers," *New Orleans Daily Picayune,* September 23, 1892.

Chapter 3
1. Albion W. Tourgee Collection, #6532.

2. Otto H. Olsen, *Carpetbagger's Crusade: The Life of Albion Winegar Tourgee* (Baltimore: Johns Hopkins Press, 1965), 8-9.

3. Roy F. Dibble, *Albion W. Tourgee* (1921; reprint, Port Washington, NY: Kennicat Press, 1968), 147.

4. Olsen, *Carpetbagger's Crusade*,14.

5. Ibid., 24.

6. Theodore L. Gross, *Albion W. Tourgee* (New York: Twayne Publishers, 1963), 19.

7. Olsen, *Carpetbagger's Crusade*, 24.

8. Gross, *Albion W. Tourgee*, 21.

9. George M. Fredrickson, introduction to *A Fool's Errand*, by Albion W. Tourgee (New York: Harper and Row Publishers, 1966), x.

10. Gross, *Albion W. Tourgee*, 33.

11. Ibid., 30.

12. Olsen, *Carpetbagger's Crusade*, 84.

13. Dibble, *Albion W. Tourgee*, 135.

14. Fredrickson, "Introduction," xiii.

15. Albion Winegar Tourgee, "Hostility to Schools and Teachers," in *The Invisible Empire* (Baton Rouge: Louisiana State University Press, 1989), 81.

16. Albion Winegar Tourgee, "The New Book of Martyrs," in *The Invisible Empire* (Baton Rouge: Louisiana State University Press, 1989), 104-5.

17. Albion Winegar Tourgee, "Hostility to Schools and Teachers," 81-82.

18.Ibid., 125-27.

19. Ulysses S. Grant, "Reasons for Being a Republican," Warren, OH: http://www.nationalcenter.org/USGrant.html, September 28, 1880.

20. Dibble, *Albion W. Tourgee*, 77.

21. Ibid., 77.

22. "Diary and Letters of Rutherford B. Hayes," Ohio Historical Society, http://www.ohiohistory.org/onlinedoc/hayes/Volume05/Chapter54/June15.txt.

23. "A Reminiscence—How Judge Albion W. Tourgee Came to Mayville," *Mayville Sentinel*, August 28, 1914.

24. Gross, *Albion W. Tourgee*, 130.

25. Fredrickson, "Introduction."

26. Gross, *Albion W. Tourgee*, 145.

Chapter 4

1. Alcee Fortier, *Louisiana Vol. 1,* 92-99.

2. Robert A. Goldwin, "Why Blacks, Women, and Jews Are Not Mentioned in the Constitution," in *The U.S. Constitution and the Supreme Court*, eds. Steven Anzovin and Janet Podell (New York: H. W. Wilson Company, 1988), 93-106.

3. "Horses and Negro Lost," *New Orleans Picayune,* June 29, 1837, p. 1.

4. "Horses and Negro Lost," *New Orleans Picayune,* June 29, 1837, p. 1.

5. "5.00 Reward," *New Orleans Picayune,* June 29, 1837, p. 1.

6. "Negroes for Sale," *New Orleans Picayune,* June 29, 1837, p. 3.

7. "$20 Reward," *New Orleans Picayune,* June 29, 1837.

8. Martin et al., eds., *America and Its People*, 408-9.

9. Ibid., 427-28.

234 WE AS FREEMEN

10. Ibid., 428.

11. *Scott v. Sanford.*

12. Bernard Schwartz, *A History of the Supreme Court* (New York: Oxford University Press, 1993), 120-21.

13. Stephen B. Oates, *With Malice Toward None: A Life of Abraham Lincoln* (New York: Harper Perennial, 1994), 134-35.

14. Schwartz, *History of the Supreme Court,* 116.

15. Richard Gambino, *Vendetta: First Edition* (New York: Doubleday, 1977), 26-27.

16. Martin et al., eds., *America and Its People,* 462.

17. Minutes of the Loyal National League of Louisiana, printed by H. P. Lathrop, 1863, Historic New Orleans Collection.

18. Ibid., 12-14.

19. "The Emancipation Celebration," *New Orleans Era,* June 12, 1864; "Emancipation Celebration," *New Orleans Daily True Delta,* June 12, 1864.

20. "Notice to the Colored People of the City of New Orleans," *New Orleans Tribune,* April 22, 1865.

21. Blasingame, *Black New Orleans,* 178.

22. "Notice to the Colored People of the City of New Orleans," *New Orleans Tribune,* April 22, 1865, p. 1.

23. Low and Clift, eds., *Encyclopedia of Black America,* 72-77; John Hope Franklin, *From Slavery to Freedom: A History of Negro Americans, Fifth Edition,* (New York: Alfred A. Knopf, 1980), 235-37.

24. Gerald Gunther, *Cases and Materials on Constitutional Law: Ninth Edition* (Mineola, NY: Foundation Press, 1975), 901-2.

25. Eric Foner, *Reconstruction: America's Unfinished Revolution 1863-1877* (New York: Harper and Row, 1988), 276; Michael Kent Curtis, "Fourteenth Amendment," in *The Oxford Companion to the Supreme Court of the United States,* ed. Kermit L. Hall et al. (New York and Oxford: Oxford University Press, 1992), 309-11.

26. "Local Intelligence," *New Orleans Crescent,* May 7, 1867.

27. "Local Intelligence," *New Orleans Crescent,* May 1867; "The Cars," *New Orleans Tribune,* May 5, 1867, p. 1; Roger A. Fischer, *The Segregation Struggle in Louisiana, 1862-17* (Urbana, IL: University of Illinois, 1974), 30-41.

28. *"The Negroes and the City Railroads,"* New Orleans Times, May 7, 1867, p. 1.

29. "Classification of Cars," *New Orleans Crescent,* May 7, 1867.

30. Reed, "Race Legislation in Louisiana," 381-82.

31. Gunther, *Cases and Materials on Constitutional Law: Ninth Edition,* 902-3.

32. Lerone Bennett, Jr., *Before the Mayflower: A History of Black America* (New York: Penguin Books, 1993), 493-94.

33. Vincent, "Black Louisianans during the Civil War and Reconstruction, 104; Perry H. Howard, *Political Tendencies in Louisiana* (Baton Rouge: Louisiana State University Press, 1971), 421.

34. Lerone Bennet, Jr., *The Shaping of Black America* (Chicago: Johnson Publishing Company, 1975), 199.

35. Blasingame, *Black New Orleans,* 119.

36. Fiehrer, "The African Presence in Colonial Louisiana," 101-2.

37. *New Orleans Times,* June 23, 1873.

38. T. Harry Williams, "The Louisiana Unification Movement of 1873," in *The Journal of Southern History Vol. IX, No. 1* (Vanderbilt, TN: Vanderbilt University Press, 1945), 359-61.

39. "Equal Rights—Unification at Exposition Hall Last Night," *New Orleans Times,* July 16, 1873, p. 1; Williams, "The Louisiana Unification Movement of 1873," 364-65.

40. "Equal Rights—Unification at Exposition Hall Last Night," *New Orleans Times,* July 16, 1873, p. 1.

41. Williams, "The Louisiana Unification Movement of 1873," 368.

42. Rodolphe Lucien Desdunes, *Our People and Our History,* trans. and ed. Sister Dorothea Olga McCants (1911 *Nos Hommes et Notres Histoire; reprint, Baton Rouge: Louisiana State University Press, 1973),* 139.

43. Blasingame, Black New Orleans, 116-24, 173.

44. Hall et al., *The Oxford Companion to the Supreme Court of the United States,* 149.

45. Fischer, *The Segregation Struggle in Louisiana,* 134-35.

Chapter 5

1. Hall et al., *The Oxford Companion to the Supreme Court of the United States,* 789-91.

2. Low and Clift, eds., *Encyclopedia of Black America,* 244-46.

3. Blasingame, *Black New Orleans,* 223.

4. Hall et al., *The Oxford Companion to the Supreme Court of the United States,* 844.

5. Ibid., 149.

6. Gunther, *Cases and Materials on Constitutional Law: Ninth Edition,* 704.

7. Ibid., 914.

8. Hall et al., *The Oxford Companion to the Supreme Court of the United States,* 512.

9. Bennett, Jr., *Before the Mayflower,* 502.

10. Franklin, *From Slavery to Freedom: Fifth Edition,* 263-64.

11. Riley E. Baker, "Negro Voter Registration in Louisiana," *Louisiana Studies* (Winter 1965): 338-39.

12. Gambino, *Vendetta: First Edition,* 26-27.

13. C. Vann Woodward, "The Case of the Louisiana Traveler" in *American Counterpoint: Slavery and Race in North-South Dialogue* (Little, Brown and Company, 1971). (www.soc.umn.edu?~samaha/cases/van%20woodward,%20plessy.htm)

14. "Constitution of the American Citizens Equal Rights Association," *Crusader,* March 22, 1890, p. 1.

15. Henry Rightor, ed., *Standard History of New Orleans* (Chicago: Lewis Publishing Company, 1900), 572-77 ; Leonard V. Huber, "River and Port," in *New Orleans: A Pictorial History* (Gretna, LA: Pelican Publishing Company, 1991) 325-36.

16. New Orleans city directory, 1890.

17. The Acts of the Louisiana Legislature 1890, 161.

18. Berthold C. Alwes, "The History of the Louisiana State Lottery Company," *Louisiana Historical Quarterly* (October 1944): 1016-25.

19. *Official Journal of the Proceedings of the Senate* (Baton Rouge: 1890): 22-30.

20. Charles L. Dufour, "The Louisiana Lottery," in *Ten Flags in the Wind: The Story of Louisiana* (New York, Evanston, and London: Harper and Row, 1967), 218-26; Joy J. Jackson, "The Lottery Controversy and Its Aftermath," in *New Orleans in the Gilded Age: Progress and Urban Progress, 1880-1896* (Baton Rouge, LA: Louisiana State University Press, 1969), 111-43.

21. *Official Journal of the Proceedings of the House of Representatives* (Baton Rouge: 1890): 62.

22. Joy J. Jackson, *New Orleans in the Gilded Age,* 125.

23. Thomas Jefferson, "Thoughts on Lotteries," in *Thomas Jefferson on Politics and Government: Quotations from the Writings of Thomas Jefferson,* ed. Eyler Robert Coates, Sr. (http://etext.virginia.edu/jefferson/quotations/jeff1320).

24. *Official Journal of the Proceedings of the Senate* (Baton Rouge: 1890): 187. This table contains a listing of levee breaks.

25. "Governor and Lottery," *Crusader,* March 22, 1890.

26. *Official Journal of the Proceedings of the House of Representatives* (Baton Rouge: 1890): 12-13.

27. "Official Journal of the House of Representatives," *Baton Rouge (Louisiana) Advocate* May 28, 1890.

28. *Official Journal of the Proceedings of the House of Representatives* (Baton Rouge: 1890): 201-3.

29. Ibid., 203-4.

30. Ibid., 201.

31. "Local Matters," *Baton Rouge (Louisiana) Advocate,* May 11, 1890.

32. Foster (Murphy J. and family) papers (box 5, folder 4), June 10, 1890, LSU Libraries Special Collections.

33. "The Separate Car Bill," *Crusader,* July 19, 1890.

34. *Official Journal of the Proceedings of the Senate* (Baton Rouge: 1890): 410, 437-38.

35. Ibid., 410

36. *New Orleans Times,* July 9, 1890.

37. "Illness of Honorable J. Fisher Smith," *Baton Rouge (Louisiana) Advocate,* July 8, 1890.

38. *Official Journal of the Proceedings of the Senate* (Baton Rouge: 1890): 421.

39. Ibid., 437.

40. "Speech of Hon. Henry Demas, on the Separate Car Bill, Delivered in the Senate, at Baton Rouge, La., July 8, '90," *Crusader,* July 19, 1890, 2.

41. "The Separate Car Bill," *Crusader,* July 19, 1890.

42. Rodolphe L. Desdunes, "Was It a Matter of Vengeance, the Separate Car Bill," *Crusader,* July 19, 1890, 1.

43. "The Separate Car Bill," *Crusader,* July 19, 1890.

Chapter 6

1. Gambino, *Vendetta: First Edition* 79-80.

2. Bennett, Jr., *Before the Mayflower,* 507.

3. Louis A. Martinet to Albion W. Tourgee, October, 5, 1891, 11, 20-22.

4. Louis A. Martinet to Albion W. Tourgee, October 5, 1891, 23-24.

5. Louis A. Martinet to Albion W. Tourgee, October 5, 1891.

6. Rodolphe Desdunes, "Forlorn Hope and Noble Despair," *Crusader,* August 15, 1891.

7. Joseph Logsdon and Caryn Cosse Bell, *Creole New Orleans: Race and Americanization,* eds. Arnold R. Hirsch and Joseph Logsdon (Baton Rouge: Louisiana State University Press, 1992), 258.

8. Rodolphe Desdunes, "Forlorn Hope and Noble Despair," *Crusader,* August 15, 1891.

9. Gunther, *Cases and Materials on Constitutional Law: Ninth Edition,* Appendix: Table of Justices, 2-5.

10. Jackson, *New Orleans in the Gilded Age,* 109.

11. Rodolphe Desdunes, "To Be or Not to Be," *Crusader,* July 4, 1891.

12. Desunes, *Our People and Our History,* 141.

13. Logsdon and Bell, *Creole New Orleans,* 257.

14. New Orleans city directories, 1890s; New Orleans voter registration records.

15. Dianne M. Baquet, Baquet family researcher, interview by author; *New Orleans Democrat-Picayune,* August 24, 1905, p. 8, col. 5.

> Rudolph B. Baquie, clerk in the United States appraiser's Office, died suddenly at his residence, No. 708 Constantinople Street of heart disease. He was an intelligent and educated colored man and had filled several positions under the Republican regime over thirty years ago. It was under his direction that the big reservoir on Canal Street and the Galvez Canal culvert were built. Two years ago he was appointed Clerk in the United States Appraiser's office and was filling that position up to the time of his death. He was a soldier in the Union Army during the Civil War and rose from the ranks to be a sergeant-major. For several years he was Adjutant General of the Grand Army of the Republic for Louisiana and Mississippi.

16. *History of the Catholic Indigent Orphan Institute School,* published by the board of directors, Earl K. Long Library Archives and Manuscripts Department, University of New Orleans, 4.

17. "1868 Louisiana State Senate," *Louisiana History,* 71-74.

18. Desunes, *Our People and Our History,* 148.

19. "An Appeal," in *Report of Proceedings of the Citizens Committee* (New Orleans, 1891).

20. "Receipts and Expenditures," in *Report of Proceedings of the Citizens Committee* (New Orleans, 1891).

21. Louis A. Martinet to Albion W. Tourgee, October 11, 1891, document #5763.

22. Ibid., May 30, 1893, notation 6998.

23. Olsen, *Carpetbagger's Crusade*, 312-23.

24. "For a Patriotic Purpose," *Crusader*, December 17, 1892, Desdunes Collection, notation 1/18/8, Xavier University Archives.

25. Louis A. Martinet to Albion W. Tourgee, October 5, 1891, document #5760.

26. Ibid., December 7, 1891, pp. 1-2, document #5737.

27. Ibid., 2.

28. Rightor, ed., *Standard History of New Orleans*, 572-77.

29. Louis A. Martinet to Albion W. Tourgee, December 28, 1891, 2.

30. "Receipts and Expenditures," in *Report of Proceedings of the Citizens Committee* (New Orleans, 1891), 8.

31. "Statement of the Citizens' Committee," in *Report of Proceedings of the Citizens Committee* (New Orleans, 1891).

Chapter 7

1. "Receipts and Expenditures," in *Report of Proceedings of the Citizens Committee* (New Orleans, 1891), 8; *New Orleans Daily Picayune*, August 3, 1888. Christopher Cain sworn in as captain of the parish prison.

2. New Orleans death index, Louisiana Division, New Orleans Public Library.

3. "Shoes," *New Orleans Daily City Item*, August 31, 1891.

4. Huber, *New Orleans*, 325-39.

5. Sanborn Fire Insurance maps, 1888-1896, Louisiana Division, New Orleans Public Library, vol. 3.

6. "Mandeville in Line—A Trial Trip Over the East Louisiana Extension," *New Orleans Daily Picayune*, May 26, 1892, 2.

7. *New Orleans Daily Picayune*, June 9, 1892.

8. New Orleans Police Department arrest books, AB-11, Louisiana Division, New Orleans Public Library.

9. *Daily Crusader*, Xavier University Archives, New Orleans.

10. "Exhibit II," *State of Louisiana vs. Homer Adolph Plessy, No. 19117, Criminal District Court for the Parish of Orleans, Section "A,"* 2.

11. *Daily Crescent*, June 8, 1892.

12. *New Orleans Daily Picayune*, June 9, 1892.

13. *Crusader*, June 1892.

14. Martin et al., eds., *America and Its People*, 595.

15. Howard, *Political Tendencies in Louisiana*, 178-79.

16. *New Orleans Daily Picayune*, July 4, 1892; "Our Natal Day," *New Orleans Daily Picayune*, July 5, 1892; *New Orleans Daily City Item*, July 5, 1892.

17. Nils R. Douglas, *Who Was Louis A. Martinet?* Archives and Manuscripts Department, University of New Orleans.

18. Ibid.

19. Louis A. Martinet to Albion W. Tourgee, July 4, 1892.

20. Ibid., July 9, 1892.

21. Ibid.

22. Ibid.

23. "Jim Crow Is Dead," *Crusader,* July 1892, Xavier University Archives.

24. "The Courts," *New Orleans Daily Picayune,* July 4–October 14, 1892.

25. General docket, Criminal District Court, Parish of Orleans.

26. "The Weather," *New Orleans Daily States,* October 13, 1893.

27. "Oklahoma's Race War," *New Orleans Semi-Weekly States,* October 4, 1892.

28. "Black Brutes Meet Death at the Hands of an Infuriated Mob," *New Orleans Daily Picayune,* October 14, 1892.

29. "Miscegenation," *New Orleans Daily Picayune,* October 15, 1892.

30. *New Orleans Daily Picayune,* September 4, 1892.

31. "The Courts," *New Orleans Daily Picayune,* October 14, 1892.

32. Gambino, *Vendetta: First Edition,* 72, 102; "A History of the Courts in the Parish of Orleans," Historic New Orleans Collection, 20.

33. *New Orleans Daily Picayune,* July 9, 1898, 7.

34. Louis A. Martinet to Albion W. Tourgee, December 7, 1891.

35. Ibid., October 28, 1891.

36. *New Orleans States,* October 13, 1892.

37. Criminal District Court, Parish of Orleans minute book, October 13, 1892.

38. *New Orleans States,* October 13, 1892; Otto H. Olsen, *The Thin Disguise: Turning Point in Negro History* (New York: Humanities Press, 1967), 14.

39. Bernard A. Cook, "The Typographical Union and the New Orleans General Strike of 1892," *Louisiana History* (1983).

40. *New Orleans Times-Democrat,* November 19, 1892.

41. *Crusader,* Xavier University Archives.

42. "The Separate Car Law," *New Orleans Times-Democrat,* November 19, 1892.

43. "Judge Ferguson and Allies," *Crusader,* notation 1/18/6.

44. "The Judiciary," *New Orleans Times-Democrat,* December 20, 1892.

45. "Separate Car Act," *New Orleans Times-Democrat,* December 1892.

Chapter 8

1. "Three Deadly Shots," *New Orleans Times-Democrat,* May 15, 1893.

2. Orleans Parish death certificates, May 14 1893, Louisiana Division, New Orleans Public Library.

3. "Three Deadly Shots," *New Orleans Times-Democrat,* May 15, 1893.

4. "Killed Himself," *Daily Item,* May 15, 1893.

5. Louis A. Martinet to Albion W. Tourgee, May 30, 1893, notation 6998.

6. Rodolphe Desdunes, *Hommage Rendu a la Memoire de Alexandre Aristide Mary,* 1893.

7. Louis A. Martinet to Albion W. Tourgee, May 30, 1893, notation 6998.

8. Benjamin Harrision, "Annual Message to the Senate and House of Representatives," December 6, 1892 (http://www.theamericanpresidency.net/1892.htm).

9. James C. Walker to Albion W. Tourgee, October 93, notation 7428.

10. Louis A. Martinet to Albion W. Tourgee, May 30, 1893, notation 6998.

11. Ida B. Wells, *A Red Record* (1895), document 4, (http://www.bing-hamton.edu/womhist/aswpl/doc4.htm).

12. Olsen, *Carpetbagger's Crusade,* 315-16.

13. Louis A. Martinet to Albion W. Tourgee, May 30, 1893.

14. Ibid.

15. Ibid.

16. Diary of Emma Tourgee (1892-94).

17. Louis A. Martinet to Albion W. Tourgee, May 30, 1893.

18. L. A. Martinet, ed., *The Violation of a Constitutional Right* (New Orleans: Crusader Print, 1893).

19. Diary of Emma Tourgee, October 29-31, 1893.

20. Albion W. Tourgee to Louis A. Martinet, October 31, 1893.

Chapter 9

1. Martin et al., eds., *America and Its People,* 282-596.

2. J. Kingston Pierce, "The Panic of 1893," *Columbia: The Magazine of Northwest History* (Winter 1993/1994; reprinted in *SIRS Global Perspectives* 1994): 37-44.

3. Joy J. Jackson, "The Cornucopia Of Wealth," in *New Orleans in the Gilded Age,* 230.

4. Logsdon and Bell, "The Americanization of Black New Orleans," *Creole New Orleans* (Baton Rouge: Louisiana State University Press, 1992), 256.

5. Albion W. Tourgee to Sen. William E. Chandler, February 1896.

6. Acts Passed by the General Assembly of the State of Louisiana (1894), 63.

7. "Senate Calendar—House Bills," in *Official Journal of the Proceedings of the Senate of the State of Louisiana (1894), 109;* Official Journal of the Proceedings of the House of Representatives of the State of Louisiana (1894), 728.

8. Franklin, *From Slavery to Freedom: Fifth Edition, 258.*

9. Daily Crusader, June 1, 1895.

10. "Mother Katherine Drexel and the Color Line," *Daily Crusader,* February 28, 1895, Xavier University Archives, Desdunes Collection.

11. Lester Sullivan, "The Unknown Rodolphe Desdunes: Writings in the New Orleans Crusader," *Xavier Review* 10, nos. 1 and 2 (1990): 10-12.

12. "Come Forward," *Daily Crusader,* March 13, 1895, Xavier University Archives, Desdunes Collection.

13. Louis A. Martinet to Albion W. Tourgee, July 24, 1895.

14. James C. Walker to Albion W. Tourgee, August 5, 1895.

15. Louis R. Harlan, ed., *The Booker T. Washington Papers,* vol. 3 (Urbana: University of Illinois Press, 1974), 583-87.

16. Olsen, *The Thin Disguise,* 80-103.

17. Louis A. Martinet to Albion W. Tourgee, March 4, 1896.

18. Albion W. Tourgee to Sen. William E. Chandler, February 1896.

19. Hall et al., *The Oxford Companion to the Supreme Court of the United States.*

20. Schwartz, *History of the Supreme Court*, 174-75.

21. Jeffrey B. Morris, "The Era of Melville Weston Fuller," Yearbook Supreme Court Historical Society, 1981, 6 (http://www.supremecourthistory.org/myweb/81journal/morris81.htm); (http://lawbooksusa.com/supremecourt/fuller.htm).

22. Hall, et al., *The Oxford Companion to the Supreme Court of the United States*, 626-27.

23. Schwartz, *History of the Supreme Court*, 177.

24. http://lawbooksusa.com/supremecourt/brewer.htm.

25. Schwartz, *History of the Supreme Court*, 178; Lerner Law Book (http://lawbooksusa.com/supremecourt/shiras.htm).

26. Lerner Law Book (http://lawbooksusa.com/supremecourt/shiras.htm), 1.

27. Hall et al., *The Oxford Companion to the Supreme Court of the United States*, 783.

28. Ibid., 345-46.

29. Ibid., 290.

30. Ibid., 291; 'Lectric Law Library (http://www.lectlaw.com/files/case24. htm).

31. Charles Thompson, "Harlan's Great Dissent" (http://athena.louisville.edu/library/law/harlan/harlthom.html). This article originally appeared in the 1996 number 1 issue of *Kentucky Humanities*, published by the Kentucky Humanities Council, 206 East Maxwell St., Lexington, KY 40508-2316.

32. Hall et al., *The Oxford Companion to the Supreme Court of the United States*, 362.

33. Olsen, *Carpetbagger's Crusade*, 334-35.

34. Hall et al., *The Oxford Companion to the Supreme Court of the United States*, 99-102.

35. Schwartz, *History of the Supreme Court*, 176.

36. Willard L. King, *Melville Weston Fuller Chief Justice of the United States, 1888-1910* (New York: MacMillan Company, 1950), 152-53.

37. Minutes of the Supreme Court of the United States, October 8, 1894-May 25, 1896, National Archives and Record Service, microcopy no. 215, roll 20.

38. Albion W. Tourgee, "Plessy Vs Ferguson. Argument of Albion W. Tourgee," Albion W. Tourgee Collection (Chautauqua County Historical Society, Westfield, New York), #6472, p. 21.

39. Diary of Emma Tourgee (1895-1898), #9900.

40. *Plessy v. Ferguson*, 163 U.S. 537 (1896). Decision by Justice Brown.

41. *Plessy v. Ferguson*, 163 U.S. 537 (1896). Dissent by Justice Harlan.

42. Charles Thompson, "Harlan's Great Dissent," 2.

43. "Statement of the Citizens' Committee," in *Report of Proceedings of the Citizens Committee* (New Orleans, 1891), 7.

44. *State of Louisiana vs. Homer Adolph Plessy*, No. 19117, Orleans Parish Criminal Court records.

Chapter 10

1. *Official Journal of the Constitutional Convention* (Baton Rouge: 1898), 380.

2. Howard, *Political Tendencies in Louisiana*, 189.

3. *Official Journal of the Constitutional Convention* (Baton Rouge: 1898), 374-75.

4. *Constitution of the State of Louisiana Adopted in Convention at the City of New Orleans* (New Orleans: H. J. Hearsey Convention Printer), 51.

5. *Official Journal of the Constitutional Convention* (Baton Rouge: 1898), 375.

6. Ibid., 384.

7. John R. Kemp, ed., *Martin Berhman of New Orleans: Memoirs of a City Boss* (Baton Rouge, LA: Louisiana State University Press, 1977), 46.

8. *Official Journal of the Constitutional Convention* (Baton Rouge: 1898), 384.

9. Ibid., 380.

10. *Official Journal of the Senate of Louisiana at the Second Regular Session* (Baton Rouge: 1898), 33-35.

11. Howard, *Political Tendencies in Louisiana,* 190; Baker, "Negro Voter Registration in Louisiana," 338-39.

12. Devore and Logsdon, *Crescent City Schools,* 117-19.

13. "Text of the Star Car Law," *New Orleans Daily States,* October 14, 1902; "New Law Is Effective," *New Orleans Daily States,* November 3, 1902; "Wilson Car Law Sustained by State Supreme Court," *New Orleans Daily States,* March 16, 1903; "Mr. Pearson Fined $1100," *New Orleans Daily States,* May 8, 1893.

14. Desdunes, *Our People and Our History,* xvi.

15. *New Orleans Times-Picayune,* November 13, 1915.

16. *New Orleans Times-Picayune,* March 3, 1925.

17. W. E. B. Du Bois, "Address to the Nation," delivered at the second annual meeting of the Niagara Movement, Harpers Ferry, West Virginia, August 16, 1906 (http://www.wfu.edu/users/zulick/341/niagara.html).

18. Mary White Ovington, "How the NAACP Began," http://www.cincinnatinaacp.org/history.html, 1914.

19. Olsen, *Carpetbagger's Crusade,* 353-54.

Index

.